Lead Me On

THE JOURNEY

Letting God and His Word
have impact on our lives, daily

LINDA LETKEMANN

 FriesenPress

Suite 300 - 990 Fort St
Victoria, BC, V8V 3K2
Canada

www.friesenpress.com

ISBN
978-1-4602-6334-1 (Hardcover)
978-1-4602-6335-8 (Paperback)
978-1-4602-6336-5 (eBook)

1. Religion, Christian Life

Distributed to the trade by The Ingram Book Company

TABLE OF CONTENTS

Life isn't from here to there,
or from this time to that;
it is from who you are,
to who you can **become,**
in *Jesus Christ.*

Forward

To say I have known the author, Linda Letkemann since the day she was born would be the truth. I have seen her grow throughout the stages of her life and I couldn't be more in awe of the woman she has become. Her passion for Jesus and His Church along with her love and commitment to her family and community is palpable and inspiring.

The Journey is written out of the story of her own life as she has sought to discover God's wisdom and leading through His Word. She shares insights from the Bible in a way that is practical and relevant to the situations that each of us will encounter in life.

This book is clearly a labour of love from the heart of a grateful daughter of the King who's greatest desire would be to pass on a legacy of faith and hope to those she is called to lead and influence. You, the reader will find much gold as you ponder the truths that have been so thoughtfully prepared from the overflow and richness of her heart.

Great is the LORD and most worthy of praise;
his greatness no one can fathom.
One generation commends your works to another;
they tell of your mighty acts.
They speak of the glorious splendour of your majesty
and I will meditate on your wonderful works.
They tell of the power of your awesome works and
I will proclaim your great deeds.
They celebrate your abundant goodness and
joyfully sing of your righteousness.

Psalm 145:3-7 NIV

Helen Burns

The Journey

The greatest single event that can happen to any individual is to be born again through accepting Jesus Christ as their personal Lord and Saviour. Many people think it ends there, but it doesn't! Yes, we are saved, forgiven, and blessedly set free from guilt and condemnation. We are now on our way to Heaven, but I for one want to enjoy the ride as well! When Adam sinned, the greatest battle in the cosmos began, with us as the prize.

This book is meant as a guide to help you live on the path Jesus Christ recommends and overcome anything that has been put in your way. Too many Christians become victims of sin instead of victors over it. My hope and prayer is that the words contained herein will be used as tools to deny the enemy his pleasure and ensure our victory. God loves us way too much to leave us the way He finds us when we come to Him, which is often in a place of deception, dysfunction, and problems. He wants us to not only survive, but thrive in life. God is no respecter of persons and what He did for me He will do for you. He allowed me to encounter Him daily in a life-changing and lasting way. The Great Love Whisperer to the heart will personally reveal Himself to you as long as you're sincerely looking for Him. Life is not always fair, but He is utterly just; life is not always easy, but He provides avenues through difficulties. We don't always get what we want, but He will see to it that we get what is best. Resisting sin is difficult, but He provides not only the strength to resist and the way out, but also the valid reasons why we should. My life as a Christian went from black and white to colour, and this is the story of why and how. My goal is to help you encounter Him for yourself and for you to become a vessel He can flow through to others.

For this to happen, God gave me a keen desire to know His Word, which led me to study the entire Bible once a year from 1998 forwards. I made extensive notes in my *New International Version Experiencing God Study Bible*, noting many of what I referred to as "CPAs" in my margin, which indicated He had busted my preconceived notions with Cataclysmic Perception Alterers. I had found that in many ways, I'd painted God in my own image, not His. I had formulated my perception of God and His actions to be comfortable for me, and not necessarily truth. I began to find the God of the universe for who He Himself said He was and is, and found that the God who expresses His wrath every day is also the God whose mercies are new every morning; that the Father of pity and compassion is also the King of power and dominion. Most of all—and I cannot overstate this—is that the God of the whole universe is vitally and passionately interested in you and me. He is not interested only in teaching us or in us serving Him, but in having an intimate personal relationship with every person on the planet. There are only two kinds of people on planet Earth: those who are in relationship with Him, and those with whom God wants to be in relationship but are not for one reason or another.

I never intended to write a book, but God had other plans, and it's been amazing how we arrived here today. On April 2, 2004, the pastor of my church, Pastor Jim Potter, approached me and asked if I would write a "kernel of truth" for our weekly church bulletin. I replied, "Who am I to minister to God's people? I'm not a minister." His response hit me between the eyes. "Linda," he said. "We are all ministers." His point was that God can minister through anyone who is willing to be a vessel. Since then, the newsletter has become monthly, but I continued to provide these kernels for each edition until last year. In the early days, people came up to me regularly and remarked how they had been helped by my writing and encouraged me to put my kernels into a book, as some were collecting and keeping them. The Lord continued to bring deeper revelation to me through His Word. I knew He was guiding me. There is no other explanation for the excitement I experienced in studying the same material for years on end and never growing weary of doing so. If God is who He says He is and He created our unimaginably complex universe and left a detailed record of Himself on Earth for me to follow, surely He could explain things if I had questions. As life brought new challenges, He brought fresh answers. I was deeply moved to realize that I, with no formal training in writing, could actually hear God speak to my heart and put it down in words. He continues to bring fresh and deeper revelation that is self-fueling and creates the never ending desire to learn more about how to bring His Word into our daily lives.

This book was born from a vast collection of over twelve years of research and kernels of truth. Each of these kernels ties the Bible's relevancy directly to the topic at hand. Often, I read a passage from the Bible and relevancy of its truth to our lives today will jump out at me. Each bears God's fingerprints because they did not come from me, but through me.

Part 1 discusses who God is and how we can know Him. These sections deal with the nature of God, how to find Jesus, and why we should invest ourselves in living life His way. Part 2 looks at how we can thrive financially, personally, and in relationships through His Word and practical applications. Part 3 deals primarily with our enemy, Satan, and his tactics to kill, steal, and destroy us. It discusses how we are meant to have victory against him and our fallen nature, our flesh. I've taken much out of my own life that has been good, bad, and ugly and hung it on the wash line for everyone to see. I describe how I cooperated with God to celebrate the good, help me through the bad, and address the ugly. I show that as long as there is breath in your body, it is not too late for a new beginning. How we begin in life is not nearly as important as how we finish. You may have had a lousy beginning, but that doesn't mean you have to have a lousy life and finish.

God and His Word are alive and well on planet Earth. Mining the depths of His Word will never fail to yield fresh, precious gems, no matter how many times you've explored the same area. At first glance, you may not see anything new, but the key is to keep looking. In the beginning, you pick the gems up from the ground that are scattered right in front of you, but later you will need to dig. It may take a little effort, but encountering beautiful treasure becomes self-motivating. If you keep searching, you will encounter the God of the ages through His Word. A life-long transformation ensues as God begins to change you into the likeness of His Son from the inside out. God's Holy Spirit brings revelation and enlightenment to all who seek it. I hope that this anointing, His voice in these pages, will speak to you. These are His words, and it is my responsibility to relay them. If one person is helped, it has been worth it, because you are worth everything to God and He desires to spread that good news. If we let God have His way with us, we will start to reflect the goodness of Jesus. We will learn to live like Jesus, lead like Jesus, and most importantly, love like Jesus. This is my sincerest prayer for every person who takes this journey.

Life on Earth brings so many challenges. That's what building a life is all about; it is a kaleidoscope of challenges. Some are won, and some lost, only to see us pick ourselves up and meet them head on again. This abundant life, which Jesus talked about, works against the enemy's attempt to destroy us. God didn't design us to fail at life, but to be victorious. It's time we allowed Him to perform that in us and then through us. He didn't write the Bible for Himself; He knows what's in it. He wrote it for you and me. It is His love letter to us, but if we don't take hold of it, we'll miss out. The Bible I once found to be boring and outdated came to life when I fell in love with the Author. I have found this Book—God's inspired Word—to be a miracle in its own right, and I hope my message will help you see that too.

A Word of Thanks and Acknowledgement

To my dear husband, Jake:
For being there with me through the journey thus far. For letting me use you as a sounding board and keeping me in balance. For letting me pick your brains and helping me see things from a man's point of view. For all your continual encouragement, and for believing that God could and would use me for His purposes. Thank you now and forever.

To my amazing daughters, Melissa, Jocelyn, and Katelyn:
For providing the raw material from which sprang many of the life lessons along the way. They were an integral part of my journey, as well as yours. Thank you for your incredible love for me and for allowing me to be a flawed mom in progress as you grew up. Most of all, thank you for drinking from the well that we brought you to. You didn't have to, but you did, and you will be forever blessed.

To my awesome sons-in-law, Mario, Neil and Jeffrey:
Thank you for your patience, trust, and love as you heard our hearts as parents giving away a very big part of ourselves—our daughters—in marriage. As we work together to create a family that is blessed and one that God can continually work with and shine through, I look forward to the future that God has planned as we live life together.

To Pastor Jim Potter, who put this train in motion by recognizing something in me and asking me to minister to the people in his church through our church bulletin. This was a small beginning that brought us to this place today. Thank you for being a part of my Journey.

And to my readers, I extend my thanks for your interest in learning how God can bring victory in all arenas of life through His Word. My heart's desire is that these kernels will be a tool in God's hands to help His children live victoriously and to multiply that. I pray these bless you abundantly above all you can ask or think.

With love and prayers,
Linda Letkemann

PART I

WHO IS GOD AND HOW CAN WE KNOW HIM?

CHAPTER 1
The Nature of God

WHY DOES GOD HIDE HIMSELF?

When I was a young girl, there were times I'd beg God to let me see Him. Just this once, I would say, please! I thought it would improve my faith in God and change me forever. If I could just get a glimpse of Him, I'd never doubt again, and I'd be a strong Christian! I couldn't understand why God didn't just show Himself to everyone. After all, if they saw He was real, surely they would change their ways and follow Him. Being young and childish, it annoyed me. Why did it have to be so tough to believe in God? You may have pondered the same thing.

God isn't hiding, He's just invisible—and for good reasons. Remember, it wasn't always this way. God walked with Adam and Eve in the Garden of Eden, and they saw Him with their physical eyes before their sin broke that fellowship.

There are reasons why it appears that God hides Himself. The first is to encourage us to look for Him. Have you ever played hide and seek with a child? Do you ever hide so well that the child can't find you? Of course not. When they've looked for a while and start getting upset, you give them clues. You make some noise or move because you don't want them to become discouraged and give up. What happens when they find you? Everyone shrieks for joy and happiness. This is how I think our Heavenly Father enjoys revealing Himself to His children. He'll let us seek and look for Him for just long enough until we become hungry to find Him. He'll even help us find Him, much like a parent. How much joy is there when you find the answer that you've been seeking? How much confidence do you place in God's revelation of Himself when you have been searching for some time? However, the reason He hides Himself is definitely not a game.

Every person ever born has been created with a God-shaped hole that only He can fill on a constant basis. People use many things to fill it: money, sex, drugs, illicit relationships, and the quest for power, fame, or prestige. Once one thing stops working, we move on to the next. In the ancient world, idolatry was their problem.

Psalm 115:2-8 sheds some amazing insight into this. Verse 2 says, "Why do the nations say, 'Where is their God?'" The psalmist replies that his God is in heaven, and that what the nations worship are idols made of silver and gold, made by their own hands. They have mouths, but can't speak; eyes, but can't see; ears, but can't hear; noses, but can't smell; hands and feet, but can't feel or walk. Verse 8 says, "Those who make them will be like them, and so will all who trust in them." If anyone turns away from the draw of the Holy Spirit and wilfully chooses to ignore God and believe in a substitute, they will have those results. In other words, their senses will become completely dull and non-responding.

We run across people every day who believe in anything but God and who vehemently defend their position. Just the other day, I heard that a group of atheists are banding together to defend their beliefs (or lack thereof) by demanding that all references to God or a deity be removed from public places. We see this at Christmas when it is no longer politically correct for us to say "Merry Christmas" but we are advised to say "Happy Holidays" instead. They feel they are being discriminated against. Ironically, we can see in the psalms what those who didn't believe in an invisible God sought after the very thing they made—a god they could see.

In our culture, we may be prideful that we're too sophisticated to believe in an idol, yet many will do anything for money. The apostle Paul likened greed to idolatry (in Colossians 3:5), and Luke 16:13 states that we cannot serve two masters, both God and Money. In the New International Version (NIV), "Money" is capitalized, indicating it is a person and not just a thing. Anything that we trust in as a substitute for God will make us blind, deaf, dumb, and unfeeling, and will hinder us from finding Him. We cannot find Him in that state; we have to choose to seek Him first.

The process of seeking God in all things is a life-long process that keeps us in faith, but not because He is a mean, elusive, stern Father who enjoys seeing us struggle. Instead, it is because He loves us so much that He wants to keep us hungry for His company: "And you will seek me, and you will find me, when you seek me with all your heart. I will be found by you," declares the Lord" (Jer 29:13–14). What a promise. I can attest to the truth of this, as you will see as you read on. If you truly look for Him, you will find Him. He's declared it!

IS GOD FAIR?

In a secular radio broadcast, the following question was asked in calling God to account for His sense of justice:

"How could a loving, fair God give you the choice to choose Him or reject Him, and then condemn you for your choice?"

In case you are unfamiliar with God and His position towards humankind, He is holy and sinless, and His relationship to unholy, sinful humans shows that each person born has a sinful nature and is already condemned to an eternity separated from Him, unless they accept His gift of salvation. If you choose to reject that gift, the question infers that God condemns you and is not loving and fair. It is a good question, to which there is no simple answer. If the question stood alone, it would seem that God is not loving and fair, but it does not take into consideration pre-existing conditions. Consider for a moment a situation in your life where events occurred, and your response was completely appropriate and fair, but if someone had walked in without prior knowledge of what went before, it would have appeared like you were anything but fair.

For example, I remember once when I disciplined my child. My little girl was in a season of testing her boundaries, and I addressed each incidence of disobedience with long-suffering patience. I tried everything short of disciplining her to give correction, but she continued pressing. The day the shoe dropped, we were at my mom's house. My mother witnessed the "correction with direction" on the padded rear section of my daughter's behind that the Lord gave for this purpose (as well as sitting). My mother said, "Did you have to be so hard on her?" She thought I was being unfair, yet she had not seen the previous times I had exercised restraint. As I pondered this question, I realized that if people are going to put God on the stand, they need to agree to the following:

- If the world is going to infer that God is unfair, the world must also acknowledge that God does actually exist in the equation; otherwise, there is no dispute.

- If the question is inferring that God is not being loving and fair, the conditions for love and fairness need to be established. In other words, we live in a moral world where there is love and hate, right and wrong, fairness and unfairness.
- If the question is holding God accountable for not being loving and fair according to the world's sense of what is right and wrong, the pre-existing moral state of the world needs to be considered. The world then needs to be at least as fair as God to accuse Him of unfairness. Wouldn't you agree? In other words, the world needs to be as moral as God is.

> The day the shoe dropped just happened to be at my mom's house where my mother witnessed the "correction with direction" on the very padded rear section of her behind that the Lord gave for this purpose as well as sitting...

God claims He is perfect, sinless, holy, loving, and fair, and does not change. He is as He has always been. Can we say that about the world? Are the world's conditions what makes something fair and equal to those of God's? Is life fair all the time? Are there no injustices in the world? Are the conditions for every person to thrive perfectly fair to everyone? If we answer honestly, the answer is a resounding no.

Therefore, we have a loving, fair God that exists, and world conditions that are grossly unfair. What happened to cause this and how does it affect us?

If we acknowledge that God does exist, we must then look at the whole picture, not just from our standpoint, but also of things that happened before us. Through the fall of Adam and Eve, we are not given the choice to be guilty; we are born guilty. Now we're back to square one. The critical question has to be filtered through the reality of events that transpired before us—namely the fall of man.

Some would ask, "If I'm born guilty, how is that my fault? If God made me and put me here in this condition, it's up to God to fix it."

True. He did. And look at what it cost Him.

Imagine you are walking down a busy street, minding your own business, when all of a sudden a car goes out of control, heading straight for you. A young man runs towards you and pushes you out of harm's way. He is struck by the car and dies. As you stand there stunned, an older gentleman runs to you, grief-stricken, and tells you, "That was my son." You stand there dumbfounded as the reality of what just happened sinks in. The father looks at his dead son and then at you. He asks you an odd question: "Do you think that my son cared about you?" As you look at the dead body and the grief-stricken father, you say, "Yes. He must have cared for me. He threw himself in front of that car and saved my life, and I didn't even know him." The father continues to gaze at you and after a moment's pause, says, "Yes. He did care. But what you don't know is that I was the one who saw the car coming, and sent him to save your life."

You see grief on the father's face, and yet you see something else in his eyes. You can feel his love for you through his pain, despite what just happened. You stand there, amazed at this incredible display of love, and you ask the father, "I don't get it. Why would you do this? You don't know me either. Why not let me die instead of your son?"

Through no fault of yours, you were in the wrong place at the wrong time. Someone just saw the car coming and did what was needed to save you.

Through no fault of ours, we were born guilty. God just knew what was coming and did what was needed to save us.

Coming back to the question on the radio show, I find it to be unfair—to Jesus at least. He was abused and crucified, though He did nothing to deserve it.

The truth is, God does not condemn us. We condemn ourselves. Wilful blindness causes judicial blindness. If we on purpose close our eyes in order to deny truth, we leave an utterly just God with nowhere to go. If we choose to reject His love in light of what happened, we choose to live separated from Him for all eternity. Some will say, "I don't believe that Christ died for me, so I'm off the hook, right?" No, you're not. Not believing something doesn't make it untrue.

God's presence and existence reveal His Holiness before which sinful people cannot stand and yet, so great is God's love for us, that He sent His Son to die in our place while we were yet sinners so we could once again experience an intimate relationship with Him through Jesus. The choice should be clear, and the consequences—utterly fair.

Do we love God for who He is, or only for what He does? We say, "I love you Lord, so very much!" But when adversity strikes, what happens to the level of our devotion? Believing that God is intimately involved in our lives also leads us to have to accept the fact that when trials and tribulations occur, they have gone by His inspection and He has allowed them for His perfect reasons and for our good. This is where the measuring line between true devotion and feelings of devotion is drawn.

When things are going well, it's easy to love God and give Him all the credit. But what happens when we've been disappointed or blown away by our circumstances? Life is full of them! Is God still so good? This is where our love for God is put to the true test, and our faith that He knows what He is doing is put through the fire. Fire destroys everything not impervious to it and what is left is something that is stronger than the fire itself. This is the material that God wants our faith and devotion to be made from.

1 Peter 1:7 says, "These [grief in all kinds of trials] have come so that your faith—[of greater worth than gold, which perishes even though refined by fire]—may be proved genuine..."

I don't have answers to all of life's questions, but one thing is for sure: Jesus Christ has always revealed Himself to me in the midst of my trial, and that has been my saving grace and comfort because He has never left me alone in it. True devotion is not displayed when we understand why things happen, but is displayed especially when we don't.

1 Peter 1:8 is further comfort. "Though you have not seen Him, you love Him; and even though you do not see Him now, you believe in Him, and are filled with an inexpressible and glorious joy." Isn't it wonderful that these words come right after a verse about the reasons we go through adversity? To me, it is a miracle in itself that we can have a measure of "inexpressible and glorious joy" when we're hurting.

The next time a trial comes along, what will you do? Will you say, "God is good all the time"? Understand that in saying that God is good, you are not saying your difficulty is good. Many things that happen in life are the result of sin and are not good, but God can and will repay us in so many different ways if we'll allow Him to lead us through. We sing the song, "Refiner's Fire," which echoes the sentiment: "Refiner's fire, my heart's one desire, is to be ... holy. Set apart for you, Lord." We are born to be about His business, after all. If you take care of God's business, He will take care of yours.

My Grandmother was a Godly woman who exemplified a life-long dedication to Jesus. She and her family endured terrible hardships under communist rule in the Soviet Union and in the years following, when she was separated from her family for many years. Her life had not been an easy one, but she never complained. She was always so full of joy one would never guess what she'd been through. I was the only one in the room other than her children when she passed away, and I'll never forget her last few hours. I know that despite all the hardships and trials she endured, she believed and affirmed that God was good, and had been so all her life. I will never forget this. Even while dying, she wasn't thinking of herself; she was thinking of her wayward grandchildren. When they came to see her to say goodbye, instead of telling them she loved them (which we all knew beyond a shadow of a doubt), all she told them was, "Be there. Get there. When I get to Heaven, I don't want one to be missing from my family. Get yourself right with Jesus." Her mouth was moving right to the end, and I know she was praying. She set the bar very high for me.

No matter what happens during our time on Earth, at the end of our lives, I am sure we will be able to honestly say, "God is good, all the time." Dare to believe it, and watch God prove it.

DOES GOD REALLY CARE ABOUT THE LITTLE THINGS?

In light of the huge problems our society and world constantly face, many find it hard to believe that God really cares about the seemingly mundane daily problems we have to deal with. There was a time in my life when I pulled back from involving God in all the small challenges of my life, though at the time they seemed large to me. As I thought about world events and the magnitude of the problems God has on His hands, it felt ridiculous to bother Him with trivialities. I didn't know to what extent God cared about my problems, and perhaps I was counting on His help when I had no business asking for it over my seemingly small issues. Did God care about my struggles at work? There were people out there trying to find loved ones in the rubble after an earthquake and here I was upset that it was raining hard and praying for a parking spot near the mall entrance.

I began to pull back from going to Him with everything and only asked for help with things after I asked myself, "Is this problem big enough to ask for help, or should I just be quiet and handle it myself?" After a while, I found myself talking to God less and less. As I relied on myself, I began to solve my problems my way, instead of God's way, which resulted in poor solutions.

I languished for a while because I didn't know where the line was. As I searched God's Word, I came across Colossians 2:6 in the Living Bible (LB). It answered my question with full assurance: Yes! God is interested in every minute of your life because He desires to be a part of you. If we exclude God from the everyday minutes, we end up excluding Him from our lives. The enemy is also interested in every minute because He seeks to cause us to fall through our daily challenges. To thrive, we need God's intimate involvement in every minute.

Colossians 2:6 says, "And now, just as you trusted Christ to save you, trust Him too with each day's problems—live in vital union with Him." What does the word "vital" mean to you? Synonyms include crucial, essential, imperative, most important, and required for the continuation of life. To me, it means that we need it to be alive. We cannot live without our vital organs, and Christ wants us to live in vital union with Him.

This tells me that God wants to be the air that I breathe. What an awesome privilege we have if we can simply believe that and live it out! When you trust Christ as your Saviour, you trust Him with where you will spend all eternity, so why would He not be interested in our daily problems? Still, the fact that He is there for us won't make a difference unless we believe that and act upon it. If your earthly father was hovering over you to see you through a daily challenge, but you didn't bother to ask for his help, what good would it do you? This verse settled it for me years ago. Many Christians miss out because they think He's not that involved, and that simply isn't true.

Another verse that reaffirms this is Psalm 68:19: "Praise be to the Lord, to God our Saviour, who daily bears our burdens." Not once, not now and then, but *daily* Jesus wants to carry our burdens as we go through life, being led by Him as He helps us. If He's carrying the burden, then we don't have to, right?

1 Peter 5:7 says, "Cast all your anxiety on Him, because He cares for you." This tells me that there is no issue too big or too small to cast on Jesus; whatever makes us anxious can be cast on Him. Notice that we are to throw all our anxiety onto Him, but not the responsibility of the problem. Often, we want God to fix it while we watch, to be delivered from our problems, but Jesus wants to develop our faith and character in and through the problems. If we pray and trust Him and they aren't immediately solved, God has a good reason, and He isn't finished molding us. We want every problem fixed on our timetable, and God isn't moved by our impatience. He's always right on time. Often, there is a period of waiting while He leads you here and there and shows you what you must do to solve your challenge. We get anxious as we wait, and we are to cast our anxiety on Him. "Because He cares for us" is our guarantee.

Today and for the rest of your life, don't cheat yourself out of an intimate walk with Jesus. Why carry a weight or go it alone when you don't have to? He is mighty enough to handle countries in conflict and, like the perfect Father that He is, tender and powerful enough to help His children through every minute of every day. That is why we were created, to do life with Him and share everything with Him. Tell Him how you're feeling—He appreciates honesty, even when it's not pretty. He knows exactly how you're wired because He made you! He knows exactly what it will take to see you through. I guarantee that as you become intimate with your Lord, He will show Himself to be faithful to His promises and richly reward you with a deeper relationship with Him.

CHAPTER 2
The Wisdom and Fear of God

WHERE IS THE WISDOM OF THE WORLD WITHOUT GOD?

Have you ever found yourself at the receiving end of a sympathetic look from a person who thinks you're a fool for believing in God? There are also people in important positions who are completely brilliant and as such command a lot of respect who genuinely pity us. These people of high position or importance often intimidate us ordinary folk who are "foolish" enough to believe the Gospel. Once again, however, God explains things the way they are, and not as they appear to be. Consider 1 Corinthians 1:18–25. They are very important in today's intellectual climate relating to the Gospel.

"For the message of the cross is foolishness to those who are perishing, but to us who are being saved it is the power of God. For it is written: 'I will destroy the wisdom of the wise; the intelligence of the intelligent I will frustrate.' Where is the wise man? Where is the scholar? Where is the philosopher of this age? Has not God made foolish the wisdom of the world? For since in the wisdom of God, the world through its wisdom did not know Him, God was pleased through the foolishness of what was preached, to save those who believe."

Not to be disrespectful to anyone, but I didn't write these verses. In a nutshell, the message of the Cross is the power of God to save those who believe it and condemn those who think themselves too smart to believe it. To better understand what God is saying, we have to first understand God's definition of wisdom. Wisdom is more than knowledge. Knowledge is information or facts that can be learned, but God's wisdom is an

> Wisdom is more than knowledge. Knowledge is information or facts that can be learned, but wisdom is understanding that must be *discerned*.

understanding or "knowing" that must be discerned and is imparted only by Him. Worldly wisdom stems from the sum of all the conclusions we draw about life and from everything we are up to this point, but will only take us so far. When we enter into a relationship with God, who is the epitome of all wisdom, we come into its fullness; He imparts His wisdom to our gut, giving us the inside track. The world's wisdom is limited. This leads to wrong conclusions. When we snub our noses at God, thinking ourselves to be wise, we fall into one of the categories in the verse above and our "wisdom and intelligence" will be destroyed and frustrated. You see, in the glaring all-revealing spotlight of truth, all other contradicting wisdom about humanity's sinful condition ends up being foolishness.

About the worldly wise man, scholar, and philosopher, He asks, "Where are they?" They cannot be found because apart from God, they don't have truth. A philosopher, for example, is deemed to be a truth seeker, but a philosopher who denies or negates the existence of God can't truly be seeking the truth. God's wisdom is not difficult to obtain; a five year old can seek and find God. Here's the kicker: the world didn't acknowledge Jesus for these reasons, so God saved those of us who believe.

You have to appreciate God's methods. As I've said many times, sight rejected is sight denied; light rejected is light denied. Who can truly see without the sight and light God gives? We need to look with these eyes. The apostle Paul, who penned these verses, was the living embodiment of them. He himself knew God's Word inside and out and was trained by Gamaliel (Acts 22:3), yet because of his incredible intellect rejected the Gospel and became spiritually blind. On the Damascus road, the Lord literally blinded him, and it wasn't until he acknowledged Jesus that he literally and spiritually received back his sight.

Pride is at the root of this; God opposes a haughty (proud, arrogant, conceited, or condescending) spirit. If we reject what Jesus did for us, we are unable to see the truth. This is right in line with 2 Corinthians 4:4: "The god of this age [Satan] has blinded the minds of unbelievers so that they cannot see the light of the gospel of the glory of Christ, who is the image of God." Does this then condemn all unbelievers? No. Only those who think themselves to be wise are actually blinded to true wisdom. Because we simply trust as a little child, God is exceedingly pleased to reveal the hidden mystery of the ages—that salvation is found in trusting in Jesus.

It's important not to let any person intimidate or belittle you when they come against the message of the cross. It's a tactic of the enemy meant to discourage us. We need to pray for them to begin seeking truth. They need our love no matter how they come against you and me. Only when they begin to embrace the light of the Gospel will they begin to see. They won't care what you know until they know that you care.

One day not too far from now, God is going to reveal everything, and everyone will see that which has been hidden. As the Apostle Paul put it in Colossians 3:2-4: "Set your minds on the things above, not on the things that are on earth. For you have died and your life is hidden with Christ in God. When Christ, who is our life, is revealed, then you also will be revealed with Him in glory."

WHAT DOES IT MEAN TO FEAR GOD?

We are told throughout God's Word that we need to fear God, and many people do not understand what that means. Are we supposed to be afraid of God? Isn't God our father, who we can go to without any fear or shame? How are we supposed to fear God and at the same time run into His arms?

Many churches today promote God's love, forgiveness, and acceptance, which are wonderful and primary, but to truly appreciate all that He is and His intrinsic awesomeness in the first place, we need to fear Him as well.

I was brought up in a conservative church that promoted the fear of God so much that we never had any fun during church services. Few people ever smiled. This is the impression that many people have of church, that it is a complete downer. Because of this, churches of late have become more liberal in their services but have moved so far the other way that we neglect the reverential fear of God.

Truth be told, we need both. God is not averse to us having fun—He knows how to party righteous as the slang goes; He's the One who mandated all the festivals and celebrations of the Old Testament. But there are times His Spirit needs to minister and His proximity deserves our full appreciation. Think of it this way: if we had an audience with the Queen of England, we'd be coached on the appropriate protocol to be in her presence. Yet, we often have an audience with the King of Kings and disrespect Him by our conduct when He is speaking to us. The best definition I've heard of what it means to fear God is this:

To fear God is to have a wholesome dread of displeasing Him.

When I first heard this, I thought, "I'm supposed to dread God?" How can dread be wholesome? But that is not correct; I am supposed to dread *displeasing* Him. We should love and respect Him so much that we dread even the thought of doing anything that would affect His pleasure with us. I see an imbalance in the body of Christ in this regard. We focus on God's forgiveness and love, but don't give it the proper place it should have. Human nature tends to treat cheaply that which is free. Since forgiveness is a gift and cannot be earned, we tend to treat God's forgiveness like a free pass, instead of placing it next to what it cost our Father and His Son.

In our services, we cry out to God for His Holy Spirit to come amidst us, and we reverentially bow our heads as we wait on Him. People respond and come forward to receive ministry from the Holy Spirit. As the service winds down, however, in the place that the Holy Spirit is still ministering, people begin talking, children begin running around, and the sounds of movement escalate. This does not sit right in my spirit. I know that it's unintentional and this is why

> I don't want to hear people chatting and laughing behind me while I'm bleeding at the altar. Do you?

we need to learn this, but I am grieved in my heart at the irreverent posture of people towards the presence of the Holy Spirit. It's an insult to Him. If you disagree, just look throughout God's Word and how He required them to approach Him. The Old Testament particularly had a clear method for how to approach Him. In the book of Acts, chapter 5, Ananias and Sapphira fell down dead on the spot for daring to lie to the Holy Spirit. Acts 5:11 says, "Great fear seized the whole church and all who heard about these events." Again, this fear was not a lack of faith, but the "wholesome dread of displeasing God." And this was the New Testament Church, not a smoking mountain on fire with the presence of God as He showed Himself in the Old Testament!

It's true Jesus came so we might come boldly to the throne of grace to find help in our time of need, but coming boldly doesn't mean irreverently. I've heard people say, "Yes, I understand that, but how do you keep a five year old quiet?" I'd like to answer this with another question: "How is a child going to learn to appreciate the reverential fear of God unless it is displayed and taught?"

There is a time for jubilation, noise, dancing, singing, and shouting in the house of God. But there is also a time of quiet introspection as His damaged, hurting children come to Him, weeping, broken, and needy. We just need to respect both the people who are humble enough to come forward, as well as the One ministering to them.

We are blessed to stand, pray, revel, and rejoice in the atmosphere of God's presence. I hope that these thoughts cause us to ponder what it means for us to truly fear God without our efforts deteriorating into a legalistic chore we have to perform. We will never fear God without the proper attitude in our hearts. Both Psalm 111:10 and Proverbs 9:10 state, "The fear of the Lord is the beginning of wisdom." Let us begin to be wise on this foundation.

CHAPTER 3
What God Will Do

GOD WILL DELIVER!

When God has promised us something, how can we proceed without evidence that it is on its way? This is when our faith is put to the test. The pressure mounts to let go of our faith and make things happen in our own way and timetable. Let's say you're waiting for God to bring your soulmate into your life, and you've been waiting for a long time. What if the path that God is choosing to lead you on in the meantime is hard? Waiting is important, but so is how we wait. In fact, what we do while waiting can have a huge bearing on the promise itself. God always has a reason for making us wait. He's getting us ready.

God will see us through the waiting process if we let Him lead. We see a good example of this in Genesis 12. God promised to make Abraham into a great nation and to give the land of Israel to his offspring in verse 7 and again in 13:15. He was seventy-five years old at the time. Abraham went on his way, and God appears to him in Chapter 15: 4, 5 and tells him again that not only will he have an heir, but that his offspring would be as numerous as the stars. After a considerable amount of time had passed, Abraham explains to God, "You have given me no children, so a servant in my household will be my heir." God responds and says that a son will come from Abraham's own body. His response to this is one of the most important verses in the Bible, Genesis 15:6: "Abraham believed the Lord." If you were Abraham, wouldn't you be elated that the fulfilment of the promise was coming? I would be.

Time passes, and they still have no child. Abraham is now eighty-six and decides that although he believes God fully, he needs to give Him a helping hand. He listens to his wife and takes her servant Hagar to be his wife. He has a son with her, to be credited to Sarah. This was a huge detour from God's plan and had monumental consequences on the nation of Israel, which continue to this day. Her son,

Ishmael, becomes the father of the Arabs, who also claim Abraham as their father, as well as Isaac and the Jews, thereby both claiming historical rights to the land of Israel. At the age of ninety-nine, twenty-four years after the promise was given, Sarah and Abraham have the promised son, Isaac.

Let's pause for a moment. Do you think Abraham thought it would happen this way? Not likely. I believe that God was teaching Abraham about Himself, His ways, and His expectations, to see if Abraham would hold on to his faith in those years. It was a long time to wait, and they made mistakes along the way too. There's hope for all of us.

> Waiting is important, but so is how we wait.

What obstacles do we face? In our instant-gratification society, we're often impatient and don't want to wait. We say, "If I have to go through it the hard way, I don't want to go through it at all." We cast down our faith and decide God doesn't know what He's doing, or we believe that He's not doing anything. Or, "I know what's best for me better than God does." Or perhaps we try to help God out like Abraham did. None of these mindsets honour God or His intentions. We need to fully understand something We are going to have to go through the challenges of waiting for things one of three ways:

1. Without God
2. With God but kicking, crying, or pouting all the way
3. Cooperating with God with Him in the driver's seat.

To gain perspective, think of it this way:

A: We can go through life with the Creator of the universe at the helm, who sees the beginning from the end and only has the best planned for us,

B: We can walk alone in charge as one who sees only from the beginning of our lives until the present in our own limited perception and knowledge.

Why would anyone choose B? Yet people do, until they realize how much harder that way is outside of God's leadership. If you're waiting for God to deliver your soulmate, it helps to remember that there are worse things than being single—being married to the wrong person, for one. Ishmael seemed like the promised heir, but in the end, wasn't Isaac. Abraham believed God. It was settled at that moment, even though he fell down in conduct sometimes. If we choose to believe God, we must act accordingly and let our lives reflect the fact that it has been settled. Trust and obedience is what God expects. We need to do what God tells us to do, when He tells us to do it, how He tells us to do it, until He tells us not to do it anymore. Lord, help us to walk this out, day by day, until your perfect plan for us is accomplished.

"PERHAPS THE LORD WILL ACT"

This is the stuff movies are made from, written ages before *The Lord of the Rings*. Huge insurmountable odds face our hero against the forces of evil, and we are faced with wondering how he will win the battle. It's a core theme and has universal appeal. It's so exciting to me that God's Word has so many accounts that reflect this theme, but far from being a screenplay for a movie, they are based in fact and actually happened. One of my favourite accounts in the Bible, which shows a wonderful example of our hero conquering seemingly insurmountable odds, is in 1 Samuel 13–14. I love this. An ill-equipped Israelite army of six hundred is facing a Philistine force of "3000 chariots, 6000 charioteers, and soldiers as numerous as the sand on the seashore." Their situation was critical, and the soldiers were hiding in caves, thickets, among the rocks, and in pits and cisterns. Sounds just like a movie, doesn't it? They were terrified!

But not Jonathan—King Saul's son and David's best friend. This account is a testament to the fact that one man with God can make all the difference. This is how he went about it, and I believe his method is also valid today when we are faced with enemies. They may not be a garrison of soldiers, but we face serious opposition by our invisible enemy nonetheless.

Imagine a valley with cliffs on either side. The outpost of the enemy is on top of the opposite cliff to where you are. Jonathan, our hero, decides to ask his young armour-bearer to go with him to check out the enemy. He says in 1 Samuel 14:6: "Perhaps the Lord will act on our behalf. Nothing can hinder the Lord from saving, whether by many or by few."

There is a world of faith in his words. God had not previously told him what would transpire like Abraham. What he said was an overflow of what was already in his heart. Notice he says "perhaps." He isn't even sure God will move at this time. In other words, if God didn't act on their behalf, he would still be okay with that. He then shows an attitude of faith by saying that if God were to act, nothing could get in his way. Jonathan already had a solid vision of the bigger picture. He faced an outpost, but Israel faced a multitude. Remember the odds?

I love this next part. His friend tells him in verse 7, "Do all that you have in mind. Go ahead; I am with you, heart and soul." It's so important to have the solid support of a loyal and close friend when we face obstacles. It warms my heart that God provided firm support for royalty going into battle. I believe He does no less for us. This soldier was, in essence, telling Jonathan he would die with him, if need be. Jonathan responds in verse 8: "Come, then; [since you are with me] we will cross over toward the men and let them see us. If they say to us, 'Wait there until we come to you,' we will stay where we are and not go up to them. But if they say, 'Come up to us,' we will climb up, because that will be our sign that the Lord has given them into our hands."

Notice how Jonathan gave God room to move and confirm His will in that situation. His statements contain two ifs. Remember, he isn't sure what's going to happen. They're still safe if they're seen from a distance. He's walking cautiously and not recklessly bulldozing ahead of God. Jonathan and his friend show themselves to the enemy, and the Philistines challenge them to "Come up to us and we'll teach you a lesson."

What would you and I be thinking if someone desiring to cut off our heads said that to us? It would be my cue to turn and run and avoid that lesson! What a sign! The enemy held the advantage of higher ground. If it were me, I would be seriously re-thinking my sign. Not Jonathan, however. He doesn't stop to negotiate how he feels about the situation. He says to his friend, "Climb up after me; the Lord has given them into the hand of Israel." He acts on his faith, climbs up with his friend right behind him, and they kill twenty men. What happens next is extremely noteworthy. God was waiting for someone to initiate the battle. Verse 15 says, "Then panic struck the whole army—those in the camp and field...in the outposts and raiding parties—and the ground shook. It was a panic sent by God." My guess is that it was an earthquake of sorts. The rest of the Israelite army comes out of hiding upon seeing the Philistines in "total confusion" slaughtering one another, and finishes the campaign.

Remember, six hundred men were initially facing a multitude, and all it took was two men and God to begin a miraculous deliverance. How did they do it? How are we to do it?

- They didn't go and hide in fear, but had faith God could save them.
- They started out small and said, "It doesn't hurt to look!"
- They considered that maybe God might use them here—nothing can stop God, after all.
- They stepped out and tested the ground by asking God to direct the way.
- They got the response, didn't talk themselves out of it, and went for it.
- God did all the rest.

How many situations could we apply this method to? What army are you facing today? Perhaps it's a big decision to move. Perhaps it's a financial problem. Perhaps it's dealing with kids, parents, or spouse. Perhaps it's a work-related issue.

We'll never know where and how God is going to provide salvation until we try. Jonathan saw in his spirit the result he wanted, but only did what was possible with his own hands, accompanied by a friend and God. God knew what He had to work with then, and He still does now. He didn't start with those that were hiding, but with those who stepped out in faith. What has God put in your hand to do?

WE DON'T KNOW WHAT TO DO, BUT OUR EYES ARE ON YOU

Do you ever find yourself in a jam where you simply don't know what to do? When there simply doesn't appear to be an avenue out of the problem? Many people don't realize it, but the Bible is full of true war accounts that are relevant to us today, both literally and figuratively. Although most of us may not be directly involved in a war, we deal primarily with the battlefield of the mind. The Bible's accounts give us many examples of what to do when we're faced with a seemingly overwhelming enemy, particularly when we're emotionally, physically, mentally, and spiritually weakened.

Although I do not necessarily agree with the philosophy of German philosopher Friedrich Nietzche, he did come up with a quote that is widely used today: "That which does not kill us makes us stronger." This is true, in essence. We are God's precious children, but He sometimes allows difficult things to pass through our lives, to burn the dross from the silver, so to speak, to therefore redefine us. I love the phrase, "The silversmith knows that the silver is completely pure when he can see his reflection in it." When Jesus looks into the smelting pot of your life, does He see your reflection or His? When people look at us and see Jesus, even though we're in the middle of going through a trial, we have allowed Him to burn the garbage away.

This is where the Israelites found themselves. In 2 Chronicles 20, they were again faced with war. They felt helpless, as we all have felt at times. Jehoshaphat, their king, cries out to God in 20:12: "O our God...we have no power to face this vast army that is attacking us. We do not know what to do, but our eyes are upon you." This was the key to their deliverance and ultimately ours, as well. They decided to rely on God and keep their focus upon Him and not their circumstances.

This account is included in the Bible specifically for you and me and is very significant. We need to do what they did. Let's break 2 Chronicles 20 down:

- Cry out to God, acknowledging our total dependence on Him, making up our mind to keep our focus on Him, and not the problem (verse 12).
- They were told, "Don't be afraid; don't be discouraged" (verse 15). We have to differentiate between *feeling* fear and discouragement and *being* afraid and discouraged. You can still operate in faith and take courage, even when you feel fear and discouragement. Take your position of faith, "and you will be upheld" and make up your mind to stand firm (verse 17, 20).
- Why can we operate in confidence and courage? "For the battle is not yours, but God's." v15. We're not the ones fighting. In saying this, we must remember that this is not a licence to do nothing. God does not expect us to do the things we cannot do, but He does expect us to do the things He tells us to.

- Stand firmly where you are. Wait patiently and watch for God's deliverance to take place (verse 17).
- Why be bored while you wait for God to deliver you? Don't give the enemy an opportunity to distract you with doubtful thoughts. Praise and worship Him for who He is, and for His love even before the battle has ended (verse 21). This puts you on the offensive in the battle in your mind, will, and emotions.

When we begin to focus on thanking God even before we have the victory, we come up higher. I can't tell you how many times I've been consumed with the stuff going on in my life, feeling burdened and heavy, only to experience a weight falling off my heart as I chose to listen to worship music and begin to sing along with thankfulness that Jesus would come through. Just as darkness exits immediately when a light is turned on, the devil can't stand a Christian praising God. Remember too that darkness in itself has no power; it is simply the absence of light. When we bring the light in, darkness exits in a flash.

> An attitude of gratitude determines our altitude.

After the Israelites had done this, God responded to that cry and not only delivered them from this vast army, but abundantly blessed them. It took three days to collect all the spoils in the enemy's camp!

It's important to note that had they not relied on God the way they did, they wouldn't have obtained those results. Each step of obedience needed to be followed to reap the full harvest. So too with us. We can't be just a little full of faith and expect to receive the full rewards. We need to decide to be sold out and commit to trusting God, no matter what happens. The next time we don't know what to do, let's make the choice to follow the example that God put in His Word for us to follow and watch what happens. It's the reason it's in there!

ARE YOU IN HELL ON EARTH?

I want to offer some healing to those of us who have experienced deep losses. My heart goes out to my brothers and sisters who have lost something dear to them. Perhaps it is a loved one, a divorce, or the loss of a relationship. The Lord spoke to my heart and directed me to offer this encouraging word. There is life after death. There are two key things I want to impress upon you:

1. Nothing is impossible with God;
2. When you're going through hell, don't stop.

In the book of Ruth, there was a woman named Naomi who lost everything, including her husband and both her sons. She didn't even have enough to eat, so she decided to go back to her homeland. All she had going for her was the loyalty of her daughter-in-law, a foreigner named Ruth. In Jewish culture, having children and offspring meant everything for the women of that time. Much of a woman's worth was determined by how many sons and daughters she had borne. Naomi's life was destitute, and she blamed God by saying, "Don't call me 'Naomi' (pleasant), call me 'Mara' (bitter) because the Almighty has made my life very bitter. I went away full, but the Lord has brought me back empty…The Lord has afflicted me; the Almighty has brought misfortune upon me."

She had no husband, no offspring to carry on the family name and historical property, no means to support herself, and no self-worth. Does this strike a chord in you? Just as hell was never intended for humankind after death, so too hell on earth was not intended by God for His children. What is hell? An existence where God's presence isn't. We feel alone and abandoned by God. Does God know how we feel? Beyond a shadow of a doubt, *yes*. Jesus experienced separation from His Father when God abandoned Him at the cross: "My God, my God, why have you forsaken me?" God shook the earth through His pain. Jesus was completely alone and abandoned, but not for long! He paid that price, so we'd never have to. You are not alone in your suffering, and God has not fallen asleep at the wheel.

Naomi also did not feel abandoned by God for long. Although there was no hope for her in the natural, God began to move in her circumstances. Ruth, her widowed daughter-in-law, went to the field of a man named Boaz to glean the leftover grain after the harvesters in order to find food for them to eat. She casually mentions where she gathered, and God prompts Naomi to recall that Boaz is distantly related to them. Through a series of God-directed events, Ruth ends up marrying Boaz, who honourably agrees to carry on Naomi's husband's family name and property. Naomi ends up holding her grandson in her lap. What happened to her circumstances? They were impossible to rectify, right? God had once again filled her life to the full.

What was God's plan in all of this? God is all about generations and legacy. Naomi is the great-great-grandmother of King David, the greatest King Israel ever had, a man after God's own heart. Who do you think taught David to love God? Most likely his mother, who heard the account of God's faithfulness passed down from generation to generation as was their custom. Ruth, a foreigner, who made the decision "Your people will be my people, and your God will be my God" because of Naomi's example, became David's great grandmother. We can assume from this account that God used all these reversals to accomplish His will not only for her, but the future of His people.

When all is gone, what are you left with? God! What would have happened if Naomi had stopped in the hellish place on earth that she found herself? She would have missed the supernatural intervention of God. There is always something or someone waiting on the other side of your obedience—maybe even for you yourself. If you're feeding off the table of mourning, it's time for you to get up. When you're going through hell, don't stop. Weeping may remain for the night, but joy comes in the morning. Whatever you've lost, God will bring restoration, and He won't leave you in despair. Just like He didn't abandon Christ to the grave, He won't abandon you to hell on Earth, either. He is the One who has made beauty from ashes for millions of people and He will do the same for you.

THERE'S ALWAYS HOPE, EVEN IN EXILE

Exile. By definition, it is: "Unwilling absence from a home country or place of residence, whether enforced by a government or court as a punishment, or self-imposed for political reasons; a citizen of one country who is forced or chooses to live in another." Encarta's Dictionary give this as a first definition under the word Exile: "Same as Babylonian captivity." Since my reference is the book of Jeremiah and spins off of the Jews in Babylonian exile, this is very appropriate indeed!

What happens when our children go through a season of continually disobeying us? The first time your son directly disobeys your instruction, you let him off with a warning. The next time, a time-out may be issued. If he continues to disobey, serious action and account-ability may need to be exacted. Human nature is not naturally obedi-ent. We test our boundaries to see how strong they are and see what will happen if we go beyond them. When our children have grown up, and they live a life that is not honouring God, the time for dis-cipline and time-outs has passed. As they are now adults, we can't make them live the way we know is right; we can't impose our will over theirs. We can give input if it's welcome, but we can't order them around. As Christian parents, we embrace the next role, which is to pray for them because they now answer to their Heavenly Father.

God is much the same with us. When we as Christians choose to live outside of His will, He lets us. He will exert pressure, speak to our hearts, and speak through people and His Word, trying and doing everything to change our minds, but He will not stop us. However, disobeying God comes with a hefty price tag that we bring on our-selves. Sin is pleasurable for a season, but the full consequence of it often manifests itself later.

Many people are in a place of self-imposed exile, far from the heart of God. If you're driving somewhere and take one wrong turn, chances are you can easily get back on the right road. If you've taken sixteen wrong turns, you become lost, and it may take a long time to get back onto the right road. Such is the case when we continually disobey God.

The book of Jeremiah gives us a powerful application of *hope* for those who are currently in this place due to the consequences of their sins. The first twenty-nine chapters give warning after warning from God, and finally, God's judgement fell on the disobedient Israelites in the form of exile to Babylon for seventy years. He didn't want to do it, but they insisted on continuing with their idolatry. But here's the great news: After they realized their sin, even while they were there, God said in Jeremiah 29:11–14:

"For I know the plans I have for you … plans to prosper you and not to harm you, plans to give you hope and a future. Then you will call upon me and come and pray to me, and I will listen to you. You will seek me and find me when you seek me with all your heart. I will be found by you, declares the Lord."

We may have to spend time in our place of exile as we wait for God to turn this thing around, now that we've put Him back in the driver's seat. God always has a plan, even though we've royally messed up what He intended for us. It is a testament to His incredible restorative power and love. There are scores of examples not only in His Word, but also in the lives of many around us. Just talk to someone who is passionate about God, and they'll tell you how He restored to them the essence of what they thought they'd lost. The truth is we all will have times in our lives when we're in exile because we didn't go God's way, but ours. The beautiful thing about the Israelites' situation was that it says that God carried them into exile, like the tender Father that He is. God carries us there too. He does not enjoy disciplining us any more than we enjoy disciplining our children. He doesn't ever leave us.

Despite all the wrong turns Israel took to get there, God still had a plan for hope and a future for His children. No matter where your feet have taken you, God can bring you back to a new plan and purpose.

CHAPTER 4
The Truth About God and His Word

LIE BUSTERS ABOUT GOD

I recently ran across seven lies that the enemy tries to use on us to get us off track. If he can get us to believe his lies, our actions will follow suit, because where the mind goes, the body follows. It's so important for us to recognize them so we can counteract them with the truth of God. He desires that His truth be established within us. All of God's truth won't do us any good unless we believe it, accept it, and act on it. His truth can be likened to a protective wall that guards our hearts and provides an environment where our souls (mind, will, and emotions) can be nurtured, and our faith can grow.

Whenever we allow one of Satan's lies to enter our hearts, we create a breach in truth's protective wall. For many years, what I'll call the wall of truth surrounding my heart had many cracks. God's Word said that I could cast all my care on Him because He cared for me (1 Peter 5:7) and I believed that, but I was afraid to put the full weight of my trust in that God would handle my problems. I would trust God, then the enemy would bring pressure to doubt, and I'd cave to it.

As long as the breach remains, our hearts will be flooded with doubts, fears, and condemning thoughts that God never intended us to dwell upon—thoughts that will rob us of our peace and steal our joy. Here are seven lies that can breach God's protective wall of truth within you:

1. God can't be trusted. So many people have had crushing disappointments that have wounded them and left scars. These could have come from a parent, a husband or wife, a child, close friend, or any number of others. This creates a wariness in us because we feel that person can't be trusted to not do it again. We withdraw and build a protective wall around ourselves. We set our expectations low to avoid more disappointment. This can make it hard to trust God with our whole life, especially if the person that has hurt us is a father figure. People that have been deeply hurt by their dad often find it hard to trust their Heavenly Father, as their only point of reference is the one they have on earth. We come to Him with reservations because we're afraid He'll disappoint us too.

The truth is: God is forever faithful.

1 Corinthians 1:9 says, "God is faithful [reliable, trustworthy, and therefore ever true to His promise, and He can be depended on]; through Him you were called into companionship and participation with His Son, Jesus Christ our Lord."

As the verse says, God Himself can always be trusted. Even when we are faithless and doubting Him, He will remain faithful, because He simply can do no less. Everything that God Himself allows in our life is for our ultimate good, even if it means going through some hard things. He can be completely trusted, and there is great comfort in knowing that when our character is being refined by hard times, we are not alone. He is aware of what we're going through. However you are being tempted to cave in, God will not allow you to be tested beyond your ability to resist.

1 Corinthians 10:13, Message Bible (MSG), says, "No test or temptation that comes your way is beyond the course of what others have had to face. All you need to remember is that God will never let you down; he'll never let you be pushed past your limit; he'll always be there to help you come through it."

2. God is against me. Many people think that when they make a mistake of any kind that God is mad and going to retaliate with vengeance. This is dangerous thinking, because as flawed human beings, we sin every day! What often happens next is that we let go of doing the right thing because "God is mad at me, I'm going to get it anyways, so I may as well just give in and sin."

The truth is: God is always for you, cheering you on.

Here's a cataclysmic perception alterer (or CPA): God is not mad at you. God may be against some of your plans that He knows won't be good for you, or against sin that you are involved in, but He is always for you, desiring the very best for you, no matter what. He loves you because you are His child, not because of your behaviour. Even when we fall down, we need to rush back into His loving arms, not run away. He'll clean us up and give us a fresh start as many times as needed, until we have victory.

3. I am not good enough to be blessed. If we say this, we are measuring our self-worth and reward based on an action-oriented belief system, not the finished work of the Cross. We will constantly feel like we are falling short, beating ourselves up and living under a continual stream of self-condemnation. We simply aren't and never will be good enough. Isaiah 64:6 says, "All of us have become like one who is unclean, and all our righteous acts are like filthy rags." What He was saying is that all our efforts to be good enough by our own merit simply don't measure up.

The truth is: Christ is your righteousness, and you have been given every spiritual and natural blessing, in Him.

"That makes it quite clear that none of you can get by with blowing your own horn before God. Everything that we have—right thinking and right living, a clean slate and a fresh start—comes from God by way of [in] Jesus Christ" (1 Cor 1:30 MSG). "In Him" is the key here. It is only "in Christ" that we have access to all blessings. The moment a person is in Christ, he or she becomes the possessor of them all. It is to partake of all that Christ has done, all that He is, and all that He ever will be. What a promise!

4. God cares about others more than He cares about me. In seeing the blessings God gives others when we are in a season of trial, it's easy to think this. However, you didn't see that person go through their own lengthy trial to arrive at a time of fruitful blessings.

The truth is: God does not show favouritism.

God created everyone to be His child, and He does not love one more than another. That would make Him biased, and our God is utterly fair, just, and loving. Remember that we are all in a different place in the journey. There have been times in my life that I have struggled in a valley with what God needed to teach me, and other times that I've been on the mountaintop. What God will do for me, He will do for you, given that it falls within His plan for our lives.

5. God really doesn't love me. Pardon my bluntness, but this sounds like someone feeling sorry for themselves. If you're a Christian, you probably already know John 3:16: "For God so loved the world that He gave His one and only Son, that whoever believes in Him shall not perish, but have eternal life." You've based your salvation on it. If God really doesn't love you, Jesus' sacrifice was wasted. If we embrace this lie, we just want a licence to sin and feel sorry for ourselves. "God really doesn't love me, so I'm going to do whatever I want. He owes me." Nothing could be further from this truth:

God loves you with an everlasting love.

Always remember: There is absolutely nothing you can do to make God love you any more than He does right now. There is also absolutely nothing you can do to make God love you any less than He does right now. We grieve Him terribly with our sinful ways and rebellion, but He is so in love with His children that He died for us, even while we were still sinners.

6. My situation is hopeless. This is a powerful lie that can cause us to give up. If you're reading this and you identify, I want to encourage you. I cannot tell you how many accounts I've heard and read that were seemingly hopeless that when handed over to God, He made a way where there was no way. I always think of Moses when he was leading the Israelites out of Egypt and was faced with the Red Sea in front of him and Pharaoh's Egyptian army behind him ready to kill them all. Drown or die were their earthly choices. Then God performed one of the most well-known miracles when He parted the Red Sea and they walked through on dry ground; He also did away with their enemies once and for all. If God needs to part a sea to get His children through, He will do it. Is our situation that impossible?

With God, nothing is impossible.

Matthew 19:26 says, "Jesus looked at them and said, 'With man [people] this is impossible, but with God all things are possible.'"

Although our situations sometimes look utterly hopeless and impossible, there are two words that we should never forget: "But, God."

"But God intervened; but God provided; but God changed his attitude; but God melted her heart; but God saved them; but God carried her through; but God healed him; but God showed himself strong; but God performed a miracle; but God turned the thing around; but God changed her heart; but God got hold of them; but God sent people to intervene." The list is endless. However, there is one thing that is impossible for God to do:

It is impossible for God to fail.

7. Things will never change. When we've been waiting for a long time for things in our lives to change, it's sometimes hard not to think this. This is when the pressure of waiting can get to us. It appears that our prayers don't go farther than the ceiling and God is silent. This is when we're tempted to give up and, sadly, many people do, even on the eve of their deliverance. If we could only see that God is not asleep at the switch and that He is working behind the scenes despite the lack of action we see, we'd be satisfied, right? Wrong. We need to stay in faith for our situation, no matter what.

The truth is: Everything is subject to change, except God.

Whether or not our situation changes, or God changes us in the situation, change will happen, one way or the other. We need to believe our beliefs, and doubt our doubts, not believe our doubts and doubt our beliefs. We need to say, "God, You said it, I believe it, and that settles it!" I have often had to confess this when all else looked to be failing. Whether it was finances or personal relationships, looking at the natural had the potential to take the wind out of my sails. Making the decision to believe, especially when we don't feel like it, is where we need to park ourselves.

Our circumstances can change around us as God brings us closer to His ultimate purpose. His ways and thoughts are higher than ours (Isa 55:9), and so we need to trust in Him.

God can be trusted, God is faithful, God is for you, Christ is your righteousness, and God has blessed you with every spiritual and natural blessing, God does not show favouritism, God loves you with an everlasting love, and with God, nothing is impossible. Everything is subject to change—except God.

With truths like these, how can we lose?

If you have allowed the enemy's lies to breach your wall of truth, begin to rebuild it today. Reject the lie and start dropping the sandbags of God's promises into that breach. Soon, there will be no opening left for the enemy's lies to impact your life. Receive the Lord's cleansing, and allow the blood of Jesus to wash away all the pollution that the lie has brought into your life. As the blood washes you, the peace of God and the joy of the Lord will fill your heart once again.

THE VALIDITY OF THE BIBLE

Whether you are coming to or considering Christianity for the first time, or are looking for guidance as you reinforce and grow in your faith, it is important to understand who some question the validity of the Bible and establish its legitimacy once and for all.

There is simply not enough paper to fully convey just how trustworthy and compelling God's breathed Word is. The Bible, in essence, is comprised of two covenants between man and God—The Old Testament or Old Covenant, and the New Testament or New Covenant. The first written records were recorded on many different materials, such as pottery shards, papyrus, parchment, and clay. Tablets found by archaeologists were written in cuneiform script, and date from the second millennium BC. A page of a Gospel written in Aramaic (a Semitic language) was found in the Church of St. Thomas, Mosul, Iraq and thought to date from the eleventh century. Throughout the centuries, it has been a huge source of art and music, from Michelangelo's fresco on the ceiling of the Sistine Chapel in the Vatican, Rome, painted between 1508-12, to George Frideric Handel's *Messiah*, an oratorio composed in 1741 with a scriptural text taken from the King James Bible.

We are living in the new millennium, and the Bible—God's handbook for living—still resonates today, just as it did to someone living thousands of years ago. I personally use the New International Version

(NIV), but I reference other translations as well, such as the Living Bible, the Message, the Amplified, and the King James. For example, the Bible is:

1. One of the very first books ever printed in the fifteenth century;
2. The first mass-produced book ever printed;
3. Multi-lingual: at least one book of the Bible has been published in 1,808 languages;
4. The number one best seller of all time;
5. One book, and yet sixty-six separate books;
6. Written by forty authors over forty generations from many walks of life under the direct inspiration of the Holy Spirit (2 Peter 1:20–21);
7. Written over a period of fifteen hundred years on three continents (Asia, Europe, and Africa) from 1400 BC to AD 100, and in three languages (Hebrew, Aramaic, and Greek);
8. The source of over six hundred fulfilled prophecies, many of which are verifiable;
9. Not contradictory. This is important, because there are many items that appear to be contradictory, but which, in essence, are not.

Since the Bible is ancient, and multiple copies have been made throughout the centuries, how do we know they were copied correctly? Although the original Jewish Scriptures were copied by hand, they were extremely accurate from copy to copy. The Jews had a phenomenal system of scribes who developed intricate and ritualistic methods for counting letters, words, and paragraphs to ensure that no copying errors were made. These scribes dedicated their entire lives to preserving the accuracy of the holy books. A single copy error would require the immediate destruction of the entire scroll. They had such reverence for God and His Word that they required wiping their pens and washing their entire bodies before writing down His Name. Imagine how many times God's name occurs in the Old Testament.

The Jewish scribal tradition was maintained until the invention of the printing press in the fifteenth century. The discovery of the Dead Sea Scrolls has confirmed the remarkable reliability of this scribal system over thousands of years, making their discovery monumentally significant in validating the authenticity of Scripture as a response to critics who dispute the accuracy of copying down God's Word through the centuries.

No one can explain the unity of the Bible. How could dozens of different authors, who lived on three different continents with radically different vocations (including kings, peasants, prophets, priests, fishermen, shepherds, scholars, tax collectors, and statesmen) set apart by 1500 years, weave the story of God's love to maintain the thread of continuity so that it reads like it had one author? The answer is that it did have one Author: God. Consider this:

- The Word of God is the only book that has ever correctly predicted the future, and documented it. Half the time, the prophets never even saw the fullness of events they were predicting. Take for example a passage in the book of Ezekiel written around 580 BC. The prophet said that God would gather the people of Israel scattered throughout the world and bring them back to "their own land." After many centuries of dispersion, hundreds of thousands of Jews returned to their ancient homeland beginning in the late 1800s. But, millions more returned after Israel declared independence in 1948, when it became a sovereign Jewish state.

Ezekiel 34:13 says, "I will bring them out from the nations and gather them from the countries, and I will bring them into their own land. I will pasture them on the mountains of Israel, in the ravines and in all the settlements in the land."

There were many that once looked at that passage who simply did not see how that prophecy could every come true, yet after WWII, it happened. Prophecies continue to be fulfilled despite criticism from sceptics. One simply can't argue with events that clearly occur and fulfil what a prophet predicted hundreds of years previous. If you study Revelation and end-time events, it's fascinating to hear John describe modern warfare with the vocabulary of a first-century apostle when he wrote it around AD 95!

- The Bible is indestructible. Throughout the centuries, this Word has been attacked, burned, and people have tried to destroy it, to no avail. The Bible remains the most widely talked about, sought after, and disputed book in the world.
- The Bible has affected the entire world, regardless of culture and language. The message translates well, as it is a universal message.

- I believe the Bible to be true and in a way I cannot explain, God's Words are containers for power. When the 10 Commandments, including "Thou Shalt Not Kill" were taken off of our school walls along with banning the Bible, Ann Graham Lotz (Billy Graham's daughter) was challenged to answer this question: "If God is such a loving God, how could He allow our children to kill each other in our schools?" She responded along the lines of this: "In 1963, the Bible was taken out of schools, and taken away from children. In essence, God was asked to leave. Being the perfect gentleman that He is, He complied. What happened in our schools next? Our schools replaced it with drugs, alcohol, sex, guns, murder, and fear." This is fact. It has happened.

Today, there are many translations of the Bible. However, a translation is not a new version of God's Word. It doesn't change the original heart and intent of the text, but merely makes it understandable for today's reader. Each uses different wording so that it can be understood and read by everyone. The first hand-written English Bible was produced in the 1380s AD by John Wycliffe, an Oxford professor, scholar, and theologian who translated it from Latin into English so the common people could read and determine what it says for themselves. People such as John Hus, one of Wycliffe's followers, paid dearly to help God's children understand His Word. He advocated that people should be permitted to read the Bible in their own language, and was burned at the stake in 1415 with Wycliffe's Bibles used as kindling for the fire. His last words were, "In a hundred years, God will raise up a man whose calls for reform cannot be suppressed." Almost exactly a century later, in 1517, Marin Luther came to prominence and went on to become the first person to translate and publish the Bible in the commonly spoken dialect of the German people.

The Bible has inexhaustible depth and is accompanied by the inner witness of the Holy Spirit. How else could one study it for a lifetime and not grow weary of it? The Holy Spirit accompanies and guides true seekers, and brings incredible life and relevancy to Scripture that bears witness in our hearts. If people go out with the express purpose to disqualify God's Word, He hides His truths from them because they seek only to discredit Him. God's revealed Word is a precious gift He gives to those who are searching. Sight rejected is sight denied. If we are closed and do not want to see, we won't. I speak more about this in the chapter "The World's Wisdom, Where is It?" Scripture that we've read many times before with no impact literally comes alive as our eyes are opened to a deeper or fresher meaning, bringing valid instruction and comfort to the problem we're facing. Many times, God's word is not a new word, but a now word.

We must remember that many people have died to place this book in our hands. That alone is a testimony to its incredible importance. What are you willing to die for? Where do you place its priority? We need to read it, meditate on it, believe it, act on it, and share it. The most valuable thing we own is our Bible.

What Love!

As I was reading Luke chapter 23 the other day, a thought jumped out and hit me like a velvet brick in the head. This is the account of Jesus' crucifixion, and as He hangs there in excruciating agony, He implores the Father in verse 34: "Father, forgive them, for they do not know what they are doing." I have always read that and pondered how great Jesus' love must have been for those who had just crucified Him. Do you think God forgave them? What do you think was happening with God the Father of His only begotten Son at that moment?

Jesus never said anything just for effect. He always meant everything He said.

God the Father would have had to have forgiven them, because there was His Son dying on a cross for them. To not forgive them for this act would have meant Jesus' death was ineffective. Whether or not they *received* His forgiveness and Christ's sacrifice for this sin, only God knows. The *Believer's Bible Commentary* by William MacDonald states, "Who knows what a Niagara of divine wrath was averted by this prayer!" Imagine if you will what you as a parent watching your child die a torturous death would be feeling towards those who carried this out.

The Bible says that when we are in Heaven, we will experience no more tears, pain, sorrow, or grief. Not so with God. We are told all throughout the Word that God in Heaven has emotions like anger, grief, sorrow, and pain. It's safe to assume that God the Father was experiencing emotions and feelings on an unfathomable scale. In Luke 23:45, Luke says that "the sun stopped shining." We tend to adopt the movie version and envision clouds covering the sun, but this isn't what the Bible says. It says that God didn't just lower the lights, He shut them off to let us know a little of what was going on with Him.

As we once again ponder this amazing love Jesus has for us, we need to fully realize that we have something in common with the crucifiers. Although they were the agents through whom Christ was physically crucified, it was our sins that put Him there. It is indeed a revered moment when the full implications of just how much He loves us, sinks into our consciousness. May this bring you to a fresh depth of gratitude. He died for you, for me, and for them.

CHAPTER 5
How to Find Jesus

JESUS, DID I FIND YOU, OR DID YOU FIND ME?

One of my core values that always warms my heart is that we serve a living God who actually desires to be in an intimate relationship with us. I don't have the capacity to fully appreciate how astounding this really is. Do you want to truly find God? Do you want to encounter and experience Him? Do you want to sense Him? When the Lord showed me this truth, the tears flowed, and I had no words. Do you know why we need to seek God with all of our hearts?

Because He will be found by us!

"You shall seek me, and you shall find me, if you shall seek me, with all your heart. And I will be found by you, declares the Lord" (Jer 29:13–14).

If you want to find Him, look for Him as a lifestyle with all that you are. He promises to be found by us, and you will know it when it happens.

It is our responsibility to do the looking and seeking. People may feel that God is being elusive, but that's not it at all. He is simply so worthy that we need to be seriously dedicated in finding Him. If you are not dedicated to finding Him, don't bother trying.

We need an intimate walk with Jesus to encounter Him, sense Him, and know in your heart of hearts that He is walking right beside you, directing your steps at all times. Finding Him in every situation is the fuel that keeps us going. He desires to reveal Himself, and so He came to us wrapped in frail humanity, entrusted to a thirteen-year-old virgin and her young husband for the express purpose of dying for us.

At Christmas, we sing, "Come let us adore Him." Do we know what that means? Make the decision to sell out to your Lord with no holds barred, and you'll never look back. The Christian life God intended for us does not consist of ritual do's and don'ts that are dreary to fulfil, but seeking our Lord has to be a lifestyle to be effective. One day, we will see Him face to face, and He won't be a stranger for we will already know Him.

JESUS, ARE YOU AWARE OF MY STORM?

Do you ever feel like you're in the middle of a storm? That your "lifeboat" is being whipped by the waves? Everything that you rely on to save you is moving and doesn't exactly feel secure. What situation have you faced that has left you feeling this way? Your panic is real, and you wonder, "Lord, where are you? Do you know what is going on here?" We can all identify with situations that cause us to worry, fret, and fear. They are the opposite of what we should be cultivating: trust, peace, and faith. Have you ever been a professional worrier? I have. The choice is ours. You might say that you can't help it, but you can. As you grow in trusting God, you'll get better and quicker at it.

In Mark 4:36–40, we see a wonderful account of the reality of the presence of Jesus in the midst of a storm. A "furious squall" came up, with waves breaking over the boat so that it was nearly swamped. Jesus was fast asleep on a cushion when the disciples asked, "Teacher, don't you care if we drown?" His response is a mild rebuke for them, and for us: "Why are you so afraid? Do you still have no faith?" I've often needed this rebuke. He questioned their fear; He didn't validate it.

We can sympathize with the disciples because they could see that Jesus was asleep, but we can truly rejoice today, because He promised to be with us at all times regardless of what is happening.

It's amazing how clearly we can see things after the storm has passed, but the challenge is to remember who is in the boat with us. Fear is faith in the enemy. You are more afraid then of what Satan can do than in what God can do. Satan derives pleasure from our fear. Deny him that! Deny him his pleasure! Choose to trust and have faith.

Jesus cares more about our suffering than we can imagine because He knows what it feels like. He is the Author of all peace, and He has given it to us. The only ones who won't experience this peace are those who don't believe or know Him. Faith is required either way. He knew that His life was in the hands of His Father, and this reality superseded everything that could threaten His well-being.

Wherever God leads us, His provision goes ahead of us. God is not taken by surprise like we are. He has already planned our deliverance.

It is not what God is going to do for you that will see you through, but that His presence is with you to see you through.

GOD, I'M GETTING TIRED OF HOLDING ON

Do you ever feel beat up by the world? That at every turn there seems to be another thing happening to discourage you from obeying Jesus and living a life that honours Him? Are you in a season of going through a refining fire? I liken it to feeling pummelled by the world. I haven't been knocked out, just beat up. At times like these, it seems easier to simply give in to the enemy, but that won't solve anything. That road will lead you to places that are even more difficult. You will find if you give up and backslide and try to go around the mountain in front of you instead of over it, that you'll end up in the very same place. In fact, you'll end up in a rut, and you know what that is: a grave with the ends kicked out. So you may as well resign yourself to the task at hand, and with God's help, climb that mountain.

What we often fail to realize is that the journey is as important to God as actually getting the victory when we arrive at the top. We want deliverance, but God is far more interested in our character growth than our comfort level. When I'm discouraged, I often let the Psalms minister to me. That's what they're there for. God knew we'd feel this way, so He recorded them for us to draw comfort from. There were many times David felt pummelled by being pursued by his enemies and his own father-in-law, King Saul, who wanted to kill him, yet it was in these awful places that God was preparing him to be king over Israel. He was getting him ready to reign. We may not be headed for an earthly throne, but

> You'll end up in a rut, and you know what that is: a grave with the ends kicked out...

God is preparing us for something. Just look at how David laments and praises God at the same time. You can just see him wrestle with his own mind in Psalms 56 and 57:

"Help me God, for men hotly pursue me and attack me all day long...but when I am afraid, I will trust in you and your Word; after all, what really can mortal man do to me? Bring them down, God! List my tears on your scroll, because my enemies will turn back when I call for help...I cry out to you, for you will fulfil your purpose for me! Be exalted, O God, above the heavens and let your glory be over all the earth! They set a trap for me, I was in deep distress, but they've fallen into it. My heart is steadfast. I will give myself a mental shake and wake up my [mind, will, and emotions]! I will praise you and sing of you to everyone, for great is your love and faithfulness."

Can you see how he switched gears? God appreciates honesty. David could be completely honest about what he was feeling, but he never gave in to despair. In 57:8, he said we need to wake up our soul. We can be discouraged or dismayed and struggling to maintain hope, but in his time of need, David praised God. This is the warfare of faith-based praise that we do in the midst of dire circumstances. It is a sacrifice of praise, as it costs us something. Did you know that your time on Earth is the only time in all eternity that you will face opposition in praising God and doing the right thing? The enemy knows how powerful it is, so he does everything to keep us from doing it. God said to give thanks in everything, so we need to, no matter how we feel.

When you are living through a tough season and know God is refining your soul, don't get discouraged. None of your tears and pain go unnoticed or are wasted. Despite all our circumstances, we can "cry out to God Most High, who fulfils His purpose for me." He will either change your situation, or change you. Either way, change will happen. God used David's trials to prepare him to be a king. Trust that God is preparing you for something too.

"DON'T TELL ANYONE, BUT GO"

Have you ever wondered why Jesus always told the people that He healed not to tell anyone? Would this not promote His cause? Would this not cause more people to believe in Him? Wasn't the supernatural healing of diseases and maladies a testimony that the Messiah had indeed come in the flesh? Why not promote it? Mark 1:41-44 sheds some insight into this. Jesus, filled with compassion, reached out His hand and healed a leper. Right after this, He sent him away at once with a strong warning: "See that you don't tell this to anyone. But go, show yourself to the priest and offer the sacrifices that Moses commanded for your cleansing, as a testimony to them."

Why did Jesus want this healing to be a testimony to the religious community, but not the average crowd? In meditating on this, I realized something. What was His message to humankind when He came? The answer gives you a clue as to why He never promoted His ability to heal.

Jesus didn't want His message to people to be that He had the power to heal— rather, that the Kingdom of God had come.

The leper represents a life that was changed because of meeting Christ. Healing in itself doesn't change hearts. If people only heard about getting healed, they would go to Christ with that purpose, not with the intent of addressing the condition of their hearts. How similar we still are, even today. We think that a bona fide miraculous healing will convince people that God is real, yet sceptics still remark that it was just coincidence, or that there's some information they're missing, even if they're witnesses to it—but certainly not a miracle. They're not seeking, so they're blinded to the truth.

The healed leper was told to go the priest for examination. Jesus showed His obedience to the letter of the law in telling the leper to do this. Many wondered, by whose authority is Jesus performing these miracles? The logical conclusion should have led them to realize that the Messiah had indeed come.

Mark 1:34 says, "and Jesus healed many who had various diseases. He also drove out many demons, but He would not let the demons speak because they knew who He was." He forbade demons to bear testimony to His identity. In our logic again, we would probably say, "Why isn't He using this to His advantage? Surely the people who saw the demon-possessed person freed from their horrible bondage would benefit from hearing the demon itself confess that Jesus was the Messiah!" Jesus, however, would not allow demons to be the herald or announcer of His arrival.

We must be seekers of God, not of signs and wonders to help us find Christ. We need to promote His truth more than His healing.

Jesus spoke to the people in parables that always required some introspection. Then and today, the Kingdom of God is here to be discovered, but you won't trip over it if you're watching where you're going. The truth is, a changed life is the biggest miracle of all.

CHAPTER 6

Don't Water Down the Stain Remover

JESUS IS THE ONLY WAY

Have you noticed how popular it has become among celebrities to be perceived as religious? Notably, they often give thanks to God at awards ceremonies for their work. When I first heard high-profile movie and music artists acknowledging God for their gifts and talents, I was shocked and pleased. My pleasure, however, was short-lived. Not long after hearing one of these stars give thanks to God for their award, I saw their new music video, which was nearly X-rated in content. After hearing some of them on talk shows, conveying what they really believe, it was evident that their brand of religion was only a form of godliness. Talk is cheap. True Christians don't need to tell people they're genuine; the way they live their lives will speak louder than anything they can say. If someone professes to be a follower of Jesus, we need only watch the fruit that follows their lives. The Bible says we will know them by their fruit. We need to become fruit inspectors.

Don't be fooled by the world's new brand of religion. It has become popular to believe in many different things at the same time, which includes God but is not exclusively God. There is a common belief out there that all religions take different trails on a very big mountain that make their way to the top where God resides. But there is one problem: All religions can't be true. It is a clever ploy of the enemy. Satan would like nothing better than to permanently stamp out anything to do with God, and goodness knows he's tried. But he also knows that intelligent people will not believe an outrageous anti-God religion. Therefore, Satan waters down true Christianity with just enough lies to keep people out of Heaven. Ironically, this is nothing new. It is the same ploy that the Israelites fell for in 2 Kings 17:33–34 well over two thousand years ago:

"They worshipped the Lord, but they also served their own gods in accordance with the customs of the nations from which they had been brought."

The Israelites at this time were in constant warfare and trouble. You can see they mixed their faith with the horrible worship practices of evil nations. When I say horrible, I mean it. Some of their customs were to sacrifice their children or "pass them through the fire." This meant heating up the arms of a metal idol until they were red hot and putting their children on them. It's too horrible to even imagine. They thought God considered them acceptable and that they had all bases covered. Not so; the Bible says God was extremely grieved over what they were doing.

Verse 34 says, "To this day they persist in their former practices. They neither worship the Lord nor adhere to the ... commands that the Lord gave ... Israel."

Didn't it say they worshipped the Lord in verse 33? If we mix truth with lies, we have no truth, period. We cannot serve two masters. If we accept Satan's version of the truth, which is faith in God mixed with modern philosophy, which master are we following? To lay the groundwork for this, Satan's attack has been to undermine the inerrancy of Scripture. God has Himself stipulated strict warnings and consequences about adding or detracting even a "jot" (a speck or dot) from His Word. We are to not add or take away the smallest stroke of a pen to change meaning. If we don't believe the whole Bible as the truth and authority of our faith, we may pick and choose the parts we like and change the meaning of the parts we don't. This creates a new version of God's Word based on what we want to believe, and not on God's inspired, breathed Word. There are major religions like Jehovah's Witnesses and Mormons who have done exactly this in the past two hundred years and still consider themselves Christians, even though they fly in the face of God by directly disobeying His Word. They are deceived and follow re-written, "updated," and altered versions of the Bible and other books, much like the Israelites did. Although they claim to be Christians, there are fundamental differences, and altering God's inspired Holy Scriptures is just one. They've painted God in their own image to suit what they want to believe. The truly tragic thing is that they're hanging their eternity on a slippery slope of deception.

There is only one true spirituality: accepting the person of Jesus Christ as God's one and only begotten Son, who came expressly to die for our sins, be raised from the dead, and to take His place at the right hand of the Father. The Bible is an account of God redeeming us to Himself. In the Old Testament, Redemption is *needed*, and through the prophets, Redemption is *planned*. Through Jesus coming, dying, and being raised from the dead, Redemption is *effected*, and through the Gospels, Redemption is *shared*. Through Acts and all the letters, Redemption is *explained*, and finally, in the book of Revelation, Redemption is *realized*.

True Christians are often viewed as being narrow-minded in that they won't deviate from what God's Word says. What people don't realize is that God Himself said the way to heaven is narrow; not narrow-minded, but narrow as in there is only one way, and that way is through Jesus Christ. It's not always easy.

How can you be kept from being deceived and help others as well? To illustrate, consider a friend of mine who worked for a bank. She was sent to a workshop to learn how to recognize counterfeit money. If you think they studied counterfeit money for an extended time, you're wrong. They spent their time studying genuine currency. They felt the thickness of real money, scrutinized it, smelled it, and held it up to the light. You

> I feel like I've won the lottery and want to share it with people.

see, if you know the real thing, you can spot a counterfeit immediately.

Study God's Word; talk to and hang out with God Himself; find a Bible-believing fellowship; learn to discern what He's saying to your heart, and measure everything you hear or read next to His Word, no matter who is giving instruction (me included). You will then be able to spot the devil's infiltration. When you are talking to lost people who believe in God and all sorts of other philosophies, you will be able to speak truth into their lives. Don't be lulled into believing they're safe. They're not. We must stand with the entire Word of Almighty God and be His voice of truth, no matter what. Don't water down the stain remover! Only the blood of Jesus can remove the stain of sin from us, and without it, we cannot stand in God's presence. Remember, they won't care what you know, until they know that you care. Love for them, not judgement, must be our motivation. The truth coming through the lens of love will bring conviction one way or another; the Holy Spirit Himself accompanies your words when you speak the truth about Jesus Christ.

Jesus says in John 14:6, "I am the way, the truth, and the life. No one comes to the Father except through me." God's Word is either all true or not true at all. Anything less than this would render God to not be God, as He cannot be untrue to Himself.

HE HAS RISEN! DO YOU BELIEVE?

I recently saw a segment on TV profiling a man claiming to have proof that Jesus didn't actually die on the cross, and that he could prove it. In my heart, I quickly prayed that his misleading words would not take root in all the seekers out there who hadn't found a personal relationship with Jesus yet, but that truth would win out. How many times have we watched a TV show about a court case, knowing in advance who was guilty and who was innocent, yet the prosecutor twisted facts about the case in such a way as to lead the jury to convict an innocent man? People can spend their whole lives trying to disprove the crucifixion, and yet the Bible promises that if you look for Jesus, you will find Him. That simply can't happen if He remained in the grave. We need to be looking for truth, not just facts. I also wondered about the man and the show itself. It struck me again that if Jesus Christ was not raised from the dead, why do they continually try to persuade everyone He is? The answer is simple: He's not dead. You would think that before making a claim that flies in the face of millions of Christians, you would take a good long look at how He ended up on a cross in the first place. The Apostle Paul faced people in his day that also did not believe in the resurrection of Jesus Christ. He answers them in 1st Corinthians 15:13–15, 17, 19, and 20:

"If there is no resurrection of the dead, then not even Christ has been raised. And if Christ has not been raised, our preaching is useless and so is your faith. More than that, we are then found to be false witnesses about God, for we have testified about God that He raised Christ from the dead. And if Christ has not been raised, your faith is futile; you are still in your sins. If only for this life we have hope in Christ, we are to be pitied more than all men. But Christ has indeed been raised from the dead, the first-fruits of those who have fallen asleep."

Jesus made a way for us to be forgiven. To be cleansed of sin. To feel the burden of guilt for every wrong thing we've ever done to roll off our hearts and onto Him. This could only be accomplished by taking the penalty we deserved and dying in our place and being raised from the dead. He made a way for us to live after we die, just as He died and lives today.

I don't want to force anyone to believe what I believe. In fact, it's impossible. No one can believe in God unless His Spirit draws them, and all we're doing is being a witness to the reality of His presence with us. I do however feel like I've won the lottery and want to share it with people.

We so need to see the bigger picture. I realize that there are many religions in the world and I do not desire to offend anyone. Respectfully, I would rather hold up the standard of my living God next to their dead leader and let them decide for themselves. This is the key difference between most religions and a living relationship with our Lord and Saviour. The message of the Gospel is as old as the earth itself. When Adam sinned, Christ knew He was headed for the cross.

What do people see in us?

Did you know that we are being watched? If people know we are Christians, they measure us against a higher standard than their other friends. God help us! I for one have not always been a great example to follow. I'm not perfect and never will be, but one thing I do strive to be is transparent and real, flaws and all. I think what gets under the skin of people is when they see a poor Christian witness who is self-righteous at the same time. I'll discuss this in more detail in Chapter 7.

Christians have to remember that God is not willing to lose anyone and to that end, He is constantly bringing every person who doesn't know Him to a point of decision to either accept Jesus or

> We need to realize that we might be the only Bible some people will ever read.

exercise their right to reject Him. The Holy Spirit is constantly behind the scenes, urging them to seek God.

Every unbeliever has said no to God more than once, but He doesn't give up. Finally, an opportunity presents itself. Perhaps they've hit rock bottom, and their hearts have begun to soften because they've tried everything else to no avail and they begin to search Him out. God is thrilled and brings them to—us. He needs us to be His voice and show them the way.

There was a time I was afraid I might offend people or that they would think I was a religious fanatic, so I compromised my witness and tried to soften the message and fit in with the crowd instead of standing out like I should have. I truly felt like I let God down and actually, I did. When God convicted me, I made up my mind that I would be purposeful and ready if anyone approached me; to take every opportunity that God presented. We don't have to be a super-Christian; all we have to do is look for a chance, open our mouths, and see where God takes it! The minute anyone asks me a question about God, I pray: "Holy Spirit, please help me." Then I relax, answer the question, and let Him do the rest.

I wonder if God ever gets frustrated with us when we water down our witness. He does all the behind-the-scenes work, and when people finally yield, we drop the ball. We need to realize that we might be the only Bible some people will ever read. What a sobering thought.

This little message is not meant to condemn us for past failures— rather it's to encourage us to press on!

The Apostle Paul's words in Philippians 4:9 challenged me the other day, and I hope they challenge you too. In speaking about his personal witness, he said, "Whatever you have learned or received or heard from me, or seen in me—put it into practice." We need to be aware of that too. People should hear about Jesus from us, receive Jesus from us, learn about Jesus from us, and see Jesus in us and coming from us. After all, Christians are to *be* good news, before they *share* good news, no?

We may not be able to live as Paul did, but every believer can reflect Jesus to the world in our sphere of influence. I'm so glad that God knows all my faults and shortcomings. To quote a favourite preacher of mine: "I may not be where I need to be, but thank the Lord I'm not where I used to be! I'm on my way, and that's okay!"

CHAPTER 7

Tell Me Again Why I Should Obey God?

PRIDE VS. COMPASSION

I really like the account of Jonah the Prophet. He was a man with personality flaws who God used despite his shortcomings, so I know there's hope for me too. There is much we can learn from this prophet's humanity. Although he disobeyed the Lord's instruction, I believe the source of Jonah's problem stemmed from pride. He was a work in progress, just as we are, and yet God still used him. There's hope for us all.

In around 800 BC, God's concern became evident over a large non-Jewish city called Nineveh (one of the most ancient cities of the world, located on the banks of the Tigris River and nearly opposite the site of the modern Mosul in Iraq). The people of this ancient city were immoral, and their wickedness had come before Him. God told Jonah to go and preach against it, as He was threatening to destroy it. Although they were wicked, God wanted to give them an opportunity to repent, like He gives all of us. Jonah's feeling towards the lost city of Nineveh was "good riddance to them," and to that end headed in the opposite direction with the intent to ignore God. He had zero compassion for these people. He clearly couldn't have cared less about them. Jonah, like God's people of that time, rested on past achievements, expected God to work out their problems, and waited for Him to destroy their enemies. Sounds an awful lot like what many people expect from God today too. Jonah strikes me as

> Jonah had painted God in his own image, and his religion was self-centred.

being full of pride, resulting in a lack of compassion. It's like he expected God to serve him, instead of the other way around.

As the book of Jonah recounts, God wasn't about to let His prophet get away with this kind of behaviour. Through God's rebuke and mercy, Jonah finally came to Nineveh and spent three days going through it, preaching and warning them that God's judgement was about to fall. As a result, the people humbled themselves and called "urgently on God." I love what happens next. "When God saw what they did and how they turned from their evil ways, He had compassion and did not bring upon them the destruction He had threatened" (Jonah 3:10). Let's pause for a minute. If these people had been prideful and stubborn (like Jonah), they would have been destroyed. Look at the deadly consequences of pride and the incredible compassion of God. This speaks loudly to me.

> We are to have compassion on the *sinner,* but judgement on *sin,* and we need to know how to convey the difference.

What was Jonah's reaction? In Jonah 4:1-2, we see pride rear its ugly head again. He pouted that the Ninevites got off the hook. Jonah's main reason for fleeing from God's command to preach to them was so that he wouldn't look foolish if God relented and had compassion to spare them. Instead of rejoicing, he said, "Oh Lord, is this not what I said when I was still at home? ... I knew that you are a gracious and compassionate God, slow to anger and abounding in love, a God who relents from sending calamity." Can you believe it? He's mad at God for those reasons! Jonah was actually upset that God didn't destroy them, and yet God's very same compassion saved his life in the belly of the fish.

Jonah had painted God in his own image, and his religion was self-centred.

We often want God to do to others what we judge to be right. I have done this, and the Lord showed me how wrong it was. How often do we quietly hope that God's wrath will fall on them, and rely on His compassion in dealing with us? Do we realize that when we sit in the seat of judging people for their sins that we have elevated ourselves to the position of being equal to God? Many Christians are despised by non-Christians for this self-righteous attitude. Are we quick to dole out judgement, except where we're concerned? We can't have it both ways.

God wants us to have compassion on the *sinner* but judgement on *sin*, and we need to know how to convey the difference.

GOD WILL NOT VIOLATE OUR WILL

Have you ever heard anyone ask, "If God is so all-powerful, why doesn't He just make people do what's right?" The answer lies in the amazing laws of creation that He set up when He created humanity. We are the only being on Earth that has been created in God's image. We need to be in awe over this incredibly wondrous thing! What a privilege! We are a spirit, have a free will, and were meant to rule. He said in Genesis 1:26, "Let us make man in our image, in our likeness, and let them rule over the fish of the sea ... over all the earth." You are a spirit, you have a soul (mind, will and emotions), and you live in a body. Three distinct parts, yet all one. The part of us that will live into all eternity is our spirit, which is who we really are.

Who's in the driver's seat? Jesus or you?

We have the God-given right to choose where we will spend all eternity. God will not violate our will, even if we choose to destroy ourselves. He will support our choice to go to Hell, even though He sent His only Son to die and be raised up so we don't have to. This is what makes rejecting this choice such a crime against God.

We also have the God-given right to run our own lives if we want. God will not violate our will if we choose to be in control of a situation, but just as there can only be one driver of a car, there can only be one person calling the shots. So often, we think we know what's best, until the whole thing falls apart. It's only then that we choose to let God take over and do damage control. Wouldn't it be better to avoid the damage in the first place? God knows how to get us where we need to go, at the safest speed, taking the best route.

I have learned how important it is to invite God into every new challenge my life presents. This has become a solid habit. If God won't violate my will, I need to surrender my agenda in the situation and give Him permission to drive, right out of the garage. It is amazing to see what happens when we say, "Lord, I invite you into this situation. I need your wisdom and guidance, and I will do whatever you tell me to do." The beautiful thing is that many times we are both headed in the same direction anyway. God loves us so much and only has our best interests at heart.

My challenge to you today is this: if you have a problem relinquishing control, let Jesus drive for a while. I guarantee that after finally giving up the driver's seat to Him, you won't want it back!

WHAT IS PRAYER AND WHY SHOULD WE PRAY TOGETHER?

Many great books have been written on this subject, as it is of utmost importance in the life of every Christian. There are countless reasons to pray, but I would like to hit what I consider the basics. In a nutshell, real prayer is intimacy with God.

Prayer is spoken and unspoken communication with God who has invited His children to communicate with Him. Prayer covers addressing and hearing God, interceding for others, waiting on Him, worshipping and petitioning Him, guided by the Holy Spirit. Prayer is spending time with God; hanging out with Him, chatting with Him, listening to him, obeying Him, telling Him how wonderful He is, asking for His help, thanking Him for His help, and sharing your life with Him.

What would happen if you never spent any time with someone you love? How well would you know them? How well would you know what was going on inside of them,

> If God seems far away, guess who has moved!

what their problems or joys were, or if they were happy or unhappy? If you never spent time with them, you wouldn't be intimately involved in their life. In fact, if you continued never spending time together, you would eventually drift apart and no longer know them as you once did. It's no different with God. He longs to spend time with you as you tell Him about your challenges and joys. We need to pray without ceasing to stay close to Jesus. If you're standing next to Jesus and familiar with His voice, it's easy to hear Him when He speaks.

Have you ever needed an answer from God after having ignored Him for a month? After being out of communication for a period of time, my prayers felt like they just hit the ceiling and went no farther. If God seems far away, guess who has moved. Prayer doesn't change God. It changes me. It clues me in to the heart of God.

Something special happens when two or more people pray together. Matthew 18:19–20 says, "Again, I tell you that if two of you on earth agree about anything you ask for, it will be done for you by my Father in heaven. For where two or three come together in my name, there am I among them." Jesus Christ is the unseen party who promises to show up every time when at least two people pray, and this is the reason we receive what we ask for. There is a corporate anointing when people unite in prayer for a common purpose in holding up the needs of the body of Christ. God is with us when we pray by ourselves, but something else happens when we gather because Jesus Himself made the distinction. We may not see it immediately, or even sense it, but by faith, we believe we have received what the Holy Spirit is laying on our hearts because He is the one who helps us know what to pray for! Then our prayer becomes full of joy and thanksgiving, as we have released our petitions into His care by faith.

Prayer is not a mundane begging, but a continual process summed up by the acronym ACTS: Adoration, Confession, Thanksgiving, and Supplication (a humble and sincere appeal for God to intervene in our affairs). It is a wonderful experience that we are privileged to enter into and interact with the God of the universe whenever we choose!

This privilege isn't cheap. The world mistakenly treats things that are free as having little value. Because we received this privilege freely doesn't mean that someone else didn't pay. Having direct access to Almighty God came at a huge cost and is a monumental privilege. It cost Him His only Son. His blood covers us and makes us acceptable to approach God; He is utterly holy, and I wonder if we'll ever fully appreciate on Earth what this exactly means.

> ACTS: Adoration Confession Thanksgiving Supplication

Can you imagine approaching God in all the radiance of His splendour, through the weight of His importance, the demonstration of His power, the very atmosphere of His presence? If we fully appreciated the magnitude of this privilege, we'd be crowding the doors to get into the prayer closet. We must remember and appreciate that reality when we bow our heads.

UNITED WE STAND, DIVIDED WE FALL

I once heard someone say, "One of Satan's greatest accomplishments is that he has broken the body of Christ into a whole bunch of small fragmented pieces." One of the first questions I get from unbelievers when the subject of Christianity comes up is, "If what you're saying is true, how do you know that your way is right? I mean, just look at all the Christian churches that are out there and all the different denominations. Who has it right?" They have a good point, don't they? In pondering this, I found Satan's strategy is this: Satan has managed to divide the church by having God's children *magnify* what divides us, instead of *magnifying* what unites us.

Just look at all the different ways we are baptized. There are sprinklers, dunkers, and those that are baptized at birth, at confirmation, or upon salvation. Churches have split over these issues; they are important to be sure, and I'm not saying one is right over the other, but in so doing, we've lost something critical. It is unity.

Let's look at John 17:20–23 to gain God's perspective. Here Jesus is talking to His disciples at the last supper. His next action is to go to the Cross, literally, and He knows it. He is just about to go to the Garden of Gethsemane to be betrayed. This is His last instruction to His disciples, so we should pay attention:

> Satan has managed to divide the church by having God's children magnify what divides us, instead of magnifying what unites us.

"My prayer is not for them [the disciples] alone. I pray also for those who will believe in me through their message, that all of them may be one, Father, just as you are in me and I am in you." The reason we need to be united as one is here: "May they also be in us so that the world may believe that you have sent me...that they may be one as we are one: I in them and you in me. May they be brought to complete unity to let the world know that you sent me and have loved them even as you have loved me."

Can we see the problem? Within our own denomination we may be one, but what about the Christian church across the street? The root of the problem isn't with our different denominations; it is with our love walk towards one another. Many Christians refer to different denominations as "them" and "us." There should be no distinction between true believers. We are all on the same side. The Bible doesn't say we will come together in doctrine, necessarily, but that we will come together in the faith. Unity does not mean uniformity. When a Baptist, Catholic, Pentecostal, Lutheran, and Mennonite can have harmony together and celebrate the death and resurrection of Jesus Christ to save the whole world and make that the main event, the world will see our unity in loving one another. The world will believe that Jesus has come when He and the Father "are one with us" and the church as a whole.

I understand the huge challenge we have on our hands in becoming a united faith, and I do not have all the answers. But one thing I do know: it begins with me and you. The next time an unbeliever asks you why there are so many different Christian denominations, share with them the underlying foundation of what unites us instead of the differences that divide us. The world sees Jesus' church as a bunch of different pieces, and it's up to us to allow God to "bring us to complete unity, to let the world know that you sent me [Jesus] and have loved them even as you have loved me." When Jesus comes at the end as the Bridegroom, will there be only one Bride?

IT SURE LOOKED LIKE IT WAS GOD'S WILL!

Have you ever wanted something so badly that the desire for it outweighed your better judgement? Have you ever squelched that voice on the inside because it contradicted what you wanted? How about ignoring good advice from people who love you? Have you ever made an important decision based on what your friends say, despite what your gut is saying?

We are experts at making what we want look like it is God's will.

How often do well-meaning friends and people of influence in your life give you good, but not-in-the-right-timing counsel? Instead of waiting for God, we filter every response through our desire, even though we know deep down it might not be best. I know that I have listened to counsel that I knew wasn't God's best, but I thought it achieved my plans better and sooner. When Jake and I got married, we jumped immediately into buying a house that put a heavy financial burden on us. My parents said to wait; his mom said to buy. The only problem was that we paid dearly for it later when we saw that waiting on and listening to God would have benefitted us far better and kept us from regret. Even though it was God's will for us to someday own a home, the timing wasn't right. Sometimes God doesn't want to keep us from getting what we want, He just wants us to avoid going over the cliff if we're moving too fast.

I knew a Christian woman years ago who desperately wanted to get married. She found a man who loved her, but she had her doubts over her devotion for him. But because she wanted to be married so badly she ignored what the Spirit was telling her. She told me that even on her wedding day, she knew in her heart that she should back out and confided in her father, who unfortunately was more concerned with appearances than her happiness and told her that she daren't humiliate the family. She went ahead and married him. After two children and a loveless marriage that was full of pain and disappointment, she and her husband divorced. I'm sure God's plan included marriage for her, as it was already in her heart. She rushed ahead of God's timing to achieve her plan, and everyone lost in the break-up. All that pain and heartache didn't have to occur.

It is so worth it to wait on God and obey His voice.

God's Word gives us wonderful examples of this in 1 Samuel 24 and 26, where David, probably the most well-known King of Israel, is given two opportunities to become king ahead of God's timetable. God had already publicly anointed David to become king, as His first choice, Saul, had not obeyed Him. How would God work this out? Obviously, Saul had to be taken off the throne.

David, however, had been nothing but consistently loyal to Saul, yet Saul relentlessly hunted him down to kill him. This became tiring and wearing at times. On one occasion, David and his men are hiding in a cave, and Saul goes in to relieve himself. Saul is now in mortal danger; David's men said: (24:4) "This is the day the LORD spoke of when He said to you, 'I will give your enemy into your hands for you to deal with as you wish.'" Okay. That was true; God had promised to give David's enemies into his hands, but was this "the day" and was Saul his "enemy"? Here was Saul, hand-delivered, by himself, alone.

Would we not think God was giving David a golden opportunity here? He crept up behind Saul and cut off a piece of his robe, unbeknownst to him. He must have been sorely tempted to end his days as a fugitive. David knew it was a sin to touch God's anointed. I often wonder if a conflict raged on the inside of him. David had to discern between what God was really allowing here, just as we should.

He was so conscious and hungry for God's will that later he was conscience-stricken that he had even cut Saul's robe. It sure appeared to be an event from God, and indeed it was, but not for the reasons his men saw (24:10).

God's plan wasn't to kill Saul here, it was to show the whole nation of Israel what David was made of, and that he was "not guilty of wrongdoing or rebellion." (Verse 11) It was also establishing David's obedience to God. I do not for a second wonder, since God was so grieved over Saul's disobedience, if He wasn't putting David to the test and teaching him to hear Him and see if he'd obey before he became king.

How David ultimately became King is a beautifully woven account of Almighty God safely leading His humble yielded servant through many emotional and physical battles to incredible blessings. David was a man after God's own heart. We need to be the same way. God does use people to give us good counsel, but that counsel should never supersede what *God is saying to us* and when we should act. Not everyone has the whole picture. God does. A wise friend will more likely confirm what God is already telling you to do and when. Our Lord, however, is incredibly good at getting us out of fixes that we get ourselves into, and He did help us recover from that very significant reversal, but it took a few years. We had learned our lesson the hard way. Since then, learning to wait on God and His timetable has made receiving just that much sweeter. It's a win/win situation. There is no regret in going with God. If there is, we need to honestly ask ourselves why. Are we about our plan, or His?

> It looked *so good,* but it *couldn't be good,* if he had to *sin* or *disobey* God to accomplish it!

If you're struggling with an issue that you really want and are sorely tempted to rush into, a prayer that I pray frequently goes like this:

"Lord, please help me listen and watch ever so carefully for your plan, and your plan alone in this situation. I want your will; nothing more, nothing less, and nothing else. I know that nothing else will satisfy me. Help me to obey your leading and your timetable."

God is *only* interested in giving us what's best for us—why do we resist?

CHAPTER 8
Tell Me Again How I Should Obey God?

HOW ARE WE LISTENING?

Have you ever tried to talk to your child about an important issue but can tell they're not listening? Or how about when we bust our teenagers over finding out they've disobeyed us but they are clearly waiting for us to wind it up and don't even intend to make a change. What is going on? They're not listening and don't see the importance of what we're saying.

Just like our kids, to learn from God, we need to listen. There have been times in my own life when my heart was as hard as rocks and unresponsive to what God was saying, even though it was an amazing word. I missed out on God's best because of it, and I hope others can avoid doing the same.

Let's say you need to plant some seed. Have you ever taken a shovel and tried to dig a hole in earth that was rock hard? How about a well-beaten path that has was more like cement than dirt? Through the constant flow of people walking on it, it remains tough and yields no growth. There are many people around us like a well-beaten path, perhaps even you. Through life's circumstances, they've been walked on so frequently they're really hard to get through to; they've hardened themselves to keep out the pain, but unfortunately this keeps the opportunities for growth out too, not to mention the love.

> We need to have our spiritual ears and eyes dialled in to what God wants to show us.

When Jesus was on Earth, He used common object lessons that everyone could understand. In Luke 8, He said something to the Israelites that we need to be aware of today as well. He likened their hearts (their spiritual centre) to four types of soil—a hard path, rocky soil, soil with thorns, and good soil—and said that the type of soil our hearts are determines how we hear. God sprinkles His message of love like seed on our hearts, and just like natural laws, seed will grow and produce new life—that's what seed does, providing the right *conditions* exist for that seed. We determine the type of soil our hearts. Similarly, our kids decide if they're going to listen to or ignore us, to their benefit or detriment. God never violates our free will, and if you don't want to hear what He's saying, you are free to ignore Him.

God's word always comes in the form of a seed, carrying in it the promise of change.

We can do ourselves a great favour by performing a self-evaluation. What kind of ground is the soil of our hearts? Is your heart's soil a hard path, so that when the seed comes, and God speaks, you resist Him and allow it to sit there until it is snatched away? I remember a time when my heart was hard. I was a born-again child of God, but I'd hear a wonderful message about what He wanted to give me or do through me, and I didn't receive it. I just let it sit there, and did nothing with it. After a short while, it was snatched out of my heart, and I distinctly remember thinking cynically, "I don't buy that—it's just too good to be true." My heart was hard, and even though the message was what God wanted to give me, I let the enemy steal it from me. Of course, I didn't see it that way at the time because I was prideful.

Is our heart's soil full of rocks so that we receive God's Word with joy, but when testing comes, our commitment fades? We hear a good message and rejoice—yes, I'll definitely receive that! Although we're happy with the seed, we don't really want to do the work to help it grow. When the smallest winds of persecution blow or the sun beats down on the tender plant, we're shallow, and there's not enough soil to let the roots get around our apathy (Luke 8:13). If we're honest with ourselves, I think that most of us have been like this at one time or another. I certainly have.

Is our heart's soil full of thorns or weeds so that worldly cares choke out what God is saying to us? How many of us have said, "I'm just so busy! I don't have time for church, personal devotions, or prayer"? I recently heard a preacher say, "We need to put the first things first, and put the second things that were first, in their proper place." This simple act will re-prioritize the heart with thorns, and get rid of them!

Finally, is our heart's soil good and ready to receive what God is saying? Every day, God is speaking into our lives, and we need to have ears to hear it (Luke 8:8). Notice that each type of heart heard the word and responded, but only one "retained it and by persevering, produced a crop" (verse 15). As Jesus says in verse 18, "Therefore, consider carefully how you listen." I'm sure every parent reading this would like their kid to do the same for them! After all, you only have their best interests at heart, right? God is no different.

Perhaps you've been trampled on by people and circumstances, and everything seems to be squeezing the joy out of life. The good news is that whatever the soil of our hearts is, Jesus can soften up that hard ground, remove the rocks, weeds, and thorns, and cultivate a beautiful crop if we'll simply open up our heart to receive the gift of what He's saying to us today. He will heal our hurts and loving change us into the garden of His delight, and ours.

DECISIONS, DECISIONS, DECISIONS.

Have you ever grown tired of having to make decisions? I sure have. It's not actually the decision making that's the problem, though; it's living with the results that the decision brings. It's interesting that as teenagers, we could hardly wait to make all our own decisions and after becoming adults and having to live with the outcomes, we wish we could go back to the carefree days of someone else bearing the responsibility of decision making.

I hate to make the wrong decision and pay for it later. I used to berate myself for making a wrong decision, no matter how small it was. This just made me feel self-condemned all the time. Thankfully, God had an answer for me. He showed me that I needed to share the responsibility of all decision making with Him.

To make the right decision, we need to use the wisdom that God gives us to discern what to do. The Bible does not give specific answers to the innumerable problems that arise in life, but does give indirect answers through following its principles. Wisdom discerns truth in a situation, while common sense provides good judgement in what to do about the truth.

For example, say you are about to buy a house that you greatly desire. You ask God for wisdom to know if this is His will at this time. You wait and listen. You and your wife go over the payment schedule and your combined incomes and realize that things are going to be tight financially if you do this. You go back to God with a restlessness in your soul that is warring with your desire and begin to sense the truth that you can't really afford this. Common sense rises to the top, and you use good judgement to make the right decision to hold off. It also helps to realize that sometimes the original plan was God's but we're out of His timetable. He may be getting us ready to make an important decision with wisdom. He's teaching us to follow His leading.

This happened to Jake and I when we were contemplating relocating our business. Jake found what he deemed was the perfect location and price, and so we began the process of purchasing the unit. However, I had no peace. Something inside just didn't feel right, and I could give him no solid reason not to go forward. It persisted, and I told him about it and since we had already looked for a long period and this appeared to be more or less perfect with nothing else available, we went forward. When the deal fell through, Jake was acutely disappointed, but I was relieved. I was so glad in my heart that even when we were about to make a mistake, God kept us from making it. I believe it was because we had truly invited Him into making this decision. Then, Jake noticed a brand new warehouse complex going up a mere four blocks from our home and mentioned it to our real estate agent. We enquired and found that not only was the price acceptable, we got to design the office space upstairs to our liking even before it was built! Had we made our own decision and ignored God, we'd have missed His best for us. We were completely elated. The peace I felt, in contrast to the previous restlessness, was incredible. We knew that we were in the right place and timing of God, and we were unanimous.

Knowledge is natural and something we gain from being taught. Wisdom is supernatural, because it is a gift from God. It tells us what we need to do with the knowledge we have. In my Bible alone, there are 217 references to wisdom. It is sprinkled all throughout God's

Word, from Genesis to Revelation. We live in a real world with real issues and need real answers. We do the seeking, and He does the speaking. But we must listen, receive, and act in accordance with God's voice.

James 1:5–8 says that if we lack wisdom, we should ask God, who will generously give it to us. When we ask, we must believe we'll receive that wisdom and not doubt, or we become like a wave of the sea, waffling to and fro. God says that we won't receive from Him if we go back and forth from faith to doubt; we have become double-minded, unstable, and wishy-washy. Instead, we need to:

> *Knowledge is natural and something we gain from being taught. Wisdom is supernatural, because it is a gift from God. Wisdom tells us what we need to do with the knowledge we have.*

1. Go to God with our circumstance; invite Him freely into the situation and acknowledge His Lordship over it. This means doing what He tells us to and when He wants us to, not necessarily what and when we want.
2. Ask Him for wisdom to know which way to go, believing that we are in fact going to get it.
3. Wait on Him patiently and listen for His voice.
4. Wait for peace. If you sense peace in going in a certain direction, inform God that you believe He has directed you, and that you are going to go forward. God can only steer a ship that's moving. Testing the waters before jumping full in is what I recommend, but if you lack peace, are out of His timing, or off base in any respect, tell God you will yield immediately, and wait a little longer. He will keep you from making a big wrong decision if you truly yield to His plan.

I have found that the amount of confidence I have in making a decision is in direct proportion to how much time I have spent in talking with Jesus about it. It's a two-way conversation, not me informing Him of what I'm going to do. We can't just make our plans, barge ahead, and ask God to give us His input after the fact. If I were to make an important decision without asking Him about it and the thing didn't turn out, I would have no one to blame but myself. If I spend some time with Jesus, He will lead me to the right decision. This is not to say that we will never make a mistake, but I have found peace instead of condemnation when things didn't turn out exactly as I'd expected. Even if I make a mistake, Jesus will catch me.

HOW DO I RECEIVE FROM YOU, GOD?

This is a question that every Christian asks at one point or another. How do we receive what God has promised us in His Word? "I've prayed and prayed, but I just can't seem to receive the thing I've asked for. What am I doing wrong, Lord?"

I'd love to say that receiving what we ask for from God is simple. Often it is simple to understand but not so easy to work out. God's love for us is unconditional, but His promises aren't. I believe that we have to live a lifestyle of obedience to fulfil God's requirements to receive. Our expectations are no different, actually. Take a spoiled child who pouts when they don't immediately get what they want. How obligated do you feel to fulfil their wishes? How about if they turn their back on you and give you the cold shoulder because you didn't give them what they wanted? I would say this child needs to learn a few things. Yet this is exactly what we do to God sometimes. In contrast, when your child is doing their best to obey and honour you, are you not more inclined to give them what they want?

1 John 3:21-22 provide incredible insight into what God expects from us: "Dear friends, if our hearts do not condemn us, we have confidence before God and receive from Him anything we ask, because we obey His commands and do what pleases Him." Let's look at this more closely.

Our heart is our conscience, and if it is clear, we'll know it. It begins with our love walk towards one another. We can see whether God is going to consider our request if we see our

"Because" indicates something that *is* happening. It is a current on-going lifestyle of obedience.

brother in need and ignore him. We are to actively love with actions, not just words. It all flows out of love for God and each other. "Perhaps we harbour unforgiveness or unconfessed sin in our heart. Have you ever asked God for something while knowing you're currently disobeying Him? In these times, I lose all confidence in asking. In my spirit, my request feels as heavy as a boulder trying to go through the ceiling to God. But if the Holy Spirit has not given us any red flags, our consciences are clear, and our hearts are clean before Him.

We can come boldly to God with no fear of unworthiness; no sense of despair or desperation; and no guilt or apprehension. We can walk up to God just like our dad who has everything we desire and need. Sometimes we don't receive because we don't ask, or ask for something contrary to His plan. I once heard: "The purpose of all prayer is to find God's will, and to make that will, our prayer!"

We must also remember that obeying does not to mean we're robots; we are not required to jump through hoops to satisfy our God's rigid requirements. Instead, it indicates a lifestyle of genuine devotion, love, and obedience to Him. In such a condition, we would not ask for anything outside the will of God. When we ask according to His will, we receive from Him the things we ask for. If we obey the greatest commandment, to "Love the Lord your God with all your heart, all your soul, all your mind, and all your strength," the rest will take care of itself. A lifestyle of obedience and pleasing God will follow, giving us the confidence to go to Him and receive what we ask.

In closing, it's really important to note why the verse is in God's Word in the first place. There are things we will not receive, if we don't ask. We can't sit back and say, "God is going to perform His will whether I ask or not." Our asking and receiving is an important part of the equation, or He wouldn't have instructed us on how to do this. You *matter* in effecting God's will on the Earth: the unsaved, your children, your loved ones, your church, your friends, and your ministry. What do you need to be receiving from God?

> You matter in effecting God's will on the Earth.

CHAPTER 9
Tell Me Again What I Need to Do

WHAT CAN I DO? I'M NOT A SUPER-CHRISTIAN

Years ago, Jake and I joked with friends of ours that we called "Super Christians—model year 2006." One friend said in the next year he wanted to be "Super Christian 2007, the James Bond model," and since the Olympics were to be held in our city in 2010, Jake wanted to be "Super Christian 2010, the Olympic Model." This way he'd have a few years to prepare. We are joking of course, but in our circles, we all know Christians that we consider full of the Spirit, wisdom, and power exemplified by their lives. We look at them with envy, thinking, "I'll never be that strong. I can't teach others or lead others; I'll just serve God in a menial way, because I could never be that spiritual."

You should never settle for that self-image. It is not how God views you. He has called every Christian that has chosen to be a follower of Jesus Christ to be a powerhouse for Him in whatever capacity He has gifted you with, be that cleaning the sanctuary in church, or preaching the Gospel. We must never adopt the world's value system of what makes people "exceptional" or "ordinary." The world acknowledges success on what we do, not who we are. God considers who we are in Christ far more important than what we do for Christ.

Let's look at a man named Stephen in Acts 6. In his era, the church had been growing, and the disciples had been teaching and tending to the physical needs of the people. This included the distribution of food, when complaining broke out that some widows were getting more than others. Since the disciples could only do so much, they concluded, "It would not be right for us to neglect the ministry of the Word of God in order to wait on tables" (Acts 6:2). They decided to choose seven men from among them "who are known to be full of the Spirit and wisdom. We will turn this responsibility over to them and will give our attention to prayer and the ministry of the Word" (Acts 6:3–4).

In essence, they found seven "Super Christians" to wait on tables. It doesn't sound like a glorious a job, but meeting the physical needs of the people required mature leaders who were considered to be very godly men. One of these men was Stephen, a man "full of God's grace and power, [and who] did great wonders and miraculous signs among the people" (Acts 6:8). In today's church body, we would probably place this man in a position of leadership, not waiting on tables. Yet, that's where God put Stephen. He had completely surrendered his life to Jesus and was happy to serve where he was placed. No doubt God had good reasons for placing him there, perhaps to let God's grace and power rub off on them through his ministry.

You may be thinking, "That was Stephen. That's not me. I wouldn't know where to begin." Did you know that God considers you His offspring? Think about that. If you are His offspring, you have His DNA. You have the blueprint of His make-up. You have His attributes and His gifts for service. Let that sink in. You are already equipped more than you think! Is there anything menial, ordinary, or unimportant about what God does? How then can your service to God be any of those? It is the enemy who seeks to demean you and belittle your contribution in serving Jesus. Stephen was an ordinary man who served in the capacity of feeding widows, and yet ended his life being so Christ-like, he asked God to forgive the people who were stoning and killing him. He was a powerhouse through God, and so became one of the first martyred for his faith.

There is no such thing as an ordinary Christian. Dare to become who God says you are in His Word. Don't listen to the enemy. If he can get you to believe you are a nobody, you will act like a nobody, ignoring the wealth of God's provision in gifts. You can't give away something you don't believe you own. God has specifically gifted you for this time in all of history for His purposes, His glory, and your benefit. Dare to begin to walk out your area of service in the fullness of what God intended. See yourself as He sees you. As my pastor puts it, we can all operate in a lifestyle that is "supernaturally natural" and "naturally supernatural." In my book, that makes us all Super Christians.

CHOOSE FAITH, NOT DESPAIR!

In the book of Esther, God uses one man's hatred of His people, the Jews, one Jew's loyalty to the Lord, and one girl's obedience to unfold a drama that affected the Jews worldwide. Here, a pagan named Haman has issued an edict supported by a Persian King, who at that time controlled 127 provinces, a vast empire, to annihilate all the Jews and take their goods. His plot ultimately failed, and the Jews were saved, but what caught my attention was a wonderful model of what we need to do when in crisis.

Where do your mind, will, and emotions go when tragedy strikes? Do we throw up our hands in despair and say, "All is hopeless, this will never get fixed," or "I give up on God," or "I don't get it. Isn't God supposed to protect me from these things?" Do you instead try to fix things in your own power, and in your own way? What reaction does God expect from us? When bad things happen, does our focus go on ourselves, or on God? I've spent many hours feeling sorry for myself before finally putting my eyes on the only One who can make a difference, my Lord Jesus.

When negative circumstances occur, the Lord will use them to teach us to have faith in Him. It sounds too simple, doesn't it? I have only felt better about things I cannot change when I've finished throwing my pity party and put my focus back on God. Look at what He can do, not on the impossibility of the situation. His Word says all things are possible with God. Hallelujah.

In the account of Esther, a tragedy struck, and they were about to be wiped out. They were just as human as we are, so they allowed themselves to react to this news with "fasting, weeping, and wailing" (Esth 4:3). This looks faithless, but that wasn't their reason. They were saying to God, "I am in extreme distress here. Please help me." Mordecai (Queen Esther's cousin who had raised her) was walking around in sackcloth with ashes on his head in intercessory prayer, crying out to God. In the same breath, he also said that relief and deliverance for the Jews would arise from another place, if not from the spot they were in. He was sure God was going to come through for them one way or another, despite the many odds against them.

There is a huge difference between desperation and despair. They were clearly desperate, but they were not in despair. Grief can be both healthy and unhealthy. When grief turns into despair or hopeless-ness, we have wandered into the enemy's camp. When our grief turns into "Only God can do some-thing, so I'm going to release it to Him," we have activated our faith. We've made a conscious decision that supersedes our feelings. I believe this is often what God is waiting for and the devil knows it.

> The only thing that should end faith is the manifestation of it; that is, the deliverance or answer that comes.

He pours it on and turns up the heat so we're tempted to stay focussed on our problem instead of God's solutions. If you think about it, the enemy wants you dead and he's enjoying your despair, so why party at his house? Why not party in God's house by activating your faith? Without faith, it's impossible to please Him (Heb 11:6). When I've done all that God asked me to do, I release my faith and leave the rest to Him. Why not entrust it to the only One who can make a difference?

The Word says, "The just shall live by faith." The only thing that should end faith is the manifestation of it; that is, the deliverance or answer that comes! The entire nation of God's people (even in exile due to their own disobedience) experienced His salvation from anni-hilation. The Book of Esther is an incredible account of good triumph-ing over evil. I think it would make a great movie. God knows how to take care of His own. Having faith is an on-going process that needs to be our default, no matter how we feel. We need to learn this over and over again until we get it. When bad things happen and there's not a thing we can do, look upwards, not inwards.

PERFECT PEACE

The words "perfect peace" make me think of a place in which I am utterly content. I don't want or need anything, and I am calm and happy. I move but not too fast and not too slow. My expression is peaceful, and my eyes radiate joy, contentment, and anticipation for life. When I'm there, I never want to leave.

Contrast this to how people often feel: Stressed, unsettled, uptight, and unhappy. We drown at the pace of our lives, barely keeping our heads above water. We've all been there at times, more times than I care to admit. It's sad that we identify more closely with turmoil than on perfect peace. If that's true with you today, something may need to change.

My challenge to you (and me) is this: Jesus Christ died to give me perfect peace, and I want it. Not just rarely or some of the time, but all the time, in every area of my life. Is this possible? Can we

> Peace and joy come through believing.

live in perfect peace? When I sought the Lord on this, He showed me Isaiah 26:3:

"You will keep him in perfect peace, him whose mind is stayed on you, because he trusts in you."

The Lord showed me something that has become a core value, and can be for you too. To experience perfect peace, I need to obey what the verse says. This is simple but often hard to do on a regular basis. Every time I find myself getting wound up with negative thoughts, I have to stop and filter my stress through that verse. When I re-affirm that I trust Him with what I'm facing, my body literally relaxes, His peace invades my heart, my problem is put in perspective, my strength is renewed, and I begin to experience perfect peace. My problem isn't gone, but Jesus' peace floods my being, equipping me to thrive instead of just survive. Jesus also said in John 14:1, "Do not let your hearts be troubled. You believe in God; believe also in Me." He repeats it again in John 14:27: "Peace I leave with you; my peace I give you. I do not give to you as the world gives. Do not let your hearts be troubled and do not be afraid."

Notice He gave us some instruction. It's up to us whether or not we "*let* our hearts be troubled and afraid." This means you give mental assent to the stress or fear, or you deny assent. God's provision of supernatural peace in the midst of a trial is supernatural "perfect" peace, for the world cannot offer that kind. The world's peace hinges on *circumstances*. God's peace hinges on keeping our minds stayed on Him and *trusting* Him in the circumstance.

> The best way to step on Satan's head when he tries to rob you of your peace is to rob him of his by trusting Jesus.

Peace and joy come through believing. It can't be any simpler than that. Surrender everything that is robbing you of your peace to God, and think about it through the filter of God's guidance. I am reminded again of an old hymn: "Trust and obey, for there's no other way, to be happy in Jesus, but to trust and obey." My desire is to come up higher in this, and I will do my best, and let God do the rest. He is available to bear our burdens and give us His perfect peace during the journey.

HOW SURRENDERED AM I?

Surrender. The word invokes thoughts of defeat and weakness. It usually means that you lost, that you weren't strong enough, and that they beat you. Humanity was created to have dominion over the whole earth. Characteristics, like ruling and managing, are aspects of God that He hard-wired into all of us. No one likes to lose or be beaten. We all like to win.

When we first sinned, we all became slaves to what the Bible refers to as the flesh. Sin beat us. Sin captured us. No matter how hard we try, we fail and sin at times—all of us. Jesus died for us and ransomed us back, so we now belong to Him if we've accepted His gift. Sin still desires to have us, but we have to master it (Gen 4:7). To do this, we have to begin by doing something that goes completely against the grain. We need to completely surrender to the *Lordship* of Jesus Christ.

Why do we fight it? To win, we need to lose; to truly live, we need to die. To truly conquer life, we need to surrender. And not just once, but daily. There are levels of surrender. Being completely surrendered all the time will constantly challenge different areas of your life. Here's a great definition of what God can really work with:

Full surrender is the definite, deliberate, voluntary transfer of undivided possession, control, and use of our entire being to the rightful owner: Jesus Christ.

How is your walk through life with Jesus going? Does He have complete Lordship over your life or are you holding back areas of your life from Him? Are you afraid of what He will require of you? Remember that God is goodness, compassion, and love, not some judgemental deity sitting on His throne waiting to club us over the head. Satan is the one who comes to steal from us, kill and destroy us (John 10:10). Don't listen to him! We are more apt to trust the one who destroys us through deception than the Lord who leads us with truth. How ironic! When the Lord encourages us to yield to Him, Satan will inject negative "what ifs: into our thinking to frighten us: "If I surrender all of myself, what if I don't like where he's taking me? What if I can't do what he's asking? What if I can't give up my sinful ways? What if I don't even *want* to give up my sinful ways? What if He asks me to go to Africa as a missionary? I don't think I could handle that."

God will take a surrendered life and begin right where we're at and help us change bit by bit. He won't give us an elephant to eat. Perhaps selfishness is keeping us from full surrender. We don't want God or anyone else telling us how to run our lives. Do we know how to run our lives better than the God who made us, and has a good plan for us since before time began? If we call our own shots and make a huge error that wrecks a part of our life, who can we blame? If we fully surrender our life, God assumes total responsibility for it. Sure, we may still make mistakes, but knowing that God was with us when we made the decision shares the responsibility of the outcome with Him. God's provision is bigger than any mistake we will ever make. He's specialized in restoration since Adam and Eve.

> If Jesus is not Lord of all, He's not Lord at all.

Full commitment and surrender. They are daunting words, but in living them out, we can truly sense God's presence with us. It is a process that grows deeper and more rewarding each day. 2 Chronicles 16:9 says, "For the eyes of the Lord range throughout the earth to strengthen those whose hearts are fully committed to Him."

Let me challenge you today to begin something fresh and new. I challenge you to full surrender and commitment daily. That means no reservations, no here today and gone tomorrow commitment, and no bargaining. You will be amazed at the level of peace and joy you'll experience as you find out that God is faithful and able to be fully trusted with your whole life. Remember, if Jesus is not Lord of all, He's not Lord at all. It's so worth it!

PART II

HOW WE CAN THRIVE, NOT JUST SURVIVE, PERSONALLY, RELATIONALLY, AND FINANCIALLY

CHAPTER 10
How to Personally Thrive: We Need to Have a Plan

DO YOU HAVE A PLAN FOR YOUR LIFE?

I love David the shepherd, psalmist, and king. He is one of my favourite people profiled in God's Word because he so often let us know what was going on with him. He was a real person that we can identify with. Despite his humanity and faults, God considered David to be a man after His own heart. Is there a bigger compliment that could ever be paid? David sought an intimate relationship with God throughout his life—whether it was defending sheep, defeating Goliath, becoming a king, going into battle, and even coming out of adultery and murder to come back into an intimate relationship with God after he'd grossly sinned. He gives all of us such hope that we're never so far out of God's reach that He can't pull us back. God truly does forgive our sins and puts them in the sea of forgetfulness. Perhaps that is why he wrote this psalm. Living a life following God doesn't just happen; we need to make some conscious choices and stick to them.

In scuba diving, they teach you that when you go down into the depths, you need a dive plan; that is, you have to have a good idea of what area you want to look at down there, and keep track of where you are in relation to the surface. A good rule of thumb is to "plan your dive, then dive your plan." This is to keep you safe, so you don't wander way off course and come up not knowing where you are; the coordinates on the ocean floor remain the same as the surface, but it sure looks different down there! We can apply that same logic to our lives. God's principles and heart are the same up in heaven as they are on Earth, so we need to plan how we are going to live, then follow that to the fullest. God's will remains the same in Heaven as on Earth, and He changes not, but will we follow it?

In Psalm 101, David formulates his life plan; he uses the word "will" sixteen times in eight verses. He outlines what he will and will not do. He decides to accomplish these things with God's help. Now we know he failed and sinned at certain junctures in his life—we all do—but the reason he was a man after God's heart is that he didn't park there. His failures were the exception and not the rule. None of us will ever have perfect behaviour, but our intent is to live according to God's will even after we blow it. He genuinely repented, picked himself up, and began again. As a king, he had specific responsibilities, but these good decisions made to rule his kingdom can be incorporated into running our lives as well. David clearly wrote these affirmations down for a reason. He was making a plan to lead a careful life and wanted it on paper to make sure he not only affirmed it, but for those around him to adhere and follow as well. Here are the things he says he will or will not do, along with the contemporary meaning of our day. These are specific to David, but what would your list look like?

- "I will be careful to lead a blameless life." *I'll do my best to live honestly and with integrity.*
- "I will set before my eyes no vile thing." *No idols for David! I will be careful to not let anything come between me and my devotion for my God.*
- "The deeds of faithless men I hate; they will not cling to me." *I will resist those sticky sins of worldly people that entice me and will give them no place in my life.*
- "I will have nothing to do with evil." *I will give no place to things or ways that are clearly wrong.*
- "I will not endure those with a proud heart." *I'll not cater to those who are full of themselves to get ahead.*
- "My eyes will be on the faithful people in the land." *I will do life with those who seek God.*
- "Only people with integrity will I allow to minister to me." *I'll be careful over what I hear and receive to keep myself on track.*
- "No one who lies or practices deceit will I allow in my presence." *I will guard myself against the counsel of liars and will state the truth.*
- "Every morning I will silence all the wicked people in the land." *When given opportunity, I'll speak truth in my sphere of influence to silence the wicked.*

I'm sure David wasn't aware of just how far-reaching his values would be. He wasn't publishing a Bible; he was being led by God. Aren't we glad he obeyed? He was mentally preparing himself for future events and challenges, so that when they presented themselves, he already had his responses in place. This is why his kingdom prospered as a result.

What will we do or not do for our lives? How will we live? Being careful to consider God's heart and living right is the first step, but considering is not enough. Deciding has to result in corresponding action. Unless we apply these affirmations to our own lives, they are useless.

Don't let life just happen to you. Plan your life, and then live out that plan for your benefit and His glory. You won't regret it.

GOD'S GIFTS: ONE, TWO, OR ALL?

Do we want all of the gifts God has and wants to give us, or just some? Perhaps salvation from Hell is the primary thing we want and nothing else. God has many gifts that He wants to give us simply because He loves us, but also because He wants to equip us to become what He needs us to be. James 4:2-3 says:

"You do not have because you do not ask God. When you ask, you do not receive, because you ask with wrong motives, that you may spend what you get on your pleasures."

Consider the story of a Christian man who meandered through life with a lukewarm, disobedient walk with God, never really expecting Him to come through and always ending up with the fuzzy end of the lollipop. His finances were a mess, his personal life and relationships were rocky, and everything around him was constantly going wrong. The blessings of God were not resting on him, as he didn't want God for anything other than fire insurance. He was a minimal Christian at best. Being the gentleman He is, God complied. After he died, he went to Heaven, and James began showing him the sights. They went to his permanent dwelling and bypassed a certain room. The man asked, "What's in there?" "Oh," said James. "I don't know if you want to look in there. It might upset you." The man's curiosity was piqued, and he insisted on looking. Inside the room were treasures galore; spiritual gifts such as joy, peace, fulfilment, harmony with God and our fellow man as well as gifts that could have prospered him physically, emotionally, spiritually, and financially. The man asked, "Whose are these?" James replied, "They were set aside for you when you were on earth, but you never asked for them."

Years ago, I too had a carnal Christian walk. I was unfulfilled as a Christian and felt far away from God. I wasn't happy sinning, or happy being saved. In desperately seeking God, He led me to recite the following prayer, which I believe changed my life: "Lord Jesus, I want everything that you died to give me." If Jesus' precious spilled blood on the cross entitles me to everything Jesus has (we are co-heirs with Christ), then I wanted it all. I wanted all of His gifts, and everything the devil was currently keeping from me. I knew there was one crucial requirement. I had to surrender. My whole life needed to be His, then and now. I wanted it all, but in exchange, God required and wanted all of me, not for my glory, but for His. It's a win/win offer.

Yet surprisingly, like the man in the story, people hang onto a crust of bread when God has a banquet prepared. God does have so many gifts for us if we seek Him and desire them, but I don't want to infer that doing this will mean a happy-go-lucky life free of suffering. This is not a recipe for a Disney-type life. To live for self means suffering as well, but with no value. When Jesus hung on the Cross and said, "It is finished," He didn't just mean His death. He meant that everything that was required for us to live in victory was now completed.

That prayer changed my life. If you pray the same thing and mean it, your life also will never be the same. As you surrender your total life and ask Him for everything He died to give you, you put yourself in a position to be blessed in every way. Something new began as God took me seriously. I am still hungry for not only more of Him, but all of Him, and He doesn't disappoint. It's an exciting way to live! When I get to heaven and pass the room of gifts that I could have had on earth, I want it to be empty!

DO WE KNOW HOW GOOD WE HAVE IT?

I have been a Christian nearly all my life, and I find that there is an attitude of mine that I constantly need to check. Do I fully realize and appreciate how good my "God-environment" is? Do I really know what my life would be like if God wasn't impacting it every day? For example, imagine you find yourself feeling surly and unappreciative towards your workplace. You chat with your friend who is in the same line of work, and their company looks so much better from the outside than yours. Then you hear them complain about their horrible working conditions that are far worse than yours. All of a sudden, you look at your work situation with different eyes. Why? You had the opportunity to look at the nice green grass over the fence and found that it was only so green because a lot of manure had been piled onto it. It may look nice and green, but upon closer inspection, there is a definite odour. Suddenly going to work on Monday isn't such a chore. Your picture has been re-framed, and you're thankful for your workplace. You appreciate what you'd grown accustomed to and taken for granted.

My parents raised us in a Christian home and since I've been a Christian from the age of eight, I've had the blessing of living in the environment of God's presence, blessings, provision, and counsel while I was growing up. All Christians, from the moment they are born again, regardless of background, have the opportunity of living in the climate of God's direct impact on the storms and stillness that passes through their lives. I took it for granted until I had to learn the hard way and realize how good I had it. For example, my parents were always financially well off because they were hard workers and gave to God's kingdom. I never had to deal with lack because God took care of us. When I got married, I thought I'd just step into the same type of provision. However, I found that it didn't quite work that way if one didn't obey God. We were not tithing, and I firmly believe we became needy as a result. I had taken my God-environment for granted and expected a great harvest even though I had planted nothing. Eventually, after God got our attention and we began to give, He began to more than meet our need and we began to build a God-environment in our home. Our picture had been re-framed, and we'd learned a lesson.

In 2 Chronicles 33, Manasseh, Judah's king, thought he could ignore God and had to learn the hard way. His father Hezekiah had been a king who wholeheartedly obeyed and sought the Lord and prospered as a result, leaving a great kingdom for his son. Manasseh simply stepped into the atmosphere of God's blessings that his father had left him, and he didn't know how good he had it. Instead of being wise and continuing in what his father had done to achieve those results, he proceeded to do the most vile things, which became a long list of sins that included "much evil in the eyes of the Lord, provoking him to anger." He was known for his brutality and even led Judah astray into these sins. Did God just ignore all this? No. He spoke to them, and they ignored Him. So God brought the Assyrians against Manasseh to get his attention and they put a hook in his nose, bound him with bronze shackles, and took him to Babylon. You can bet he was re-thinking what he'd done and his life's choices.

But once again, we see just how immense God's love and mercy is for His children. "In his [Manasseh's] distress, he sought the favour of the Lord his God and humbled himself greatly before the God of his fathers. And when he prayed to Him, the Lord was moved by his entreaty and listened to his plea; so He brought him back to ... His kingdom. Then Manasseh knew that the Lord is God." Manasseh knew the odds of returning were slim. After this, he cleaned up his act to prove his about-face was genuine. Why is it only after God has cleaned up the mess that we realize He was there all along, desiring for us to avoid it in the first place?

CHAPTER 11
It's Not a Life of Dreary Servitude

CHOOSE TODAY WHOM YOU WILL SERVE

Until we graduate into glory, we will be faced with a never-ending flow of choices and decisions that will build our lives. The decisions you make today will affect your tomorrow. One decision stands above them all: who do you serve? Whatever you pour your time, energy, resources, and life into is the thing or person you serve.

In our universe, creation demands a Creator, design demands a Designer, intelligence demands an Intellect, and a building demands a Builder. One does not have to look far to see the fingerprint of intelligent design. The God of creation and incomprehensible order is passionately in love with you, His highest and most important creation—a person, like Him. You are a spirit that will live for all eternity, and He has given you the monumental privilege of choice. This amazing God has already paved the way for you to have a victorious life, no matter what. No matter what you've done; no matter what has happened to you in the past; no matter what will happen in the future.

> We are just not good enough at running our own lives. Just take a look around at those trying to do so. Is that working for them? Things may go well for a season, but eventually we will see the losses running our own lives cost us.

With God, we can always gain the victory over and through our circumstances. How?

In the book of Joshua, Chapter 24, the ancient Israelites were on the verge of finally going into the Promised Land after Moses had died and they had spent forty years wandering the wilderness. Does their situation feel familiar? We've all blown it at various times during our lives. However, the truth is that God specializes in restoration and He recycles garbage. God can take the garbage that has happened to us and recycle it into something useful and new. In fact, most people would never even know that it came from garbage!

How is this possible? Joshua confronted the Israelites and reiterated their past, about how they messed up by worshipping idols and when they turned back, God delivered them time and time again. Now they needed to make a solid decision over this choice:

¹⁴ "Now fear the LORD and serve Him with all *faithfulness*. Throw away the gods your ancestors worshipped beyond the Euphrates River and in Egypt, and serve the LORD. ¹⁵ But if serving the LORD seems undesirable to you, then choose for yourselves this day whom you will serve, whether the gods your ancestors served beyond the Euphrates, or the gods of the Amorites, in whose land you are living. But as for me and my household, we will serve the LORD" (Josh 24:14–15).

He gave them a choice: serve God, or serve a God substitute. Idolatry was a big temptation of their day. They were on the brink of going into the Promised Land, and they would live or die by their choice. He knew they needed to be the ones to consciously make that decision. God would support their choice, and if they told Him that they were going to serve other gods and to go away, He would have.

We don't have the gods of the Amorites or those their ancestors worshipped beyond the Euphrates River. In our society today, the biggest God substitute is our ego. If we spend our lives serving ourselves, we need to know that we are not good enough at running our own lives. We do not see the beginning from the end. In looking back at our lives, how many things would we have done differently if we could have known what was coming in the future?

The things we do apart from serving God and His leadership may lead us to places we do not desire, and He will let us because He has given us free will that He will not violate. Things may go well for a season, but eventually we will see the losses that come from running our own lives.

> "But as for me and my household, we will serve the Lord."

When the Israelites served God, all went well for them, as God knew what they were going to face and helped them defeat every enemy. He blessed their efforts to prosper while they served Him. The same is true today. Serving any substitute for God will not give you the abundant life that Jesus came to give us. By abundant I don't mean perfect; I mean fulfilled in ways that are far from my understanding. God takes us from a place that is between a rock and a hard place, and somehow brings us into a spacious fertile valley in His perfect timing. When we are about His business, God takes care of our business, and the result is joy and peace. He did it for the Israelites, and He'll do it for you and me too. All we need to do is make the right choice.

HOW DO WE SERVE GOD?

Do we consider serving God a privilege or an obligation? There is a big difference between the two. There are many Christians today serving God but their motivation to do so is not necessarily pleasing to Him. They are "do" oriented instead of "be" oriented. Because I've accepted Jesus' sacrifice for me, I am a child of God, but not because I'm good enough by what I do. Christianity is the only religion in which our God did something for us to save us, instead of a lifetime of servitude the other way around. We don't have to do anything to merit salvation; it has already been done. It's done versus do. Jesus didn't create us so we'd work for Him; He created us to fellowship with Him; He created human beings, not human doings. Is that then to mean it doesn't matter if we serve Him or not? No, but how and why we serve Him matters.

How are we to serve our Jesus? 1 Thessalonians 1:3 says, "We remember before our God and Father your work produced by faith, your labour prompted by love, and your endurance inspired by hope in our Lord Jesus Christ."

So, faith produces work, labour is prompted by love, and endurance is inspired by hope, not guilt produces work, labour is prompted by obligation, and endurance is inspired by fear.

Does that sound familiar? It might, because as long as we're on Earth, we all still have the lower nature to deal with. I'm sure we've all identified with these motivators. If they do describe us, all our work will be for nothing. If we work from a selfish vantage point with impure motives, all our righteous acts of service are like filthy rags (Isa 64:6). Of course, there are times when serving becomes difficult or tiring, but our core motivation is what is of key importance.

What did Paul mean when he said that faith produces work? Jesus said, in John 6:29, "The work of God is this: to believe in the one He has sent." If you were to ask the average Christian what they think the work is that God wants from us, I'm sure you'd get a long list of everything from evangelizing the world to being the caretaker of the local church. These are all important, to be sure, but God knows us far better than we know ourselves. We would quickly turn working for God into a long list of chores. The expression "work of faith"

> It makes the work far easier because it's a debt of love that you don't mind paying.

also includes the life of faith that follows conversion. When we've truly encountered His incredible love and accept His sacrifice, He begins the work of transforming us from the inside out. One of the first things that people often notice about someone who's been born again is that they're now different. One of the most common statements made by friends and family is "you've changed." It is a natural progression to want to begin to be Christ-like. If we believe in God and that Jesus died for us, it should make us desire to serve Him.

That leads us neatly to what prompts our labour for Him: love. How much easier is it to work for someone you love to make happy? This is a huge reward. It makes the work far easier because it's a debt of love that you don't mind paying. I'm reminded of Jacob in the Bible when he worked for seven years for the woman he loved, but the time seemed like just a few days to him because he loved her so much (Gen 29:20). I absolutely love writing this book, but truthfully, it's time-consuming and a lot of hard work, but not burdensome. Just the other day, I sat down to write and three hours later looked up and was shocked to see the time. It honestly felt like a half hour. I get so excited by faith in Jesus and the tremendous gift that we can all have, that it naturally creates work. I have to share this with others.

God expresses the importance of a heart of love towards Him throughout the Old and New Testaments. I love 2 Chronicles 16:9: "For the eyes of the Lord range throughout the earth to strengthen those whose hearts are fully committed to Him." God even energizes us when our hearts are full of commitment towards His cause and purposes. God is looking for people who will labour for Him because they love Him.

Finally, hope in our Lord Jesus Christ is what inspires us to endure until the job is done and our purpose is fulfilled. We are to live and do everything as unto the Lord for His glory (1 Cor 10:31). Even our jobs can be service to our Lord, providing seed for us to give and showing His love to people who desperately need it. At the end of a long day's work for wages or for our Lord, it's sometimes hard to remember what should be motivating us. It helps me to remember that only that which is done for our Lord will last forever. Why not make all of it count?

CHAPTER 12
God Provides Quality Materials

CAN OUR BUILDING MATERIALS STAND THE HEAT?

What kind of materials are you using to build your life? If you believe in Jesus Christ, every single believer is building a special structure that is unique to each individual. When you accepted Him as your Saviour, you laid down a foundation. You were spiritually born again. You received a new beginning. That foundation is what will allow you to enter Heaven based on what He did for you and me.

However, we need to realize that the materials we use to build on that foundation are up to us. Some people believe that after one is saved, it doesn't matter how lazy or diligent a Christian is, we all receive the same reward of eternal life. This is true, but according to 1 Corinthians 3:12-15, there is much more that we should be aware of. It says:

"If any man builds on this foundation using gold, silver or costly stones, wood, hay or straw, his work will be shown for what it is, because the Day will bring it to light. It will be revealed with fire, and the fire will test the quality of each man's work. If what he has built survives, he will receive his reward. If it is burned up, he will suffer loss; he himself will be saved, but only as one escaping from the flames."

You and I have a choice of building materials, including gold, silver, costly stones, wood, hay, or straw. They represent our service to our Lord while we are here on earth. If the Bible gives me a choice, then it's my responsibility to choose well. And, God doesn't want quantity; He wants *quality*. Jesus made this clear when He saw the rich putting their gifts into the temple treasury. He also saw a poor widow put in two small copper coins and remarked: "this poor widow has put in more than all the others" (Luke 21:3). She gave all she had. Imagine a house made of straw in comparison to one of gold. Which will be more durable? Which of these houses, when put through a fire, will come out intact? If God puts a house built of gold or silver through a fire, not only will it come out intact, it will be refined. All the garbage, wrong motives for our service, or anything that can't stand up to fire will have been purged out of it.

Notice that the verse says the "Day," with a capital D, "will bring it to light" (or will reveal the quality). This is capitalized because this is no ordinary day. There will come an event when what we have built on the foundation of Christ will be tested for quality. If what we built is burned up, it will be evident, and we will suffer loss and feel regret. If we've been wise, we will receive our reward. I don't want to suffer loss on that day. I want to receive my reward, whatever that may be.

Jesus also said that before a man builds a house, he needs to first count the cost (Luke 14:28). I love the account of the jailer in the sixteenth chapter of Acts. Here we have Paul and Silas thrown in jail after being "severely flogged" (Luke 16:23). God sends a violent earthquake that shakes the foundation of the prison, whereby all the prison doors fly open, and everybody's chains come loose. The jailer, who was napping, suddenly wakes up and draws his sword to end his life because he knows he'll die anyways if these guys escape. Paul and Silas call out and reassure him they're all still there. The jailer rushes in and falls before them and asks them what he needs to do to be saved, and they tell him to believe in Jesus. He takes them to his home, where he washes their sore, tender, and torn backs. In the next verse he "was filled with joy because he had come to believe in God—he and his whole family" (Luke 16:34). This guy was genuinely saved, not only because he witnessed a miracle at the jail, but because he saw their stripes. He had counted the cost, and still was filled with joy. This challenges me, and I hope, you too. The jailer's foundation was laid, and he had no delusions on what it would take to use gold, silver, and precious stones to build on it.

As you ponder your own life, what materials do you feel you've been using to build on the foundation of your salvation in Jesus? If you are considering this passage and feel that what you've been using won't stand up to the heat, rejoice today! There is still time to upgrade your building materials.

In our society today, gold, silver, and precious stones are hard to come by, but God is not going to require us to use building materials that are inaccessible to us. We can rejoice that we all can use gold, silver, and precious stones like the widow who gave two copper coins out of a heart of love for her God. Leave the hay to the donkeys.

WE WILL NEVER PLEASE GOD WITH PRETENCE

Have you ever wandered away from God in your heart but still wanted Him handy in case you got into a jam? I have. It's like a marriage that starts out full of joy and intimacy, doing things for each other out of devotion, but for one reason or another it cools off. The two become cold and distant toward one another, but because they're still married, they continue to do things for each other out of obligation, thinking that will keep all bases covered. The thing is, those bases really aren't being covered, and eventually there will be a breakdown. The same can be said about our relationship with God.

So often, when our circumstances begin to change negatively, God allows events to occur that He didn't want to happen in the first place, but will use to get our attention

The Israelites had grown cold towards God. Their moral condition deteriorated and they quit honouring Him in their midst. They worshipped idols but still wanted God handy when they needed Him. They had fallen away from the devotion of their first love and were simply going through the motions mechanically. They now faced war, and the army went out to fight the Philistines, whereby four thousand Israelites died (1 Sam 4:2). This struck me. If God would allow so many to die, He would have had to have a good reason.

They should have asked God over why they lost, but they only asked themselves: "Why did the Lord bring defeat upon us today before the Philistines?" They didn't get it. They blamed God and decided it was because His ark hadn't gone with them. They said, "Let us bring the ark … so that it may go with us and save us from the hand of our enemies" (1 Sam 4:3). Notice they were relying on the ark itself, not the God whose presence went with it. You can see where their hearts were. They thought going through the motions would obligate God to help them. The ark had gone out in the past and given them huge victories, so they reasoned this must have been the problem. Out they went again, but this time with the ark, and thirty thousand more died, and the ark was captured. This was a big deal. God clearly was not acting on their behalf, and was using a megaphone to speak loudly to them.

We are never going to please God with pretence. Ritual will never replace relationship. We are only fooling ourselves if we think that God will move on our behalf because of an outward show of Christianity, when inside we're far away.

No amount of procedure could replace obedience. Their idolatry dishonoured and disobeyed God; they made their own plans and didn't bother to consult Him. I think this is a good example of people putting their reliance in a formula instead of in God Himself. They figured they were covered and thirty-four thousand slain soldiers later, they realized they weren't.

We drift away from God and put our devotion on other things instead of Him, but still expect God to bless our plans without asking Him if we should be doing them. In everything we do, He needs to be first in our hearts. In the past, when my relationship with my Lord had grown cold, the first evidence was that He was no longer in control. I was, and as such, I began to fall off the path of His best for my life. Israel losing all those men was a result of their moral decay and was supposed to be a wake-up call. They finally understood that God was using this trial to draw His people back into total devotion. This shows just how important our love is to Him. God is jealous for our love because He loves us way more! (Ex 34:14)

The Israelites remained under the oppression of the Philistines for twenty years before they smartened up (1 Sam 7:2-4). They mourned and came to Samuel, who told them, "if you're returning to God, prove it." Again, we see that God doesn't buy appearances. They could wail and weep until the cows came home (which actually happened in 1 Samuel 6:12, and with the ark, to boot), but being sorry needed to result in action. They repented, tossed out their idols, and "served the Lord only." With a show of His power, "...the Philistines drew near to engage Israel in battle. But that day the Lord thundered with loud thunder against [them] and threw them into such a panic that they were routed before the Israelites." When God shows up, the enemy leaves.

It's important to note that God never desired for them to die. We can be certain He tried to get their attention many other ways before this. If you feel you are successfully "doing: Christianity, that is, performing the outside evidences well while your heart is far away, I implore you to ponder this: the Lord is interested in what's going on in our hearts, and it won't take long before we're faced with a situation that will show both us and God where we're at. He allows this because He loves us too much to leave us deceiving ourselves.

Partial Obedience is Not Obedience

Imagine you ask your teenager to clean his room. When you go to see, you find the bed is made, but piles of dirty clothes are still on the floor. He claims he did what you asked, but the room is still a mess. Did he obey you?

There's a good example of this in 1 Samuel 15. God commands Saul to attack the Amalekites and to "totally destroy everything that belongs to them," as God was using Saul to effect His just judgement on them. It goes on to say that Saul and the army spared Agag (the Amalekite king) and the best of the sheep and cattle, the fat calves and lambs, to sacrifice to the Lord. He kept everything that was good.

Here's the thing. It all looks good, doesn't it? We might look at that and say that Saul did destroy the wicked people, as God told him. He only kept the best animals, which he wanted to give to God anyways. What's wrong with that? The problem is that God was testing him. At the end of that day, Saul had not obeyed. By disobeying, he dishonoured Him as the God of Israel. Remember, this was Israel's first king and God tentatively placed the kingship in Saul's hands. Saul put his agenda ahead of God's. He says he saved the best animals to sacrifice, but that doesn't excuse disobedience. No matter what he was given to do, he came short of complete obedience. He redefined the Lord's commands, doing what seemed best to him rather than what God commanded. I've seen people do this for many of God's direct commands, me included. We take His direct commands and paint them with our brush and what suits us best.

This was a serious infraction where Saul was concerned. It lost him the kingship, as God said, "I am grieved that I have made Saul king, because he has turned away from me and has not carried out my instructions." God simply does not consider partial obedience to be obedience at all. In fact, He does not even acknowledge that Saul had obeyed. When Samuel confronted Saul, he said, "If you obeyed ... what is this bleating of sheep in my ears? What is this lowing of cattle that I hear?" Saul responds much the same way a teenager would: "But I did obey the Lord. I went on the mission the Lord assigned me. I completely destroyed the Amalekites. It was the soldiers who spared the best of the sheep and cattle to sacrifice to the Lord." Saul thought he could get around God's direct command due to a technicality. But God never told the soldiers what He expected; He gave orders directly to Saul.

Samuel's response is a frequently quoted truth that still applies today: "To obey is better than sacrifice." If you ask your teen to clean up their room, and they buy you a cup of coffee and skip the room, are you impressed? The coffee is great, sure, but the room is the real issue.

If God commands us in His Word to do something and we knock ourselves out to do everything just short of it, we haven't done it at all. Or perhaps we make a half-hearted attempt to obey to relieve our guilt. We are only deluding ourselves if we think God will be satisfied with the half-finished job when we are fully aware of how unsatisfied we are when our kids try to pull this on us.

At the end of the day, the reason God wanted obedience in the first place is the same as the parent with the teenager. He wanted to bless Saul with a "well done! Now I can trust you to obey Me." Let's learn from Saul and not lose out.

CHAPTER 13
How to Thrive Relationally

WHAT MEN AND WOMEN WANT – INTRODUCTION

The next three chapters look at what men and women want from one another. This section was inspired in part by a message I heard a few years ago at Relate Church by Pastor John Burns. It includes much of my own growth as a marriage partner through personal experience and study of God's Word. After all, He is the one who saw that men and women need one another, created marriage, and knows how to make it thrive.

Many of today's marriages and relationships are in serious peril when they don't have to be. I know this grieves the heart of God because relational problems don't have to end up in divorce or with His children in pain. I've been married for over thirty years and have learned much from personal experience as well as observing God at work, making my marriage shine as I obeyed Him. Investing in the relationship with your mate will be a lot of work, but I know it pays great dividends! In the end, don't we want to have joy, peace, and harmony with each other?

> Investing in the relationship with your mate will be a lot of work, but I know it pays great dividends!

If you're married, has your marriage thus far progressed smoothly, or has it been a bumpy ride? If you could do it over, would you marry your significant other again? Why or why not? The goal is for you to have the best marriage with your mate that God has planned, and if you're not married, to plan for the best to come. Joy and pain stem from whether our relationships are thriving or barely surviving. We can see the effects that our daily interchanges have on our children, our families, our work life, and our state of happiness. Through the leadership of the Holy Spirit and better understanding of how men and women are wired, I believe we can truly enjoy rather than just endure the ride. In the following chapters, we will look at the differences between how men and women think, what each of us needs from marriage, and how to work together to make a happy and healthy marriage.

MEN THINK IN A STRAIGHT LINE. WOMEN THINK IN A SPIDER WEB

Do you remember a movie with Mel Gibson called *What Women Want*? It was about a man who was given the ability to hear the thoughts of every woman he met, which gave him a distinct advantage in every situation. It was humorous for us to see his own shock at how wrong he had been about women before he received his ability. I know what you men out there may be thinking: "How much easier would my life be to simply understand what my wife wants without my having to struggle to figure her out!" It may not be quite like the movie, but we can learn to understand how men and women are different and what they want and need from one another. For example, men are not mind-readers like the guy in the movie. Ladies, we're often reluctant to tell our mate exactly what we want and we're famous for giving hints, but men generally hate hints or don't pick up on them. They want us to tell them plainly what we need! Why do we do this, and why do they need to be told?

Women are complicated—I admit it. We process our thoughts and emotions by talking. Women talk with the express purpose to talk some more, to really figure things out. In fact, they enjoy talking. Men, on the other hand, talk in order to stop talking. Have you ever noticed during a discussion how quick he is to agree with you in order to steer the conversation to a close, once he's figured out that a simple response won't satisfy you and this is going to be a long, drawn-out thing? Of course, not all men are like this, but by nature, they tend to be. Even though times, ideas, and cultures are

> Men are natural conquerors and fixers; they are goal oriented. Women, on the other hand, are analyzers. One won't work well without the other. We need each other!

vastly different from one another and are constantly changing, the basic blueprints God initially created man and woman from haven't changed.

I always say the following, with no offence intended towards men (I'm married to one too): men think in a straight line; women think in a spider web. It's so true. She gives voice to what she's thinking as she works it out. She begins by discussing an issue or problem, which quickly digresses down a myriad of different and interconnected paths to cover all potential aspects. All the reasons are interwoven, which leaves the poor guy bewildered and wondering exactly what the initial issue was. It makes sense to her, but he's lost. He just wants it to stop, so he'll talk to end the conversation, not to get at the root of the problem.

Imagine the problem is a tree in a forest. The man says, "I'll go straight to the tree and chop it down, and everything will be fine." The woman says, "No, you're going to pass dense foliage, and there's a ravine, a raging stream, and big boulders. You have to locate the right tree, and then look at what's wrong with it. You have to address the root—that's the problem! You just can't go straight in and chop it down! That won't fix anything; it will just start to grow again. This is going to take some time. You don't even know which tree it is!" Men are natural conquerors and fixers; they are goal oriented. Women, on the other hand, are analyzers. One won't work well without the other. He can't find the tree, and she can't chop it down. Both are needed.

It makes you wonder what God was thinking when He created men and women. I once heard a female preacher say that getting married to her husband was easy. It was the "becoming one" that God stipulated when He said, "a

> It isn't my job to change him; that is exclusively God's responsibility.

man will leave his father and mother and be united to his wife and they will become one flesh" (Gen 2:24). God didn't make any mistakes. In fact, He did this on purpose! It helped me immensely in understanding my husband to find out that what I once considered were his flaws were actually his God-ordained makeup. I had no business trying to change them, and God showed me that as his wife, my role is to complement and enhance his life experience, not make him like me. It isn't my job to change him; that is exclusively God's responsibility. Why would I want to be married to another version of myself? That would be terribly boring, not to mention that we in ourselves are not the complete package. That's why He gave you your significant other. We are meant to fill each other's gaps. In the following sections, we'll take a close look at what those gaps are.

WHAT MEN NEED FROM WOMEN: RESPECT

In today's society, it appears that being courteous, polite, and showing respect to others has become outdated behaviour and is simply not as important as it once was. Particularly, there appears to be a decline in respect towards the positions of authority that God instituted and deems worthy. I believe this can be a root cause for the breakdown of the marriage relationship as well. While men also need to respect women, I was surprised to learn just how important respect from women, are to men.

We often see examples of disrespect by couples towards one another. Just a few weeks ago, we were at the beach on vacation, and there was a couple in the water near us. The husband was in a little deeper and was coaxing his wife to wade in farther. She found it cool, so she was going in slowly, and his attempt to coax her repeatedly irritated her. She voiced her irritation by calling him a name. I was in the water near them, and immediately flags went up. Instead of expressing irritation with her husband over what he was doing, she directed her irritation at his person, directly. The lack of respect she showed him was clear and I thought, "They are headed for major trouble." There are times when we slip up, and an apology is in order, but when putting down our partner becomes our default behaviour, something needs to change. My daughter also noticed their interchange and later expressed surprise at the woman's verbal attack on her husband. It just shows that when people develop a habit of treating everyone with respect, it's easy to recognize when it's absent. Every person on the planet has inherent value because they're God's child and as such that position deserves respect for that fact alone.

For marriage partners, God gives us instruction in the book of Ephesians. I begin with this because almost everything else builds on it. Being respected is important to men and is commanded by God. He addresses the husband first, and then the woman in Ephesians 5:33:

"However, each one of you also must love his wife as he loves himself, and the wife must respect her husband."

Look at the commands God uses: "must" love and "must" respect. This leaves no room for discussion. God is saying something for good reason—He knows what's coming if this is ignored. When God uses an emphatic command, it's always for a good reason and our good. I don't know how many times I've said this, but we need to hear it repeatedly to get it into our heads and hearts: God's commands are not electric fences that will zap us if we stray too far; they are loving boundaries put there to keep us from going over cliffs.

By doing these two things, respecting and loving each other, we avoid a lot of strife. I love God's sense of balance of responsibilities. If both parties adhere to obeying that verse, it's easy for each of them to do. If a man loves his wife to the degree that he loves himself (in a right and balanced way), he'll be sure to take care of her needs as surely as he takes care of himself. It's easy for a woman to respect a man who lovingly takes care of her. If a wife shows her husband respect in how she relates to him, it's easy for him to love her. Sadly, we often treat people we barely know better than the ones we love the most. When we live with one another, we see each other as we are, warts and all, and this can make us disrespectful towards one another. However, God gave that man to you, and even if he's acting ugly and doesn't deserve it, we need to respect the God-ordained position of husband. We have to separate their "who" from their "do." We need to respect them because of who they are as the authority God has placed over the wife, and not just based on what they do.

Look at where it leads if you don't respect your husband. It starts to erode your relationship and becomes a forced obligation.

> We have to separate their "who" from their "do." We need to respect our husbands because of who they are, and not just based on what they do.

> God's commands are not electric fences that will zap us if we stray too far; they are loving boundaries put there to keep us from going over cliffs.

God helps us by giving us this command. We respect our mates because He told us to, not because they deserve it. Remember that what we sow, we will reap. Jesus is pleased with us if we obey Him in the tough places and He will help us. Don't forget that He is watching out for and will reward those who obey Him.

Respecting your husband builds him up and shows him you value him; it creates the desire for him to fulfil your high opinion of him. Love and respect are hard to resist!

WHAT MEN NEED FROM WOMEN: UNDERSTANDING AND PATIENCE

This is often where men and women get frustrated because they can't seem to get on the same page. Like I mentioned, women think in a spider web and men in a straight line. Women need to get better at clearly conveying expectations in a way that men can understand. I heard Pastor John say it this way: "We need you to spell it out, ladies!" Many times, women think men are mind-readers and expect them to know inherently what they want without them having to say so. In fact, I used to take it personally when Jake didn't know what I needed. Men simply aren't wired this way. We call it being left-brained and right-brained. Men are lateral in their thinking, which means they tend to use one side of their brain at a time, and tend to favour the left side of the brain where logic operates. Men tend to think logically, sequentially, rationally, objectively, and look at parts. Women, on the other hand, are right-brained in that they are bilateral in their thinking, which means they tend to use both sides of their brain at the same time, but favour the right side. They tend to think emotionally, intuitively, spiritually, and holistically (looking at a whole system that must be analyzed rather than parts before a decision is rendered). When I finally understood this about Jake, I didn't get upset with him for not knowing instinctively what I needed all the time. Now I just respectfully spell it out, not because he's inferior or lesser in any way, but because God made him like that. In fact, if you want to be fair, women should be even more understanding with how their husbands are wired, because God already made them more intuitive.

Being patient is key. I've seen women try to explain something to their husbands and if they didn't immediately understand what they were getting at, they became quickly frustrated. I've seen the man's confidence shrivel up as his wife made him feel stupid in front of friends. I've done it myself, and no one wins. The funny thing is, if I was talking to another woman and she didn't get it, I'm sure I'd patiently explain it again. Maybe we're just not that great at expressing ourselves. Being patient means not throwing up our hands and giving up. We have to be creative and think about explaining our issue from a different perspective.

When I was a young mother of two, the job of keeping the house tidy was a big challenge at times. If I could have been paid a nickel for every time I picked something up and put it back in place, I'd have been a millionaire. When Jake came home from work, he'd toss his clothes on the floor because he was finally home and could relax. As you can imagine, this set me off. I explained that it was extra work that I did not need and he couldn't understand what the big deal was. It was a few items, after all. I finally concluded I had to approach explaining it a different way, as getting mad was getting me nowhere. Since he is a plumber, I decided to draw a parallel from his work relating to mine. I asked, "How would you like it if you had to go into the same home, day after day after day, and make the same repair? It wouldn't matter that you'd already fixed it; the next day the same thing would be broken." Then he finally understood. It wasn't the picking up of the few items; it was the redundancy of picking up after kids and trying to keep the house neat. He understood and began to make an effort to pick up after himself.

I believe the Lord gave me the way to explain my feelings. This is where God's wisdom comes in. He knows, and often shows us what to say and how to say it. At the end of the day when I've become frustrated, I've gone to my Lord and asked Him to help me express myself in such a way that Jake can understand. God always comes through. He greatly desires that couples have intimacy through understanding one another. The reward is that you both grow closer through understanding one another with patience.

WHAT MEN NEED FROM WOMEN:
FUEL HIS DREAMS AND CHALLENGE HIM

I mentioned that women are naturally more intuitive than men, but I'm not talking about the weak brand of "women's intuition" that we sometimes joke about. I'm talking about the way God has gifted this amazing creature called woman. I believe that women are innately aware of things without having to discover or perceive them. But even before a relationship is established a woman has the ability to see and recognize potential in her potential mate, and she is to let him know she's interested. In essence, she is to chase him until he catches her. Girls figure this out at an early age. Men were created to be conquerors. Women are to be conquered, but only at her say-so. Jake jokes about how I tricked him into marrying me. "She tricked me," he says. "She said she liked me." Women are able to recognize the good qualities our husbands have that could be great qualities, and bring them forth without nagging or correction, but by creating the desire in him to catch the big vision she sees. I remember in the early years of my marriage how key this was. I did it without even realizing it came from my God-given ability and by His direction. We were struggling financially being a young married couple during dire economic times, and Jake wasn't getting enough hours of work to pay the bills. I simply asked him why he didn't start his own business. He looked at me with doubts, but I believed in him. In fact, I think I believed in him more than he believed in himself at that time. I saw in him a great potential, and he heard and believed me. We've had our own business for over thirty years now, and it all began during a terrible recession with a seed of vision that God planted in him through me.

Be a woman who fuels his dreams.

Men were created to be conquerors and rulers. God told Adam in Genesis 1:28 to "fill the earth and subdue it. Rule over the fish ... and the birds ... and over every living creature that moves on the ground." I believed in Jake's ability to start a plumbing business with no experience, but he was the one who went out and conquered the world to accomplish that. I could never have done it, but that was not my role. It's sad to say that I've seen men trying to rise up and do something great, and their wives keep them down because they see all the reasons not to take risks. This is woman's holistic view of things actually getting in the way. Because she looks at the whole thing, she's already worked it out from beginning to end, and it looks way too hard. The man, however, who looks at parts and not the whole thing, doesn't see the obstacles as barriers, but as challenges to be conquered. His eye is on the prize. If God is leading, being a woman who fuels his dreams is not just jumping on the bandwagon each time he has an idea, but allowing God to use your natural instincts and insight to guide him. God is the one whispering in a wife's ear when her husband needs encouragement and direction. This is also an important reason why husbands should consider carefully what their wives are saying, and why wives should be careful about what they are saying. If we flippantly agree over something questionable our husband is considering doing, don't be surprised if he does it and blames you for poor results. There has never been a dream of my husband's that hasn't been my dream also. I don't think there is a greater joy for a wife than for her to see her husband not only surviving in this tough world looking after his family, but thriving despite it.

Be a woman who challenges him to become complete.

We are all on a journey—not from here to there, but from who we are to who we are becoming in Christ. The more you become Christ-like, the more you become the truer you—the person God intended you to be in the first place. You were never designed to be marred and disfigured due to the curse of sin. God knows what it will take to get us there, and we can't rush growth. We can, however, impede or enhance it.

Take a potted plant for example. If you neglect it and leave it in a dark room with little water or light, how well will it do? How much better will it do with plenty of attention in the right way at the right time? Similarly, the way that we nourish our husband matters. Nagging doesn't work. We will never do right in being a woman who nags him to become complete. As wives with Godly insight, we need to be wise when something about our husbands flags in our spirits. I don't want to make this exclusive to men either. God points out our stuff to our men too. Pointing a self-righteous finger never ends with our mate becoming complete and Christ-like. Rather, giving voice to the issue that God has shown you with love, with you being fully on his side supporting him with his best interest, is the way to go. It would be far better to start the conversation with, "I'm concerned about something and it's been bothering me for a while. Can I share it with you or is this not a good time?" This way, you've prepared him, and you're asking for his permission to speak into his life. When you're given the opportunity, go for it and don't water it down. The woman who knows who she is and has heard from God will also be heard by her man.

WHAT MEN NEED FROM WOMEN: BE HIS REFUGE; DO LIFE WITH HIM

Men were given by God the primary responsibility of ruling the world. I'm sorry if that offends the female gender, but I didn't set up the order of things, God did. But who generally moulds the minds, outlooks, personalities, and characters of little boys in their formative learning years? Women. There is a saying that merits consideration: "The hand that rocks the cradle is the hand that rules the world." It sounds like a contradiction, but both statements are true. Women throughout the ages have been the primary caregivers of children, so, in essence, women rule the world too, but perhaps more indirectly. Their role is the most important because they have the charge to fashion those little minds and raise self-confident yet fully-reliant-on Godly sons. This takes years of a consistent labour of love. A mother is crucially important to a little boy, and her support and guidance can do much to direct the course of his life. Many little boys want to marry their moms when they grow up. Here is an invaluable peek behind the curtain for every girl considering marrying a guy: if you want to know how you'll be treated as his wife, look at how he treats his mother. If that mother has done her job well, that young man will respect her, love her, be considerate towards her, and honour her. You should have no problem.

Be his refuge, comfort, and confidante.

Where do little boys go when they've skinned their knee? To mom. She kisses it and makes it all better. Moms can fix anything and know everything. When he comes home from school after a fight with his friends, she's there to listen and empathize with his problems. The same can be said for men where women are concerned. He's looking for a refuge and comfort after a hard day's work. When he unloads all the day's problems, the last thing he wants is to be told is where he was wrong, even if he was at fault. Jake has told me clearly that regardless of the situation, he wants to be told he's right and the other person is wrong when he comes home from a stressful day of work. He knows that he shares responsibility in the situation, but at that moment, he just wants somebody in his corner, not more opposition or correction. After he's eaten and watched some sports to relax, he's far more objective and is open to considering my slant on the issue. And ladies, from personal experience I recommend you never offer an opinion that might upset him when your man is hungry!

"The hand that rocks the cradle is the hand that rules the world."

Be a woman who will do life with him.
Be his companion and helper.

After the world was created, God brought all the animals to Adam to see what he'd name them. Genesis 2:20 says, "So the man gave names to all the livestock ... birds ... and beasts of the field. But for Adam no suitable helper was found ... so the Lord God caused the man to fall into a deep sleep; and while he was sleeping, He took one of man's ribs." We know that from that rib God created Eve. Adam said, "This is now bone of my bones and flesh of my flesh; she shall be called 'woman,' for she was taken out of man." In Adam's view she was the same as he was, but with a womb—hence woman. Why did God use Adam's rib to create Eve? Verse 24 says, "For this reason a man will leave his father and mother and be united to his wife, and they will become one flesh." It's interesting that the first woman came out of the first man, and from that time, all men come from women. One interpretation implies that the reason a man leaves parents and unites with his wife is to get his rib back. In other words, she completes him, as he needs her. They become one flesh because she is the missing piece of his life. A man wants a woman who will unite herself to him for the purpose God has designed for the two of them together.

I'm sure you've heard of marriages that ended in divorce the people claim they "just grew apart." It's too easy for two spouses to grow in opposite directions. This is not to mean that, as an individual, a wife or husband has to lose their identity or be stifled from being all they can be; it just means you grow together in the same direction and not apart from one another. It is a conscious decision to do life together, and that means supporting one another at specific times through the journey.

Companionship also means you enjoy hanging out together. Have you ever seen couples after a few years of marriage that have absolutely nothing in common? He has his friends, she has hers, but it's a chore to hang out together. It makes me wonder what drew them together in the first place. If you used to have things in common but don't anymore, you'll need to be more purposeful in doing things together. For example, as a woman you might not like golf, but take it up so he can teach you how to play. The goal is to be together, not to become a pro. As a man who might not like opera, you need to go with her because she does. She knows you dislike it, but if you go, the sacrifice will show her you love her and want to be with her. As we grow, we need to find new ways of doing life together as our situations constantly change. Many times couples divorce after the kids leave home because they were the only glue keeping them together. A continual effort to spend time together and do life together needs to be a priority.

> Do life with him; do not just be two strangers that have keys to the same house who once shared an emotional moment when you got married.

WHAT MEN NEED FROM WOMEN:
BE A GREAT MOTHER, A TREASURE WORTH DYING FOR, HIS GREATEST DEFENDER

I was eighteen when I married and had given Jake no indication whatsoever that I would be a good mother for his children. He didn't even know if I really liked kids. I asked him one day after we'd started our family if when we were dating he had ever considered if I would be a good mother, and he shocked me by emphatically saying yes, he knew I would be. Just like I saw potential for greatness in him, he saw my potential to be a good mom. He also said he wouldn't have married me if he didn't think I would have been a good mother. No one instructed him to look for that quality; he innately desired it. God has designed men and women with the desire to procreate. It stands to reason that they'd want their progeny well looked after. If his mom did a great job nurturing him, he'd expect nothing less from his wife, regardless if she's a stay-at-home mom or working outside the home. It is a tall order for women. If we as women make life-long sacrifices for our husbands and children for the welfare of the home and family, that husband has indeed found a treasure. She has understood her responsibilities but also recognizes the responsibilities that God has placed on her husband.

Be a woman who understands and respects the responsibility God has put on him and be a treasure worth living (and dying!) for.

Ephesians 5:25 says it far better than I can: "Husbands, love your wives, just as Christ loved the church and gave Himself up for her." God has placed the responsibility of lovingly looking after woman on man, as she is an extension of his own body, just as the church is an extension of Jesus. God gave woman to man to be his treasure, soul mate, confidante, and helper. It is her role to understand the responsibility God has placed on him, and so respect him and make his willingness to sacrifice for her well worth it. How tragic would it be for Jesus to love and die for the body of believers who didn't respect

> Marriage is not to be a life sentence; it is to be a love sentence, for life.

that sacrifice? The church's attitude towards Christ is one of eternal gratitude and love in accepting and understanding what it cost Him. The wife should reflect that same attitude. A man wants a woman who makes his life and sacrifice a worthwhile effort.

My husband Jake has a dry sense of humour and often tells me jokes. "Why do married men die younger than women?" he asked recently. "Because they want to." We laugh and can identify, but sadly there are men whose existence is miserable, largely due to their wives. How opposite is God's intention for marriage! It is not to be a life sentence as in prison. It is to be a love sentence, for life.

Be his greatest defender.

We as women sometimes fall short in this area, especially when we verbally put down our mates to other women. Many women will only defend their man to other people when they agree with him. I believe a man wants a woman to defend him no matter what because she loves him. She should always be on his side, that is, the side of his best interest. Even if he's living wrong, you should always defend him, hands down. This doesn't mean denying the reality of his current state, but defending someone we love is completely separate from defending wrong actions.

My aunt exhibited this beautifully. My uncle for a long time wasn't living right but I never once heard her put him down. She didn't agree with his life choices but loved him completely anyways. She went to the Lord about him and pleaded for the Lord to touch her husband's heart, and through her *living, loving example* my uncle responded one day, and the change was, to say the least, dramatic. He was so incredibly changed he became a different person. He became a loyal and devout advocate of the Gospel, and I would have to say that few people I've known throughout my life exhibited the joy of their salvation to the degree my uncle did. I was humbled and amazed at God's faithful goodness all around. Her source was her God, and it never shone so brightly as in that moment for me. She never nagged him; she *upheld* him and reaped the huge reward of having a close and wonderful relationship with her husband for the last thirty or so years of their marriage together.

Because man and woman are to be "one" as ordained by God, we are actually hurting ourselves when we don't defend our husbands. I say all this not just for the men's sakes, but for the women as well. We are a part of one another. If your husband sees and hears you defend him, it will foster closeness and intimacy where everybody wins.

CHAPTER 14
What Women Want

WHAT WOMEN NEED: HEALTHY COMMUNICATION

Healthy communication is one of the most important tools in every relationship, and if neglected, it can cause a marriage to fail, and if regularly maintained, a marriage to shine. I compare it to the gas we put in a car; without it, you ain't goin' nowhere. Without healthy communication, neither is your marriage. Many times, men have poor communication skills, only communicate when they absolutely have to, or won't communicate at all. As I mentioned earlier, women process by talking and men talk after processing. The only problem is if he won't give her feedback, all she can do is dissect the problem and give voice to it over and over, which results in nagging. Relationships never remain static because we don't remain the same through life. This is why we sometimes run into problems, which can actually be a good thing. What wasn't a problem two years ago now is because our needs have changed. It is a constant challenge for husbands and wives to address what comes up and grow together to enrich their relationship. Because we're always growing and changing on the journey, so is how we relate to each other.

Communication is key to this growth. Just as women have to apply to the logical, rational, non-emotional mind of men, so too do men need to understand the emotional, intuitive, holistic mind of women. To illustrate just how important communicating is, let's look at the absence of it. Have you ever had a fight with your spouse ending with both giving each other the silent treatment? Did the issue get resolved? In the early years of my marriage, I would get so mad at Jake I'd clam up to punish him, which for me was difficult. (Looking back he was probably glad I was quiet for more than five minutes!) The problem was, though, that until we talked it through, we both ate off the plate of anger, frustration, and bitterness. I found it draining to stay mad at him. Sinning is a lot of work! After a day or two, I was usually tired and would broach the subject. There was only one thing that made me even more upset, and I'm sure many women can identify: I'd finally talk, but he'd remain quiet. I was trying to resolve the issue but getting no feedback. He was punishing me for starting it. Is there ever a good outcome to this behaviour? There's a reason why God says that we shouldn't let the sun go down on our anger (Eph 4:26–27). It causes our anger to grow roots and lends it strength by building on it, giving the devil a foothold. There's a saying: "Give the devil an inch and he becomes a ruler." After a week or two of keeping our anger on the back burner, the original issue is no longer even the only problem, and other offences are now in the pot too. However, resolving an issue or staying mad are both a lot of work. The only way things will change is if we address all the issues by communicating. Healthy communication is far more than just words.

> Relationships never remain static because we don't remain the same through life.

For example, Professor Albert Mehrabian PhD is known for his pioneering work in the field of nonverbal communication (body language). In 1971, he published the highly debated book *Silent Messages*, which concluded that prospects studied assigned 55% of their weight to the speaker's body language, including posture, gestures, facial expression, and eye contact; another 38% to the tone and music of their voice; and a mere 7% by actual words. What is the 93% of our body language and tone saying? We need to understand that how we talk to one another is just as important as what we say. I've seen men speak in a condescending manner to their wives, and that conveyed a whole lot more than the words they were using. Women are good at this too. In fact, we've all done it. Here are some simple ways to keep our body language and tone in check to build up our mates instead of tearing them down. The minute your mate does something that you recognize as negativity towards you:

- Give yourself time to think before reacting, even if it's just five minutes to calm down. The "knee jerk" reaction is usually the wrong response.
- Give yourself a warning flag and understand that your partner's anger is likely tied to something else and not necessarily caused by you.

- Don't talk to your mate while you're emptying the dishwasher or doing another task. It's too easy to speak negatively when you're not making eye contact.
- Pull up a chair, sit down, maintain eye contact, and don't cross your arms or slouch. This will help you see each other clearly and hopefully diffuse the bomb that's about to go off.

If you as a man find it's too much work to figure out what your wife is trying to say, you are doing yourself no favours. Women do not forget. Sweeping it under the carpet won't make it go away. If she doesn't feel in her heart that she was heard and you capitulate because sports are on TV in five minutes, she'll know it. A woman's need to be understood drives her need to communicate. A husband understanding his wife's point of view is even more important than if he agrees with her. My goal in communicating is that we're on the same page and Jake understands my point of view, not that he agrees with everything I say. God desires a mutually satisfying, growing, thriving interchange between man and woman in all areas of marriage and truly communicating and understanding your mate even if you disagree with them brings a depth of appreciation for each other that only mutual respect can bring.

> Jake said he married Mrs. Right, which made me feel great, until he said that he didn't know my first name was "Always!"

WHAT WOMEN NEED FROM MEN: INTIMACY

When couples begin dating and fall in love, they enjoy going everywhere and doing everything together. They are giddy just to be together, whether it's shopping, cooking, going to sports events, or to the movies. You can see the intimacy that they enjoy. They get married, and through the daily grind of life, the relationship can look quite different a few years later. We say, "the honeymoon is definitely over." What happened? The reasons can be any number of things, but I'd be willing to bet that maintaining intimacy wasn't high on their priority list, and I'm not just referring to the sexual relationship. At one point during my marriage, I realized my relationship with Jake had stagnated and wondered how we'd arrived there. Somehow, we had grown apart. Separation and divorce were not an option, so that door was closed. Either we had to fix this thing to make it better or live with it the way it was. I said to myself, "Am I going to settle for this? Is this as good as it gets? No way. I want a great marriage. In fact, I want it to be spectacular. What do I need to do?" I was willing to do anything to restore the intimacy between us, and Jake said the same. We recognized the problem, talked with one another, and took action. As mentioned in chapter 13, we needed to make a conscious effort to grow together. The chasm between two people who once loved each other enough to marry can become so wide that the reason for divorce becomes irreconcilable differences.

God created every creature on earth in pairs. Why weren't Adam and Eve created at the same time? When I posed the question to Jake, he responded, "Because God wanted Adam to have a little bit of time where he could know what it felt like to be right all the time." He went on to say about me that he married Mrs. Right, which made me feel great, until he said that he didn't know my first name was "Always." He loves to joke, which I love, and despite the reference, we both thought it was pretty funny.

I believe one reason Adam and Eve weren't created at the same time was the Lord allowed Adam to come to the self-realization that he needed fellowship, friendship, and intimacy with another person. The same is true today. Little boys have no use for girls except to aggravate and tease them. When they grow older, it's like a switch is turned on and all of a sudden they become dialled into them in a big way.

A woman wants a man who understands her need for intimacy.

Earlier, I mentioned that a woman's need to be understood drives her need to communicate. Many men think that women always have to have the last word, to hammer home her point until he agrees with her. I believe she wants something else. She wants a man who understands her need for intimacy. This doesn't mean just sexual intimacy, which is the usual connotation we relate to the term, but a more comprehensive application: "a detailed knowledge resulting from a close or long association or study." This nails it on the head.

When Jake doesn't understand where I'm coming from, I feel there is a gap that separates us. I can't live that way, and I will not let the matter rest because I don't want distance between us. We have chosen to remain close to one another, and so we take the time and effort to really hear and understand each other. If he wouldn't take the time to try to understand my heart, we would drift apart and not have that same closeness and unity. I would also be less inclined to trust his instincts and decisions because I would always feel he didn't understand me, so my inclination to go with his direction would be lessened. It will greatly help to understand this by looking at the model that Jesus Himself gave us. This is a bit lengthy but well worth the read as everything flows from this passage. The Apostle Paul says, in Ephesians 5:21-32:

> [21] Submit to one another out of reverence for Christ. [22] Wives, submit yourselves to your own husbands as you do to the Lord. [23] For the husband is the head of the wife as Christ is the head of the church, his body, of which he is the Savior. [24] Now as the church submits to Christ, so also wives should submit to their husbands in everything. [25] Husbands, love your wives, just as Christ loved the church and gave Himself up for her [26] to make her holy, cleansing her by the washing with water through the Word, [27] and to present her to Himself as a radiant church, without stain or wrinkle or any other blemish, but holy and blameless. [28] In this same way, husbands ought to love their wives as their own bodies. He who loves his wife loves himself. [29] After all, no one ever hated their own body, but they feed and care for their body, just as Christ does the church— [30] for we are members of his body. [31] "For this reason a man will leave his father and mother and be united to his wife, and the two will become one flesh." [32] This is a profound mystery—but I am talking about Christ and the church.

In verses 31 and 32, the Apostle Paul was clearly not referring to sex, but something much more. Jesus as the bridegroom wants intimacy with His church as the bride in a pure, holy way. He doesn't want to be casual or even close friends with us, but desires intimacy on all levels. He gave us the model of marriage to understand and follow. Women look at this as the formal beginning of intimacy and men often look at the event as culminating in intimacy. They've "wooed" her, "conquered" her, and so have won her. They can now retire all the mushy gushy emotions. However, it isn't over, boys, not by a long shot. We are to become one and intimate in body, soul, and spirit. You are a spirit, you have a soul, and you live in a body.

> Intimacy: "a detailed knowledge resulting from a close or long association or study."

One in Body

Q: How does God view a married couple as one flesh?

To begin, Scripture often uses metaphorical language to describe the essence of what God is trying to convey. In this case, Christ is the head, and His body is the church, which consists of all believers. Marriage is pictured as a husband being the head and his wife, the body. I realize this may offend a lot of women as it sounds like God has made woman inferior to man, but that is not the case. When I was younger, it bothered me but then I finally realized why God did this. When God made both man and woman, He called them man, as they were both created in His image to be equals (Gen 5:1). When Eve sinned by taking the forbidden fruit, God made man the head of the wife, his body, in Genesis 3:16. It should also help to remember that God requires man to love his wife to the degree that he'd die for her. I've no further problem with that. Headship has to do with oneness. This head-body picture shows why God approves only of monogamous, heterosexual marriage. Two heads (two men) do not equal one flesh, and two bodies (two women) also do not equal one flesh. This is why polygamy is wrong as well. Any other model than the one God instituted is a slap in His face as it is an insult to Christ as the head, and we as the body. It mechanically doesn't even work. As the passage in Ephesians tells us, a husband is to love his wife as his own body and lovingly care for her as she is an extension of his own body. Although we each will give an accounting of our lives to our Lord, He still views us as one. Remember the wedding vows?

"Whom God has joined together, let no man separate." This is why it is so important for husbands and wives to relate to one another as God has told us to. When we hurt each other, we're hurt ourselves. When we love each other, we're blessing ourselves. It is a solid model that works to our mutual benefit.

One in Soul

Our soul is our mind, will, and emotions. Our reasoning, will, and emotions play a big part in meeting the needs of our marriage partner. Acts 4:32 in the Berean Study Bible says this in referring to how the early church members had their needs met: "The congregation of believers was one in heart and soul. No one claimed that any of his possessions was his own, but they shared everything they owned." They gladly gave anything and everything for the good of the assembly. They didn't even want recognition for it, so great was their love for their Lord and each other. To be one in soul relationally is the voluntary surrendering of our will, our desires, and emotions for the well-being of the other, with a glad heart and good attitude. The beautiful result of both parties surrendering their agenda for the sake of the other is that both husband and wife will become one, having their needs met through the debt of love they each don't mind paying to the other.

One in Spirit

Look at the perfect "one-ness" Jesus Himself described was possible between Him, the Father, and us in John 17:21: "...that all of them [us] may be one, Father, just as you are in me and I am in you. May they also be in us so that the world may believe that you have sent me." Jesus was talking about having a relationship with humankind that was so intimate that the Father, the Son, and us are literally viewed as one. When the world looks at us, they should see Jesus. I believe this may be the most important aspect of being one as husband and wife. If we truly believe we are on a journey from who we are to who we are becoming in Christ, it is vitally important that we grow together spiritually. We are all in different places spiritually at times, but the point isn't that we're always unanimous, but that we're both gaining spiritual maturity in whatever level we're at. If we don't take the time to understand God's heart, we'll never understand the depth of the intimate relationship that is ours in Him or the depth of His love for us. The best way for a man to achieve this is to invest himself in an intimate relationship with his Lord Jesus. He will empower him to become a man of God that he never dreamt was possible. When God gives us the inside track about our mate in such a way that we ourselves know we could never realize on our own, we know that God Himself is strengthening the intimacy between husband and wife, which results in heartfelt gratitude and love along with stunned amazement at His intervention.

God did not create Eve from Adam's head so he would lord it over her; He also did not create her from Adam's feet, so she'd be trampled on. God created Eve from Adam's rib, from his side, so she'd be equal to him, from under his arm so she'd be protected by him, and from near his heart so she'd be loved by him.

WHAT WOMEN NEED FROM MEN: A MAN WHO KNOWS HIS ROLE

Many years ago, Jake (at that time my boyfriend) and I went to a youth seminar in our city, where the preacher taught core values to thousands of young people that were interested in learning how to live according to Christian principles. In that seminar, he said something that caught Jake's attention. It forever changed his perception of his role as the man, husband, and father of his future family. He said that the man was to be the umbrella of the family; that he was responsible for the spiritual welfare of the family and act as the family's protection, and that at the end of the day, God would hold the man accountable for his role as the leader. This was modeled by Adam and Eve. Although Eve was the first to take the forbidden fruit and gave some to her husband, God held Adam accountable as the head of the pair in asking what he'd done before He addressed Eve. (Gen. 3:8-11)

God is the same thing, although he obviously answers to no-one. When we accept Jesus, we become His child and come under His covering, His protection, His leadership, and His guidance. When we move out from under God's umbrella, we wilfully subject ourselves to the elements—Satan's precipitation, if you will. So too the man is to be the umbrella for his family. Jesus loved us enough to die for us; He forever became our high priest, interceding for us before the Father. A man is the priest of his home. As such, God holds him accountable for the spiritual welfare of his family in certain respects. As a man who loves his wife as Jesus loves His church, he is willing to sacrifice his own desires for the welfare of his family. This is the man she willingly and wholeheartedly submits to. We all are individually responsible for our relationship with Jesus, but the man in the home is that spiritual umbrella that the wife and children are to flourish under. He is their protector, their refuge, and their leader. He sees to their welfare in the following ways:

- He cultivates his own intimate relationship with Jesus and maintains a regular regimen of prayer and Bible study to learn what God expects from him.
- He models his own relationship with the Father to his family. His children model their walk with Jesus after seeing his example.
- He makes praying together a priority and makes sure his wife and family receive biblical instruction both in the home and in taking his family to a Bible-believing church.
- He takes the initiative when spiritual things come up as God will hold him accountable in this area. He doesn't neglect this aspect of spiritual leadership even though his wife may be just as inclined towards delving into the deeper aspects of spiritual things.
- He knows who he is in Christ and what is expected of him. As such, his wife and family have confidence in following his leadership.

From this list, it's evident that the bar is set high for the man of the home. These points are meant to let us know what God expects and encourage us to attain His best. It's important to note that if men do not understand where they stand with God, or what He expects of their role, it will be difficult to lead their family in the fullness of all the good things God has in store for them. Satan has targeted families. He knows that the breakdown of the family weakens a nation, but even more so, it hurts people and the heart of God. In today's society, now more than ever, men need to be closely in tune with their Heavenly Father for guidance in how to be the priest of their home; in a lesser but similar way Christ is the High Priest of his body, the church. What better model could a father emulate than the Heavenly Father?

WHAT WOMEN NEED FROM MEN: A GOOD FATHER, PROTECTOR, AND PROVIDER

When I was expecting our first child, something dawned on me. As a mother, I was going to be responsible for looking after the life growing inside of me. We were independent young adults and up to this point had only been responsible for ourselves, which was no big deal. All of a sudden, the sense dawned on us that God was entrusting to us the stewardship of a life that would live forever! As the enormity of the task dawned on me, I felt vulnerable and overwhelmed with the prospect of having to handle all of life's challenges in addition to this person. It was then that I felt extremely glad that Jake was there to look after me and the baby. When the impending birth drew near, and I was as big as a house and not looking forward to labour, I said to him, "You men are so lucky you don't have to go through giving birth." Jake responded, "Yes, but now all I have to do is to take care of you and this child, and support you for the rest of my life." Touché. He was already preparing in his mind the equally heavy burden of providing for the family. The economy at that time was in sad shape, and I was clearly focused on our baby. I never forgot what he said, because it corrected my perception. Yes, as women we are the child bearers, but without the continual solid monetary support of men, even if we are collecting maternity benefits, it's infinitely more difficult (as single moms can attest). I realize that in this day and age, the trend is moving towards including dads as the stay-at-home parent, but for the sake of clarity I'm taking the position that women largely held this role until recent times. God has made woman wholly focused on her infant in a different way than men and later on her dedication to nurturing the children as the primary caregiver needs to be a high priority. I'm not saying that men have a lesser role in any way, but let's face it, she usually spends the most time with them and is more keenly aware of what's going on with them. Rearing children and meeting the physical needs of a family takes large amounts of time, energy, and resources.

In addition to all this, women want their men to be great dads. I always marvelled at Jake when our girls were little. He'd come home from work after a twelve-hour day, exhausted, and still play with them after dinner. He'd toss them around with their shrieks of delight, chase them around the house, and even play Barbies with them. He always got to be Ken. He was and is an amazing father. Our daughters are all married now and have children of their own, but when we're all sitting around the kitchen table, they'll still go and sit on his lap. It's a place of familiarity and safety where they still connect to their dad as they did when they were younger. He never quit giving them his bear hugs. This is just one way to be a great dad. Never stop physically touching your kids, whether it's a rub on the shoulder, a hug, a little pinch on the elbow. As a mother and wife, it gives me incredible joy to see that our daughters know they are loved beyond any shadow of a doubt by their dad—not for what they do, but for who they are. To be a good dad will mean lots of sacrifices, including time, money, emotions, patience, and more.

I've already talked about men as the spiritual protector of the home, but women also need physical protection. I believe that men are wired by God to be protectors of women and children. I saw it clearly in Jake when the girls were little and then especially when they became young ladies. The young men who came knocking at the door were definitely a little afraid of Jake, and he wanted it that way. If anyone was going to hurt his girls, they'd have to go through papa bear. It may be viewed as an outdated or old fashioned concept, but regardless of whether you're married, a mother, or single, women need protection at times, often more in other countries than here. Just look around at the young women of the world in foreign countries. The abuse and suppression of women was never God's idea. Where are the brothers, dads, and husbands who should be protecting them from the wolves that are out there? Let's face it: men are physically stronger than women, and that's not about to change. He has been equipped to rise up and stand up to the threats.

Times may change, roles may change, but the way God has created man and woman hasn't. Most girls on a date want a boy who shows he can provide for her, take care of her, and be her protector. God is setting the stage for the future. He is teaching that young man what she expects in that brief evening, and later on in a big way as a provider and protector of his wife and kids.

WHAT WOMEN NEED FROM MEN:
TO SUPPORT HER GREATER PURPOSE

Here are two jokes that are designed to press women's buttons: Why do women wear white at the wedding? So that they match the other appliances.

Or how about: What does W.I.F.E. stand for? Washing, Ironing, Fetching, Etc.

Here is what wife really stands for:

Wonderful Influence For Eternity.

Men can greatly benefit from a wife who is dialled into her relationship with her Lord. This phrase evokes a gentle spirit that is not weak, but shows strength under control. I've discussed a woman's role as a man's helper (Gen 2:18) and the mother of their children, but what about her other purpose? What if she has something great in her heart that she wants to achieve in addition to her commitment to children and family? Do the purposes, dreams, and goals of a woman end when she becomes a mother or when the children are raised? Clearly not. What women want from men in this regard is that he supports the full purposes God has for her at all stages of her life.

Many women who have shelved their personal dreams and goals temporarily to raise their families are now looking to new horizons, and they need the full support of their husband to help achieve those new goals. I believe there comes a time when a man needs to give back to her what she gave him. She needs him to:
- Take her seriously
- Understand the new or different responsibility that God has placed on her
- Fuel her dreams
- Challenge her to become complete in the further purposes God has for her
- Support her and do this new chapter of her life with her
- Take on some of the daily responsibilities to give her the time she needs to invest herself in a new goal.

Life is all about balance. We risk becoming set in our ways and inflexible especially later in life if we aren't willing to try new things. God has given women the primary task of raising children, but that certainly is not all she is meant to accomplish. Since we have a lot of living left to do while they're young and after they're raised, it only stands to reason that God has other magnificent tasks that He intends to bless us with. That will look different for every woman. A woman's husband needs to be aware of this, and that may mean making some changes. I really believe that God has much more in store for women during child-rearing years as well as after the kids leave the house. We must never forget the people in the Bible who were well along in years when God called them, like Abraham and Sarah. Age does not present a hindrance to God's purposes. He's not looking to overload us, but He has a plan that will further accomplish the reasons we're here.

CHAPTER 15
What Men and Women Need Together

THE GOD TRIANGLE

Volumes have been written on what men and women need from one another in order to have a mutually fulfilling relationship, but it's time for a balancing thought: no one person, be that man or woman, is meant to be the whole package in meeting the needs of the other.

Here's where many relationships get out of balance. Many people get married with the expectation that their spouse is supposed to make them happy. The fact is, we don't have the capability to make someone else happy all of the time, and for good reason. God is the only one who is able to completely satisfy us, and He designed us that way. Men and women sometimes look for years for the perfect mate. The reason they can't find them is because they're not out there! For us to expect all our emotional needs to be met by another human is impossible. Sure, they make us happy, but they are not meant to be the source of our happiness, or be responsible for it. This truth is freeing. A marriage will face a myriad of difficulties if the two parties look only to each other to keep them propped up emotionally. A good marriage is like a three-legged race: a woman's leg, a man's leg, and God keeping the other two legs bound together. If we stay connected and in step with all parties, everyone can win.

God's perfect plan for marriage is a triangle, with Him at the top, and the bottom. The truth is, your mate will disappoint you, and not just once, but many times. God's perfect plan for marriage is that He is both the foundation we build on and the top of the triangle calling the shots.

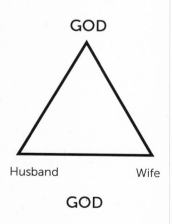

GOD

Husband   Wife

GOD

This diagram puts things in proper perspective. Our motivation for everything we do for one another needs to stem from pleasing God first, and each other second. That way, when our mate disappoints us, our reason for responding in the right way is because God instructs and expects us to, and not because the other party merits it. It stops grudges from forming because our motivation and enablement to forgive comes from God, not from whether or not we feel like forgiving each other. As plainly as I can say it, having a great marriage will involve work in doing what you know is right, but it's the last thing you feel like doing when your emotions are running rampant. We often feel like lashing out, but that will only make the problem worse. If you don't agree with working to make your marriage great, imagine how much work it will be to either fix it when it begins falling apart, or doing collateral damage control if it deteriorates altogether. Being proactive to have something great, fixing something that is breaking down, or beginning again with someone else all entail commitment, effort, and work. Leaving your mate might not even solve your problems, because you take yourselves into the next relationship.

I remember a woman from a conference who had been married and divorced several times. At the end, the speaker asked if anyone wanted prayer and she went forward. She explained to him that all the men she'd married were terrible to her. She was currently on her fifth husband, and that wasn't working out either. He spoke with her for a while to get a sense of her situation and then told her something she didn't want to hear: she was the common denominator in all the marriages. He gently told her, "Maybe it's time you started looking inward instead of outward." We're not going to get around those prideful areas in ourselves that God desires to address and fix by ignoring them and changing the landscape. We must acknowledge that change begins with acknowledging and taking ownership of our own actions and attitudes, and work from there. Speaking of actions, here is a golden key for anyone wanting a great marriage:

> Don't work at making him or her happy. Work at
> making God happy, then everyone will be happy.

It really is that simple. Not easy, but simple. If pleasing Lord is your primary goal, you will treat your mate in a way that will automatically build an amazing marriage. God has busted me so many times when I've talked ugly to Jake. If I wanted to please my Lord, I had to apologize, or I had no peace. When Jake has disappointed me, I have forgiven him; not because he deserved it, but because God commands me to. I do not desire to live in a mediocre marriage till I die, so I may as well do all I can to make it spectacular, right? That is not only possible, but God's perfect will! And what He wills, He enables! His grace is available to all who want it.

I want to inject hope into marriages that may be mediocre, struggling, on the verge of collapse, or have failed altogether. All things are possible, with God. We simply have to do things His way. People may balk at surrendering their pride and obeying Him, and I found that I rarely felt like doing things God's way when I was mad, but I was always rewarded when I exercised forgiveness. As we practised forgiveness (and marriage will give you plenty of practise), it became easier. Satan wants us to stay mad at each other and have tension and bitterness in our relationships. It brings him pleasure. We need to deny him his pleasure! Slugging through the difficult times brings a marriage relationship to a fresh and new place. My husband and I worked out the kinks as they came along, when they were still small issues, before they became big issues.

Once you bow the knee to the Holy Spirit and acknowledge that He is the boss, He whispers to your heart what you need to do in every moment. Marriage was never meant to be stagnant. It's always growing and changing with fresh challenges, and if both parties have determined to follow Jesus with all their heart,

> Biblical love is not a warm sentimentality, but a calculated pattern of conformity to the revealed will of God.

soul, and strength, God's goal for marriage will be accomplished. Are things perfect? No, and they never will be this side of eternity. But there is love, fulfilment, and joy despite our imperfections.

This is not to bring condemnation down on those whose marriages have failed. I realize there are extenuating circumstances that I won't even begin to address that are valid reasons for marriages ending. I just want to offer tangible and real hope that since God is alive, take comfort in knowing that His ways work! Keeping God at the top of the triangle and the foundation you build on will reward you with His best.

MARRIAGE IN CRISIS:
IS THERE AN EASY OUT? WHAT CAN WE DO?

Let's face it, many people are in difficult and painful marriages. Perhaps you're in one. Perhaps you're in a marriage where you will obey God, but your spouse won't. However, if God has called you to hang in there, you need to do what He says, keep on doing what He says, until He tells you to stop. There's a wonderful movie called *Fireproof* with Kirk Cameron that conveys this and is a great resource to help strengthen and affirm marriages. It parallels the fireman's motto, "Never leave your partner behind." The truth is so poignant when applied to marriages today. It's easy to stay with your partner when there is nothing threatening your marriage, but what happens when it bursts into flames and everything you've built is about to burn to the ground? Do we leave our partner behind? In a world of disposable relationships, just what does God expect from us where marriages are concerned?

If you feel you've married the wrong man, once you said, "I do," he became the right man. End of story. God has given us the responsibility of choosing. He won't choose for us, but He does expect us to support our choice. We place too much emphasis on our feelings. If we believe God can completely transform us, then the same is true for the difficult person we live with. As Christians serving a Covenant-keeping God, we need to acknowledge the covenant we made in His presence that He also expects us to keep. He was, and is, listening. I was saddened when I heard the new trend for some getting married is to alter the marriage vows to say they would be together "as long as we both shall 'love,'" and not "live." At least they were being honest, but what low expectations they were already bringing to their marriage! It was an agreement with a trap door out, which makes no sense to me. You can't follow your heart because it can be deceived (Jer 17:9); you have to lead your heart in obedience to what you promised God. Love that costs us nothing, is worth nothing. Real love will always involve sacrifice. Biblical love is not a warm sentimentality, but a calculated pattern of conformity to the revealed will of God. When we said we'd love them until death do us part, then we ourselves agreed that death is the only thing able to part us, according to God and our promise.

If we believe we can get out of our current situation by leaving, we might not actively embrace God's solutions. If you yourself decide there will be no way out, your attitude to fixing it will be completely different. You are then leading your heart. People often say, "I just can't do it," but my question then is, "If your life depended on it, could you then do it?" If the answer is yes, then let's be honest and say the real reason we're failing is that we *won't* do it. There is a world of difference between "can't" and "won't."

God doesn't hand out divorces for who you now deem a mistake because character traits that weren't there before are now evident, or they bother you now when they didn't before. We exercise our God-given authority in marrying the person we choose, but the flip side of authority is responsibility. It is our responsibility to see it through and do what we can to make it great, and with God's help, I don't believe that there can be irreconcilable differences.

> We need to keep doing what God tells us to until He tells us to stop.

If your marriage has or is breaking down, there is good news: God can and wants to re-create something new that will fulfil both of you and bring Him glory. Often, God allows the wheels to come off just so He can put it back together in such a way that is new and far stronger than before. He often achieves far more than simply restoring a marriage; He refines and redefines our character along the way. The areas that your husband lacks in are not there for you to pick on and nag him over. They are there for you to fill, or to help him fill. The same goes for men.

God desires to bring both of you out of the fire of past hurts, disappointments, and dysfunction. He desires to build a new structure with the same people, but with materials that will fireproof your marriage as He transforms both of you. Good Christian marriage counsellors have much in their arsenal on how to repair areas that we may deem totally irreparable. There are many resources to turn to as well. God will bring everything you need together to strengthen what remains or rebuild.

The truth is, that we grow in the likeness of our love for each other. If you don't like the look of your love for each other, chances are you won't like what your marriage looks like. This is first and foremost.

What are you willing to sacrifice and give to make it not only better, but the best? Jesus gave His life for the church, and the church is in complete submission to His lordship. This is the model for marriages too. Galatians 5:13 says, "You, my brothers, were called to be free. But do not use your freedom to indulge the sinful nature; rather, serve one another in love." The last phrase of this verse was the theme at our wedding, but the first part is extremely applicable to marriages as well. I can attest that it has worked well for many years, giving us sweet freedom, not bondage. We simply won't have it any other way. Serving one another, in love, works.

NEW GROUND RULES

There are a hundred reasons why marriages break down or become strained, but from what I've seen in others and learned from my own relationship, we often fall into avoidable traps. Many times a solvable problem will present itself, but the way we deal with it actually creates a bigger problem. For example, we've all played the blame game. Your spouse repeatedly does something irritating, and you address the issue by saying, "You always do A," or "you never do B." This rarely produces good results. The corresponding comment will most likely be, "You never do C for me," or "you always do D." Something that was not a big problem has now dragged another issue into it, and it becomes a competition to see who is failing who, more. It may end up that your husband won't leave dirty dishes in the sink as much, but he'll probably do the dishes grudgingly and not out of love. A subtle wall has been put up, and there is coolness between the two parties. One problem has been solved, but it's created another.

If we can identify some key ways we've been handling challenges that rarely end up with good solutions, it's time to change our method of operation and learn how to deal with them in a different manner. Healthy and regular communication is the beginning to working things out. Here are some practical ways to improve the way we interact.

- Acknowledge our part in the equation.
This begins with yourself. Often, we have what we feel is a clear picture of our mate's shortfalls and a distorted view of ours. Hence,

we only have an opinion on their need to change, and not ours. The biggest and best changes happen when we acknowledge that it takes two to have a spectacular marriage—and two to have a bad one. You can't have a fight by yourself. The first step is being willing to change ourselves and to invite God to change us. We need to go to Him in prayer with our pride surrendered and acknowledge that even though we don't think there are areas we need to change in, we want Him to show us the truth. We all have them. If you're honest about wanting a better relationship and doing this, He will show you in a convincing but loving way what things about yourself you are blind to.

• Take ownership of our own actions.
We've all seen people who remain in a state of self-pity all their lives because every bad thing that happens is always someone else's fault. If we do not take ownership of own actions, we never have to acknowledge our need to change. We adopt a victim mentality, and this stunts personal growth in a big way. Acknowledging out mistakes is key to taking ownership of our own actions.

> We were set free to love, not to demand our rights.

• Acknowledge that there is or are problems.
Take a step back and look at their concern. If you think there's nothing wrong but your spouse is unhappy, there is something amiss. We can't dismiss those things because we don't think they're important, even though he or she does. There's usually a lot more at the heart of it. Ignoring your spouse's concerns tells them that you don't put any validity into their feelings and therefore you don't really care about those things that they care about. The problem will never get solved if you don't agree that it exists.

• Recognize our true enemy and decide to stay on the same side.
There are keys to relating to one another that end up with the problem getting solved. If both parties can agree to be on the same side, much more can be accomplished. Remember, you married your mate because you love them and wanted to be around them until one of you dies. He or she is not your enemy. You didn't marry them so you would have a constant opponent. This realization was a turning

point for me in the pattern of arguing that Jake and I had at one time fallen into. Strife was creeping into our marriage. Slowly but surely, we were bickering more over everything. I began to see a pattern of behaviour emerge that was not pretty on both our parts. When we decide that we are right and refuse to budge, no one wins.

The Lord showed me this, as I had gone to Him in despair over our constant head-butting. He showed me that our problem wasn't the disagreements; it was how we were handling all of them. The minute some problem came up, we took opposite camps. The day I finally recognized this repetitive damaging cycle and cried out to God, I was ready to do anything He told me to fix it. He spoke right to my heart and told me what was wrong. He said, "You're fighting Jake. You need to be fighting the ugly way you handle problems. He is not your enemy; he is your husband. You need to each be on the same side fighting the thing that steals your love and peace." I knew immediately that God had spoken to my heart. Satan comes to rob us of our peace, love, and joy. Don't let him!

I'll not forget that day. The next time a disagreement arose, and we fell into the old pattern, I remembered what God had told me. I said, "Look, I love you. We've got a problem, but I'm on your side. I'm not against you. I want this solved so we can have something great together. I don't want us to be in opposite camps anymore. Can't we work this out?" Jake's attitude towards me immediately softened, as he knew I wasn't blaming him or telling him to change, but was willing to do whatever it took to solve it because I loved him. It was like a death grip had loosened. We were being set free to love, instead of demanding our rights. I believe that moment broke the enemy's hold that he'd had on us. It again proves that God's methods work. For me to win the argument, I had to yield my agenda. Did I lose? Not at all. We both won. It was Satan who lost. To be honest, I can't even remember today what we were disagreeing over, and that moment set a precedent. Thirty years later, we still maintain a unified front in fighting problems that arise, but never each other.

Disagreements are a part of every relationship. It's unrealistic to think you will never disagree. It is far better to have a good method of solving disagreements that builds and strengthens a marriage fighting and causing the union to weaken.

- Agree to disagree, agreeably.

It's amazing how simple this is to read and understand, yet how hard it can be to put into practice. If peace and harmony with your mate are your goals and you've decided that strife and discord will have no place in your marriage and home, this is mandatory. We can disagree with one another in a way that is not ugly. It doesn't mean you acquiesce and give up your opinion; it means that if you are at odds with your mate, you agree to respecting their right to be wrong.

The truth is, no one is ever right all of the time, and we've all been wrong. When you've been wrong, especially when you were sure you were right, wasn't it nice if the person you'd disagreed with respected your right to your own opinion? This is showing respect for one another. People who have differing opinions can still have fellowship until the truth over who was right becomes evident, and even if it doesn't, having respect for each other is more important than if we're viewed to be right. As Christians, we don't have any rights if we've surrendered them to Jesus. God can be trusted to bring justice if an unbelieving judge can. When you made Jesus the Lord of your life, you put Him in charge, correct? Just look at the rights He as the Son of God laid aside in order to love first!

Loving your mate should supersede your right to be right. When we disagree, we need to leave room for God to change our opinions. When I have a strong opinion that differs from Jake's, I surrender it to Jesus. I pray, "Lord, show him if he's wrong about this, and please, show me if I'm wrong." If my real goal is truth, then I want that even more than my being right. I can then easily disagree with him in an agreeable fashion. I'm respecting him as well as myself. God knows the truth and will reveal it to both of us if we seek Him for it. When we surrender our rights to ourselves, we surrender our wills in wanting His will above ours. After all, our desire to be right above all is actually pride disguised, which God hates. I should also add that the times I released the issue and was proven wrong, I was extremely glad I hadn't demanded I was right. It's far harder to eat crow later and sheepishly admit I was wrong after throwing a hissy fit. God's way is far better.

- When we disagree, are we more concerned over making our point or hearing theirs?

For her: Really listen to him when he's talking; don't be formulating what you're going to say next or multi-task in your mind while he's talking. He may quit talking because he can tell you're not listening. Drop your point and really listen to what he's saying. Put yourself in his shoes and make understanding him your goal. Even if you still disagree, if he can see you're really invested in trying to understand him, it will go a long way. When we flippantly disagree without seriously considering their point, we're telling them their issue doesn't matter enough to us to make the effort. This will make their resolve firm to oppose you in the issue.

For him: Don't figure out how you're going to defend your position to do what you want to do anyways while she's talking. Because women tend to delve into matters that go deeper than the surface, men often get tired of listening, and they switch off. We joke about this a lot. One of our closest friends told us once that his wife was extremely frustrated with him because he didn't appear to remember what she'd said. She finally asked, "Don't you remember? I told you!" He responded, "Oh, you must have told me when I wasn't listening." She blew a gasket, but we laugh at it now and can all relate.

- When talking about the issues, avoid using the word "you."

Saying "you always" or "you never" rarely end up with good results. If you are both on the same side fighting the true enemy, you can't accuse each other that way. When I first heard this, I decided to try it the next time Jake annoyed me over something he did repeatedly. It was hard at first, but it challenged me to identify the root of the problem and put a completely different spin on my approach. Think of the last disagreement you had with someone and eliminate the word "you." It forces you to relate how you deal with something without blaming the other person. It is entirely possible to talk about a problem without laying blame.

For example, say the problem is that a wife is feeling neglected and feels she doesn't see her husband enough. If she says, "You're never home and never make time for me. You don't care about me anymore, and this is all your fault!" As you'd imagine, this only puts him on the defensive. He might be dealing with multiple demands on his time at work, with a family member or buddy in trouble, or working overtime to buy you that vacation he wants to surprise you with. Blaming him for not spending time with you only causes him to strengthen and defend his reasons about why he's not around. You achieve the opposite of your goal.

It would be far better to say, "I've got a problem: I miss you. I'm feeling lonely and that we're drifting apart. I don't see you enough anymore. I love you too much to do without you."

This is not meant to give him a guilt trip if she really means it. People can rarely resist love. She simply desires to be with him because she loves him. She has conveyed the real reason for her heartache without laying blame. Let's not forget one monumentally huge factor: where there is lack, God desires to fill it. If He is moving a wife for all the right reasons, the Holy Spirit is involved and will bring gentle conviction to the husband. They'll find a way to meet in the middle.

- Don't put things under the carpet.

Jake and I have always enjoyed having date nights and going out for dinner. During dinner, we were each allowed to ask this question: "If you could change one thing about me, what would it be?" This might seem like a bad idea, but there were ground rules. We weren't allowed to get upset, and we both agreed this was to benefit each other, not be a platform to identify failures. The comments were coming from a place of love. You may think I'm crazy, but it was so much fun! The answers I got from him astounded me, as I had no idea he felt a certain way. Because the boundaries were clearly laid out, it was a safe place to discuss things. The same went for him. Because marriage doesn't stay static like I'd mentioned, there's always fresh new quirks or challenges we all face about ourselves and each other.

Sometimes the things he'd change in me ministered right to my heart. He said, "I would change that you aren't so insecure about yourself. It bothers me when you put yourself down." What woman wouldn't love to hear that? It was an ideal opportunity to broach a delicate subject, perhaps something that had been bothering one of us for some time, but we were just waiting for our date night to bring it up. I highly recommend this, if the couple agreeing to this can stick to the boundaries. We left the restaurant full in more ways than one—in our tummies and hearts.

If going out for dinner doesn't suit you or the issue is too serious to discuss in that context, pick a place to talk where both of you can be relaxed. Remember that our frame of mind has a huge part to play in receiving correction or problem solving. Wait until the guy has had his dinner, or for a time when the gal hasn't just stepped off the scale. Address the issue with full candour and honesty. It's not going to simply go away. If left, it can fester into something even worse. Sparing his or her feelings by not being honest is a big trap. If the issue is deep and of a sensitive nature, realize it may be painful and will take time to unravel how things got so bad. My pastor once said, "Pain without purpose is torture; but pain with purpose is a doorway to healing and new growth." Going to God is an absolute must. He knows exactly how to navigate through unsettled waters to get you both safely to the other side of resolution and wholeness.

Marriage was meant to be more than a life sentence. It was meant to be a love sentence, for life. With God, all things are possible.

CHAPTER 16
The Hardest Job in the World

IS DISCIPLINING OUR CHILDREN WITH GOOD BALANCE TOUGH, OR WHAT?

There are vastly differing opinions when it comes to the discipline of children, and these often change from one generation to the next. What was popular and worked for our grandparents was not necessarily appropriate for our parents or us. Having reared three daughters who now have children themselves, I can tell you I've seen, heard, and considered a lot of opinions and methods over the years. This is a touchy subject to be sure because many are passionate that their methods are the only correct way. We know that establishing boundaries in the early years of life are critical to the relational health of our kids in respects to all forms of authority—be it a parent, teacher, professor, employer, or even God Himself. Everyone has to learn to respect and conform their actions to that authority. If they don't, the groundwork is being laid for a lot of problems down the road. When all the differing opinions became one big noise in my head, I decided to search out what the greatest authority on child-rearing that I knew had to say. I really hope that you will give God a chance and hear what He says in His Word and let His instruction ring through and enrich your parenting skills. If you don't agree, that's okay. I am hopeful that this message will help to give balance to an important subject whereby our children will be blessed. Years ago, I heard a statement that I believe is true:

"There is no job in the whole world that requires more experience and training than parenting, and most parents are the least prepared when it happens."

When expectant parents tell me they don't feel prepared, I often tell them that no one is ever completely ready. We don't immediately become a great parent the minute we have a baby; we have to grow as parents as they grow as kids. It changes your whole world on so many levels. Talk about on-the-job training! I'm glad that God is there to help us raise the next generation and to help us when we mess up.

As the parent of grown children, looking back I've concluded that I was (and still am) as much a work in progress as they are. I have found that children will bring out the worst in a parent, but also the best. They will test their boundaries until you feel like pulling out all your hair. They will also inspire you to love them on such a deep level that you'd die for them. Is this what we do to God? I know that this is what God did for me. I am convinced that God gave us children for us to realize how deeply He loves us, and how deeply we have the capacity to grieve Him as well.

Next, you can use a lot of discipline if it is balanced with a lot of real love. Some people discipline their child without making a spit of difference. The kid remained unchanged in behaviour and character. Real discipline should be uncomfortable and result in a change in behaviour and ultimately character. Real love, which is difficult to model when a conflict arises, needs to be shown to our kids when they push their boundaries and make us angry. If administered early and consistently, discipline establishes respect and boundaries for all future exchanges, and saves you major headaches down the road. I have seen a huge imbalance in this in parenting. From a desire to have well-behaved children, I've seen parents who maintained strict discipline to the point of fear, but didn't equally offer gentleness and love, thinking that their children would interpret that love as a show of weakness and a loss of resolve. The children became bitter and resentful adults as a result. We must understand that being loving does not constitute being weak.

On the flip side, I've seen parents who give in to every hissy fit their child throws. Giving in to their fit does not constitute love but is actually teaching the child that throwing a fit is acceptable behaviour to get what they want. I've seen a three year old behave completely differently with her mother than with others. I've seen this child throw herself to the floor because her mother was simply talking to me and the child demanded her attention, yet the mother did nothing to address the fit. I assumed this was how this child usually acted, but when I spoke to another woman who occasionally took care of her, she said, "When Jane [not the child's real name] is not around her mother, she's an absolute angel. The minute her mother walks in, she starts behaving badly." I asked her why she thought Jane behaved well with her and not her mother and she responded, "Jane knows I won't put up with it. She stands and holds my hand as she quietly waits for her mom to come and pick her up, and she's actually really sweet." Can you see the problem? I feel bad for both of them. The child flounders around, unhappy in looking for a boundary around her mother, and may feel happier around strangers who give her the discipline she needs.

> If administered early and consistently, discipline establishes respect and boundaries for all future exchanges, and saves you major headaches down the road.

Balancing love with enforcing boundaries provides security for children because they begin to realize that behaving is to their own benefit. Also, you are not allowing them to sin without consequences. If you think a two year old can't sin, consider this: If they're old enough to display ugly behaviour and disrespect you, they're old enough to be taught that that behaviour is wrong and that if they continue, punishment will ensue. I'd like to add that when we discipline a child, we should not immediately swoop in right after to make it all better. We will waste all our effort and the teaching moment. Discipline is not to look like an apology, but something that will occur again if the child disobeys. There should be no doubt about that. When I disciplined my girls, I had a plan to make sure we all received value from the experience. I wasn't quick to go into their rooms and ask if they understood. I waited several minutes, allowing my children to process their behaviour and my reaction.

If we as adults are allowed to live a spoiled, selfish lifestyle, it affects our joy level. Why would it not affect theirs too? God disciplines those He loves, and we should too. That means paddling them on the rear from time to time as well, in my opinion. We are merely stewards of His kids and should follow how God says to discipline them.

When I was young, I always felt happier after my parents gave me God-directed "correction with direction" (a spanking). I had received punishment in direct response to my actions, and it relieved the guilt I was feeling, allowing me to feel light-hearted and better inside. We were never created to be sinful beings and every person on the planet has a conscience that tugs at them when they do wrong. A good cry from a spanking relieved stress and tension. I'm thankful I was disciplined this way. My parents never beat me, nor did I ever think that I was being abused. A few curt swats on the padded part of our bottoms is not abuse, which I would never advocate. We've become vastly out of balance in this regard because of the abuse that does, unfortunately, happen when a parent unleashes anger instead of administering God-directed discipline.

> Discipline is not to look like an apology; it is to look like something that will occur again if Johnny or Susie disobeys, and there should be no doubt about that.

I am not knocking time-outs as an alternative, but I frankly don't think they're that beneficial to a child under three. I've witnessed it. Ten minutes is an eternity to a three year old who doesn't have a concept of time. As far as they're concerned, they've been put there forever. Very young children are just beginning to be able to express themselves in more complex ways. I've seen a three-year-old child put in a corner who verbally spewed angry comments, not making any sense about her situation, becoming more angry. I thought to myself that this cannot be emotionally healthy. She may eventually internalize her anger, not knowing how to deal with it, and as we know now, anger turned inward with no outlet becomes depression. Yet venting emotions by slamming doors or throwing things is allowed in some homes and not seen as inappropriate behaviour when a young child is given a time-out. Something is definitely out of balance.

There are reasons God advocates spanking. We seem to have lost common sense when it comes to this. The Bible isn't quiet about this issue either. Fifty years ago, spanking was not only okay, but the norm and expected. Nowadays, we've become so "civilized: in frowning and looking down at spanking that we allow young children to display brutish behaviour towards their parents and elders. Here are verses to back this up that I'm sure many will have issues with, but I didn't write them, God did.

Proverbs 22:15: "Folly is bound up in the heart of a child, but the rod of discipline will drive it far from him."

Proverbs 13:24: "Whoever spares the rod hates their children, but the one who loves their children is careful to discipline them." Another version says: "He who spares the rod, spoils the child."

Some use the phrase "spoiled brat" to describe a child which I think is very unfair. The child is that way because he or she has been allowed to behave that way. In the original interpretation, the word "spoil" in the verse above was meant to indicate fruit going bad. In that case, the child literally suffers if the rod is spared. In case you believe the "rod" is metaphorical and not literal, Proverbs 23:13,14 says, "Do not withhold discipline from a child; if you punish him with the rod, he will not die. Punish him with the rod and save his soul from death."

His soul—his mind, will, and emotions—are hanging in the balance. This is why I believe that spanking is easier on a young child, with better results than a mental punishment. Please note that I'm not advocating spanking with a rod; the point is the form of punishment, not the administering agent. My parents used a belt, Jake's mom used a slipper, and Jake and I spanked our three girls with our hand only, and always only on their bottoms. All three have turned out to be beautifully balanced, respectful, and thoughtful women of God. We disciplined them with spanking until such a time that it was no longer the best method. God showed us on the inside when the time was right to move to other forms of discipline.

Let's take some comic relief from a difficult subject. In talking about this with a friend, she relayed what her parents did to discipline them when they were in grade school. If they needed punishment, her parents would place a chair in front of the TV but have it face the opposite wall. They would then have to endure only listening to their favourite TV program but were not allowed to turn around to watch it! In those days, there were no VCRs, DVDs, or other means to catch the program later. Once it was over, it was over forever, unless you were lucky enough to catch the re-run. I'm sure many parents have created creative disciplinary measures that work for their children.

When our children challenge any boundary we've set up, they are asking two core questions: "Do you love me?" and "Can I have my own way?" The answers are of course: "Yes, I love you" and "No, you cannot have your own way." In every interaction with mom and dad, there is a fear of not being loved and a wilful demand to "get what I want now." Both questions need to be answered well and at the same time, which is difficult.

I remember a time when I yelled at my child when she richly deserved it, but I felt bad inside. I went to God and said, "Lord, you know she deserved that, but why do I feel so bad about it now?" The Lord spoke immediately. He said, "It wasn't what you said. It's how you said it." I learned something important that day. As a parent, God has put us in charge. We cannot lose our cool over things our children say or do. We must remain in control despite our anger and not use it as a reason to vent inappropriately. We often lean too far to one side or the other, trying to make up for whichever we feel is lacking. As a parent, we too are learning self-control. If we can't maintain it, our kids will do as we do, not as we tell them to. This is why we need to be a good example. Like I mentioned, our daughters are all grown up and well-adjusted, confident young women. In writing this, I asked them if they would change how we raised them where discipline was involved. They said, "Absolutely not. We are going to raise our kids the same way you and Dad did with us."

Being a good parent is one of the most difficult jobs in the world, and frankly, we don't have what it takes in and of ourselves. Go to God when you're running on empty, and you feel like you're losing and failing; He'll pick you up and show you how to get the job done and feel rewarded at the same time. Remember, the most perfect parent in the Universe, Father God, had rebellious kids. God knows what we face daily. You will see a harvest of good character, peace, and joy in your child and it will fuel your resolve to stay consistent in administering real discipline and real love.

In closing, please take a moment to meditate on Hebrews 12:9–11.

"Moreover, we have all had human fathers who disciplined us and we respected them for it. How much more should we submit to the Father of spirits and live! They disciplined us for a little while as they thought best; but God disciplines us for our good, in order that we may share in His holiness. No discipline seems pleasant at the time, but painful. Later on, however, it produces a harvest of righteousness and peace for those who have been trained by it."

The Lord desires to reveal Himself to us through our kids as much as He wants us to teach them to know Him and His ways!

CHAPTER 17
How to Thrive Financially

GOD'S ECONOMY

Did you know that the Bible has much to say on finances? Peter Grandich is convinced it is. He is the co-founder of Trinity Financial Sports & Entertainment Management Co., a firm that specializes in offering guidance from a Christian perspective to professional athletes and celebrities and claims to get all of his financial guidance from the Bible. "Money and possessions are the second most referenced topic in the Bible," he says. "Money is mentioned more than 800 times – and the message is clear: Nowhere in Scripture is debt viewed in a positive way." Grandich, who says his years as a highly successful Wall Street stockbroker left him spiritually depleted and clinically depressed, says the Bible is an excellent financial adviser, whether or not you're religious, and that answers to all sorts of money issues can be found in the good book.

God's Word has much to say on how to prosper and it's a good thing—this world has money problems. I feel for the many who struggle financially, as we once did. The good news is, God wants to bless you and me, and He has given us specific instruction on His expectations. Just as good parents will not simply throw money at their children but instead teach good stewardship through life-lessons, so too our Heavenly Father desires to teach us. God does have answers and has personally shown us how to get out from under the burden of crushing debt. It has always been my desire to share this with other people. I hope and pray you'll benefit from our journey.

Did you know that God delights in prospering His children? If we don't believe that God wants us to thrive financially, we'll have no faith in everything that follows. Psalm 35:27 says:

"Let the Lord be magnified, Who takes pleasure in the prosperity of His servant."

If we're struggling financially, God is not the one keeping us from prospering. His economy is based on sowing and reaping principles, and not just with money either. For example, if you want a harvest of friends, God doesn't just rain them out of the sky. Instead, we need to sow friendship with someone. If we want a harvest of love, we need to sow love. So too, if we want a harvest of financial gain, we need to sow finances. This is the cornerstone of His economy. If you are one of many people who struggle financially, I want to share good news: God never experiences lack. He owns it all, because He made it all. Then why do His children so often experience lack? One reason is because they've tied themselves to the world's system of economics and we can see what a state it is in. If we operate by those methods, we will get their results. They don't have the answers that will allow everyone to thrive despite their circumstances, but God does. An elderly King David said in Psalm 37:25–26:

"I was young and now I am old, yet I have never seen the righteous forsaken or their children begging bread. They are always generous and lend freely; their children will be blessed."

Doesn't that sound great? David lived in perilous times, yet he could confidently make that statement near the end of his life. This is my goal also.

FINANCIAL LACK: HOW DID WE GET HERE?

This subject is close to my heart because landing in a position of serious financial lack when Jake and I were young was the avenue that God used to show us that He is a real God revealing Himself to His young, inexperienced kids. He became a personal God to me. He dealt hands-on with us and began to teach us about Himself. He showed us that He was and is faithful to His promises. This wasn't just head knowledge; it became heart knowledge. He provided a way out of a financial wilderness.

When Jake and I got married at the ages of twenty-one and eighteen, we assumed we'd leave our parents' homes and continue to operate on the level of prosperity that they were currently enjoying. The economy crashed, Jake lost his job, we had a new baby, first and second mortgages, a huge personal loan that included paying interest to parents, and a car payment—all with no money in the bank. We woke up to a sobering reality. What happened? What are we going to do? Where did we go wrong?

Why do so many Christians struggle with making ends meet? There are many natural reasons to be sure, but if God is our Father and supposed to take care of us, why do we end up broke? We hear a message that if we tithe (that is, give one tenth of our gross income to Him), God will make sure we always have more than enough; however, I can tithe and be as faithful as ever in believing God will meet all my needs and still end up broke if I spend money foolishly and without discrimination. If we buy or invest in something costly without including God in the purchase, He is not obligated to pay for it.

Common sense dictates that we have to work and that more has to be coming in than going out. When my adult children obtained their first credit card, I held up the card and said: "This is not money. This is *debt*. The minute you use it, you owe." There are natural and supernatural causes to ending up in debt, but when we arrive at this place, we usually end up going to God and ask Him what happened.

In the big picture, if Satan can keep us financially needy, he can keep our eyes on our own needs and circumstances instead of concentrating on God's purposes for our lives. How many times have you wanted to help someone financially but simply couldn't afford it? We are often so busy and worried making our own ends meet that we simply don't have the resources and emotional energy to care about the other guy, because we ourselves are suffering. If Satan can keep the church as a whole poor, how can it meet the huge needs of the world? There seems to be more people in need, Christians included, than those who are providing the resources to help.

If we as the whole body of Christ would put God first in our finances and find Him to be as faithful as He says He will be, we would enter a prosperous cycle. We can get this thing turned around if we obey, and with His help, I believe the world's wealth as a whole would shift as a result. Twelve men turned the world upside down with God's message of salvation and love. What would happen if every Christian had enough to give liberally to the

Yet there are and have been millions of believers who have dared to trust God's system of finances, stepped out in faith and found him to be faithful.

poor and hurting people in the name of Jesus? The compounding results would be staggering.

Jake lost his job due to the poor economy of the early eighties. There wasn't enough work to go around, and since he was the last hired, he was the first to be laid off. He was a qualified plumber, but there was no demand for his services. We wound up in serious trouble and had to face some hard facts. We had over-extended ourselves with monthly payments. Yes, we needed a place to live, but in calculating what it would cost to own a home, have a new car, and raise a new baby, we did not leave any margin for saving for a rainy day. We were living from paycheque to paycheque. We were young and just starting out, but we hadn't been cautious enough in respects to incurring debt. Like many others, we saw something we wanted to buy and barged ahead. We had to face the fact that we had gotten ourselves into this mess and it was our fault. We had to take responsibility.

We could not exclude God from all of our financial decisions up to that point and then shake a fist at Him about out dire financial state. I went to my mom and asked her what we should do, and she told us to start our own plumbing company, as my father had started his own heating company when they immigrated to Canada many years before. I told her it was too hard, but she said: "Sure you can. We did it. You can too!" Looking back, I believe this was God preparing the way. We latched on to her optimism and gave it a shot during the worst recession in recent memory up to that time.

IF YOU LOVE ME, OBEY ME

As good parents, our expectations from our kids are no different than God's directives for us. If my kids continually said they love me but never gave me any other indication like obedience or listening to me, I would begin to wonder. When they really wanted something, I'd say, "Prove it!" Right behaviour would be rewarded with my blessing on their lives.

God is no different. We will never have perfect behaviour towards God because of our fallen nature, but when we're doing our best to listen to and obey Him, He is pleased.

When we started a plumbing company, Jake was overwhelmed. The Lord graciously provided a partner, who was a good friend and a plumber. To begin, we needed a truck, so we borrowed another $3000 from my parents to buy a beat up old truck and some basic materials. We began to bid on providing plumbing systems for new houses, but the competition was cut-throat. I remember that the material and fixture costs alone to plumb a regular home at that time was around $3300. We were bidding as low as $3500, meaning our gross profit was around $200 per house. Fourteen hour days were the norm to make ends meet. During this time, God was getting our attention. We began to pay close attention to what preachers had to say, especially on how to prosper. We needed real answers for real problems. I've said this many times before and will probably say it again: the love of God is unconditional, but His promises aren't. There are often conditions that God requires for us to meet to receive what He has promised. Even salvation requires our acceptance of His gift, right? At this time, we heard a message on tithing and were convicted that we had been disobedient.

Historically, the tithe was a religious duty and existed even before biblical times. When God approached Abraham, it was certain that the giving of tithes had already been recognized as a holy deed. Dividing the spoils of war with rulers and religious leaders was widespread. Abraham, way back in Genesis, had just defeated four kings and gave God full credit by giving Him "a tenth of everything" (Gen 14:18–20). Later, when God brought the Israelites out of Egypt and began to teach them about Himself, He required the tithe to provide for the running of the temple and the means for Levites and priests, who ministered there, to have an income.

I believe we are to tithe, that is, to give at least 10% of our gross income back to God, but if you decide that that number is different for you, please don't miss the essence of this series. I don't want us to lose sight of what is really important, but understanding God's requirements in centuries past, present and future, is very important and helpful in deciding what the Lord wants from us, today. We are to give generously, humbly, and with the proper attitude.

We, however, had not been faithful in regularly giving to God any specific amount, never mind a tenth! We had been careless with our giving, and God said this portion was holy because it indeed belonged to Him. We had kept His portion and used it for ourselves, and as such God's blessing was not resting on our finances. The tenth we withheld became a curse.

We had become careless and indifferent in our relationship with our Lord. Just as the Jews had drifted away from God through idolatry in putting other gods before Him and had ended up in exile after countless warnings from God, we too were in a self-imposed financial exile. God did not cause the Israelites to go into bondage, but after they'd returned, He finally had their attention and used it to bring them back to Him. God didn't cause our debt, but He definitely used it to bring us back too.

THE TEN PERCENT

And so, Malachi 3:6–9 MSG spoke clearly to us:

6-7 "I am GOD—yes, I AM. I haven't changed. And because I haven't changed, you, the descendants of Jacob, haven't been destroyed. You have a long history of ignoring my commands. You haven't done a thing I've told you. *Return to me so I can return to you*," says GOD. (My italics)

"You ask, 'But how do we return?'

8-9 "Begin by being honest. Do honest people rob God? But you rob me day after day.

"You ask, 'How have we robbed you?'

"The tithe and the offering—that's how! And now you're under a curse—the whole lot of you—because you're robbing me.

Firstly, God implored them to return to Him in their hearts first and foremost. The first step was theirs, and subsequently ours as well. We must realize our true spiritual state as viewed by God. We all have blind spots when it comes to a critical self-analysis of our hearts. If God is far away, guess who has moved?

> If your desire is to honour Him and give Him what He requires, you will find a way, and He will make a way.

Secondly, how exactly were they to return? God viewed those who kept the tenth as robbing from Him. So how does my giving Him my measly tenth show that I am "returning to Him?" It conveys where my level of devotion to Him is and where I am putting what He commands me to give as a priority.

Chances are if you wait to see if there's a tenth left over, there won't be. I know because I tried it.

Also, giving represents the very sweat of our brow, so to speak. It is our labour, our toil, our work, our effort; our "crop," and a tangible chunk of our lives and we are giving the first tenth of that toil away to the Lord who enables us *to* work.

The first tenth is His. If we keep it, it won't do us any good; it becomes a curse in our pocket, as Malachi stated. Have you ever seen people who are stingy towards God who actually make a good income but just can't seem to hang onto it? It seems that everything is flowing against them. They miss a great financial opportunity, or their investment goes sour. If we hang onto God's portion, we're putting that money into pockets with holes. It just gets lost in places. God's blessing and favour won't rest on your labour. I have personally witnessed the unmistakable favour of God on our labour, because He is first in our hearts, our lives, and our chequebook. God's portion can do a world of good, but only if we give it where it belongs.

The first step is ours.

Contributing financially to His body, that is—giving our money to God's vehicle to effect His will in the earth, the church—is a touchy subject for many. Preachers even shy away from preaching it, because they don't want to give the impression they're after our money. This is not meant to pressure anyone to give or condemn them for not giving, but to educate and enlighten. God knows our needs and desires to meet them and to that end has created a System whereby we can operate in God's economy and have those needs met, as well as effect God's will throughout the earth. He has set forth some specific guidelines, however, that don't make sense to the world. For example:

The world says: "Get all you can, can all you get, and then sit on that can."

God says: "In order to receive, you need to give." How can I get more if I give away the little excess that I have? God loves to fill a need. As we give to meet a need, He, in turn, will pour out more to meet our need, because our hands are empty. How can God pour out blessings into fists that are tightly clutching "my stuff"? Have you ever heard someone say: "You know, I'd love to give more and I know I'm supposed to tithe, but I simply can't afford to. I don't know why God doesn't give me more money, especially when I'd give more, if I had more."

The truth be told, in God's economy, we can't afford *not* to give.

We've got it all backwards. We think we own 100% of our income, and God's asking a lot of us to give Him 10% back, when in actual fact, He owns the entire 100%, and lets us keep 90%. He makes us the stewards of 100% to see what we'll do with it, and asks us to give back to Him 10% out of obedience and love, to put us in the position to receive His provision and blessing according to His own Word. If giving 10% sounds outrageous, consider this: how much more money would we need to be able to afford to give God 10% of our income? If God gave us that 10%, would it go to Him? Chances are, there are needs and wants that would suck up that 10% too, so what is wrong with our system of finances?

How much money does one need to be able to afford a cup of specialty coffee? If a mocha costs $5 and we have one every work day, that amounts to $100 a month in specialty coffees, alone. I'm not telling you to give up your Tim Hortons or Starbucks, but the point I'm making is that we afford what we want to afford. If we want something badly enough, we will pour our time, energy and resources into obtaining that thing, correct? God, on the other hand, doesn't need our money. As mentioned, He owns it all, full stop. He wants relationship with you, and wants to show you He'll take care of you, if you'll obey Him and put Him first.

Now I can hear many of you echo the same sentiment we did: "Lord, we just can't afford to give you a tenth of our income. We'll really go under!" But God didn't tell us to give if we could afford it. He told us to give in order to obey Him. John 14:21 puts it very clear:

> "Whoever has my commands and obeys them, he is the one who loves me. He who loves me will be loved by my Father, and I too will love him and show myself to him."

This verse has two very important parts: obeying Jesus shows we love Him, and we will not only be loved by Him and His Dad, but we will see Him! This is what happened to us; we returned to the Lord in our hearts and decided to try to obey him and see what would happen. We didn't begin by giving Him a ten percent tithe of our gross income, but we did make a quality decision to give regularly with the little we couldn't really afford, with the intent to give more as God provided.

I've heard people say, "I can't afford to give anything, period." But everyone has something to give. Remember the widow in the Bible who gave a few copper coins? We decided to give to God first, and then make purchases for our needs with what was left over. We wanted to show Jesus we loved him by being obedient in this regard and boy did it ever hurt! It cost us to begin to be obedient.

"ARE YOU GOING TO BELIEVE IN 'IT,' OR IN 'ME'?"

As mentioned we were making a grand total of $200 – $300 per house in profit and it would take roughly a week to complete one house in stages. Our tiny company would try to get as many jobs lined up as possible so that they could finish the first stage and then move to another house that was now ready for the second stage, and then go to a home that was ready for the finishing. It was a difficult cycle to be in when the return was so minimal. Jake and his business partner were working 12–16 hour days, six days a week, in order to provide for their young families. Since God seriously had our attention, we heard and latched on to a promise pertaining to God's sowing and reaping principles. Jesus Himself says in Luke 6:38:

> "Give, and it will be given to you. A good measure, pressed down, shaken together and running over, will be poured into your lap. For with the measure you use, it will be measured to you."

We basically understood that if you give God a teaspoon of your finances, He'll pour out a heaping teaspoon back to you. If you use a pail, He'll pour out so much blessing that the pail overflows. If you use a wheelbarrow—you get the point. 2 Corinthians 9:6 also says:

> "Remember this: Whoever sows sparingly will also reap sparingly, and whoever sows generously will also reap generously."

We'd returned to the Lord and had begun giving, but when we understood the preacher said that we would receive because we gave, we bought right into that formula hook, line, and sinker. We decided to try it.

Well, I'd like to tell you that things got immediately better, but they didn't. In fact, they got much worse. We would receive draws for our work, but there was never enough left over at the end to fully pay our monthly supplier bills. Eventually, we incurred a large supplier debt amounting to roughly $60,000. Now we were broke *and* owed an additional $60,000.

Remember what I said initially: We had first and second mortgages, personal loans from our parents, a car payment, new baby, and now a $60,000 supplier debt, *and* we were regularly giving. I went to God and asked: "Lord, what is going on? We're doing our best to give, and things are worse than ever! It didn't work!"

The Lord immediately impressed on me the following words so clearly that I'll never forget them. He spoke directly to my heart and gently asked this question: "Are you going to believe in 'it,' or are you going to believe in 'Me'?" I knew that was God's voice. I went to Jake and told him what He'd said. We had to make a decision to either pull back from giving because it hadn't improved our situation, or continue to believe that God would somehow provide. In the natural, we could see no way out. We came full circle and said: "Lord, where can we go from here? Are we to quit obeying You? You cannot lie. We believe your Word. We don't understand why we're not thriving, but if we're going to go down financially, we're at least going to go down doing the right thing. You said it, we believe it, and that settles it." It was this point God was waiting for. It taught me an incredible life lesson: whenever I hear people say that "it" didn't work referring to any of God's promises failing them, I always say: "You had better believe 'it' didn't work—because God wants your faith in Him, not in 'it.'"

God is no formula.

Please understand dear people: God has some specific requirements He needs us to meet in order to operate in His economy to be sure; but the motivation to obey Him needs to be out of a heart of devotion expressed in obedience, and not a desire to "get." God showed us very clearly that we were to seek His face, not just His hand. We were to seek Him, not just what He could do for us.

Shortly after we reached this point, things dramatically began to turn around. When we made the decision to trust God and obey Him even though our natural minds couldn't understand how things could change, He gave us favour by allowing us to land a contract that due to our inexperience we should not have landed. A building contractor who was building a custom home took a chance on two very young, scruffy-looking plumbers. In the natural, we do not know why he did that. I know beyond the shadow of a doubt that it was the favour of God. You see, God wasn't limited by the limitations we saw. All it took was for God to crack open the door of prospering, which we ran through and pulled wide open through faith and hard work. We *saw* Him begin to be faithful! The timing of this was poignant. It came right on the heels of our stepping out of the boat and trusting God hands down to walk on water—to simply take the next step towards Him with our eyes glued on Him, no holds barred. We had decided to sink if Jesus wouldn't save us, because we simply decided to trust Him. When God is all you've got, God is all you need.

This contract opened the door to other such contracts, and within roughly six months we paid off that $60,000 supplier debt. We were utterly astounded at what God did in just six months, when we couldn't even make our personal ends meet within the previous two years. God was faithful to His promises! The floodgates were opening like God promised in Luke 6:38 and we'd discovered that the journey to get out of debt wasn't relying on a formula, but fully relying on and obeying, Him.

It is a solid gold principle that has sustained me for the last thirty years not only in regards to finances, but in all other areas as well. If there is ever a time I can't understand why God does or does not do things, I begin to press in and seek His face, and not His hand, and I *always* find Him. In thirty plus years, He has yet to fail me.

If we look to Almighty God for who He is, instead of what He does or does not do, we will never shipwreck our faith.

BRING THE WHOLE TITHE

Since everyone's financial situation is different, I'm certain that the previous sections on God's economy have left many with comments or questions when it comes to our giving. You may say,

- "I don't believe that I have to tithe 10% of my income. That was Old Testament. The New Testament doesn't say anywhere that the amount has to be 10%."
- "I really love God, but obeying Him in this will cause me and my family to suffer."
- "I believe in giving, but why does the number have to be 10%?"
- "If I give, how can God bless me? I have a set income and don't see how He can increase my harvest with my job."

We need to renew our minds to what is possible, with God.

- "God knows what I need. I'm just waiting for Him to bless me more so I can give more."
- "I told someone that God was abundantly blessing me because I'm obeying Him, and they told me I was mistaken. They told me that I was blessed because I'd worked hard and a natural harvest occurred, and God had nothing to do with it."

Let's look another section of Malachi, beginning with the first part of 3:10:

> "Bring the whole tithe into the storehouse..."

God required a whole tithe; that is, a full tenth of all the Israelites' grain, flocks, oil, and crops. It goes against our grain to give so much. Does God know how much money that is? We need to renew our minds to what is possible with God. Consider Proverbs 3:9–10:

"Honour the Lord with your wealth, with the first fruits of all your crops; then your barns will be filled to overflowing, and your vats will brim with new wine."

> God is here to solve our money problems, not increase them.

Notice the "then" is after you've honoured God with taking ten percent off the top and giving to Him. Remember, God is not going to require from you what He hasn't already provided. Our problem may lie with a fear of lack to provide for our families, a lack of faith that God will come through, or perhaps we want some material thing to the exclusion of everything else. Perhaps money has become our god. When the highest goal of our lives is to obtain wealth, we will service that goal on a regular basis, no?

I realize that for a great many people, giving 10% seems like an impossibility, but God specializes in making the impossible possible. In talking specifically about the dangers of wealth owning us versus us owning wealth, Jesus said. in Matthew 19:26:

"With man this is impossible, but with God, all things are possible."

As we grew in God's Economy, we made a quality decision that we were not going to come off of, to build it up to the full tenth as God blessed us. I say quality decision, because as sure as anything, Satan will bring pressure on that decision. He knows full well that we will never out-give God. God is no man's debtor. He owes no one anything. He is an extravagant God, not a cheap, stingy God. Once our giving was established, it became easier to give as He enabled, with excitement along the way as well as the reward of feeling spectacularly fulfilled through obeying Him. The apostle Paul confirms exactly this in 2 Corinthians 9:10–11:

He's just looking for people that will be channels, not reservoirs.

¹⁰Now he who supplies seed to the sower and bread for food will also supply and increase your store of seed and will enlarge the harvest of your righteousness. ¹¹You will be made rich in every way so that you can be generous on every occasion, and through us your generosity will result in thanksgiving to God.

Whatever you sacrifice for becomes dearer to you. If you sacrifice to give God what is His, He will not only come through in meeting your needs and more, but I guarantee He will become dearer to you, and will reward you with the greatest gift of all: intimacy and relationship with Himself. You will know first-hand that you have had hands-on dealings with the Creator. When God turned our situation around, I was more moved by the fact that Almighty God had actually intervened in our lives than having our needs met. That became a good foundation to build our house on. It can be for you too.

WHY DOES GOD NEED FOOD IN HIS HOUSE?

Malachi 3:10 stressed the importance of giving God the first whole tenth of our income but here is the reason why:

> "Bring the whole tithe into the storehouse,
> that there may be food in my house."

Why did God want the Jews to give? A storehouse is meant to store commodities. The temple of Malachi 3 was empty. God had originally designed the temple to have rooms to store what the people gave. The people were meant to give a tenth of their grain, oil, livestock, or the equivalent in money, etc. so that the Levites could bring the required sacrifices; the priests would receive enough to meet their own needs, freeing them to care for the Temple and perform their priestly duties, as well as have ample supply to give to the foreigners, orphans, and widows who were in need. There was no governmental Social Services at that time. God always meant for the needs of these to be met by Him—His temple, His church, His people.

Whenever the people neglected their giving, the Levites and priests had to leave the temple and go work the land in order to have their own needs met, and so God's temple fell into neglect in the process.

> The Gospel is free, but the pipeline that brings it to people isn't.

The church today, also needs "food" in its house. I've heard of preachers so worn out with trying to save the church money by taking extra part-time jobs, painting fences themselves, fixing church roofs, etc. that they themselves become completely burnt out after a few years. Surely this is not how God wants us to treat our shepherds. Our shepherd is God's chosen vessel to keep us in line. It stands to reason that we should financially support the people whose job it is to teach us about following Jesus, if we expect God to bless us. They too have children who need braces on their teeth. God also wants our churches to have their storehouses full, to meet the needs He's put us there to meet in the first place. Sadly, we hear more often the church begging for bread, instead of being the stewards handing it out. This is not the all-supplying God who owns the whole universe I know.

If every Christian regularly gave an amount corresponding to their income, the compounding interest and financial windfall that would occur would amaze us. We would be astounded if we did the math—the church, in general, would then become what God intended—a source and not a need in this regard. And I'm extremely glad to say that this is actually happening in various places! As the body of Christ obeys, God is corporately rewarding them according to His own Word.

As we release our money and give to God, we break money's hold on us, in our hearts, and in our wallets. When we consciously share the responsibility of having our own needs met with God, we no longer have the sole responsibility of meeting our own needs!

The Gospel is free, but the pipeline that brings it to people isn't. Churches need to keep the lights and heat on and in our case keep the Food Bank going that operates out of our church. Ministries on TV need to buy expensive air time to compete with the garbage that the world spews out. Preachers need to have enough to give, need to eat, have periods of rest to reflect and provide for their families, and I firmly believe that if every Christian regularly gave according to their income, the stranglehold of debt that Satan holds people and the church in would loosen. And, there is another lovely side-effect:

We don't have to cling to every dollar, as God is now involved with blessings us with what see He sees fit. God can only pour out blessing into hands that are empty through a cycle! If our hands are hanging on so tight to our money, how can God give us more? Money isn't the only thing meant here, either. The same is true with all of God's gifts. Give them away to where He directs you to, and He'll give you more, be it knowledge, revelation, teaching, or money. Here's an incredible reality: When you give to God what is His, you are *partnering* with God and financing the Gospel, and you have a share in the harvest of souls that are reached! And, you are building up treasure in heaven, where it will last for all eternity.

TEST ME IN THIS!

Sometimes God packs so much information in a single verse! The last part of Malachi 3 verse 10 had special significance for us when our finances were rocky all those years ago:

"Test me in this," says the Lord Almighty, "and see if I will not throw open the floodgates of heaven and pour out so much blessing that you will not have room enough for it."

I believe that this is the only place in the entire Bible where God tells people to test Him. This is noteworthy. We are told elsewhere that it is wrong to put our God to a foolish test, but in this capacity, He commands us to! Caution is warranted here, however; I've heard this taken so grossly out of context, that people think they can tithe, sit back, and quit working, expecting God to drop money out of the heavens. Not so. You have to work hard, but God will bless your efforts and give you favour all over the place.

This was a time of serious growth for us as God's children. We made some mistakes and fell down, but God picked us up, brushed us off, and we began again. We can never fall down too many times. It still amazes me to think that in the beginning hard years, as well as all the years that have passed since then, we got out of being in debt to our eyeballs, broker than broke, by the act of giving to God through devotion and obedience. It just doesn't make worldly sense. I've heard it said that God's economy is backwards. Earthly standards say that to become wealthy, one must accumulate wealth. God says, what you want to reap, you must sow. It shouldn't work, but it does! I'm not just saying this; I've lived it, and I will continue to live by God's economy until I graduate. We have found God to be utterly, completely faithful to His Word. I challenge you to find out for yourself too.

HOW CAN GOD BLESS ME?

Here's something that's always puzzled me. It amazes me how often people resist good news! Throughout the years, some people have responded to our testimony with scepticism that God was directly responsible for our success. I remember hearing, "Sure God could bless you abundantly—you had the perfect vehicle for Him to bless you through: your own business!" In the early 1980s, the economy was the worst it had been for many years. Established companies were going under, and we were young, inexperienced, and just starting out, so that just didn't wash.

In the last segment, we saw God tell His people to test Him by giving and watch Him open the floodgates of heaven and pour out blessings. Perhaps you're thinking, "Even if I give God my tithe, how can He bless me? I'm in a dead-end job with a deadbeat boss. I know what I'll be making tomorrow, the day after, and next week. How can God increase that?"

God is no respecter of persons.

What He did for us, He will do for you. He loves you as much as He loves me. For example, He may give you favour with your boss, who will begin noticing your stellar work attitude as you "do everything as unto the Lord," and you may receive a promotion or raise. Giving is a lifestyle that is not limited to money. When you begin serving and loving others as you serve and love Christ, people begin to notice. When you couple that with obedient stewardship of God's tithe, you can't lose.

> We may as well believe big or go home. Nothing is too hard for God.

God has placed you in a certain vocation. He will bless you to the maximum that vocation can allow, and perhaps even more. God is not restricted by anyone or anything getting in the way of His agenda to bless one of His faithful kids.

God doesn't take orders from your boss; rather, He influences your boss. If your boss won't yield to God's influence, He will move in another way, hallelujah. Nothing is too hard for God. If you are limited for the time being by the resources you receive, He may open other avenues to help you save resources. Malachi 3:11–12 tells us that not only will blessings come, God would protect them when they came: "I will prevent pests from devouring your crops, and the vines in your fields will not cast their fruit."

However, when we sow seed, there is usually a time of waiting between the time seed is sown and a crop coming up. The Bible says we will reap a harvest "if we don't give up." When we began to regularly give, we began to plant good seed. When we were still learning, going through our growth pains and waiting, God saved us money in many other creative ways: I was in the right place at just the right time to get a great deal on a child's coat, or groceries, or a household need. It happened so frequently that I could not help but link this to God's promise of favour on our income.

Our business prospered and steadily grew. We began to acknowledge God in all our big and small decisions over what to buy. I can't tell you how many times we invited God into a situation where we were going to buy or invest in something, and we heard that still, quiet voice impressing us to hold off. I remember one instance, particularly when we were given the opportunity to bid on a lucrative plumbing project, which we did not get. We were disappointed but acknowledged that God was in control, so that was that. As it turned out, the project ended up going sideways where various trades were stiffed for their services and not paid with a long, drawn-out legal battle. Boy, did we thank the Lord that we didn't get that project! Our seed to give wasn't poured into a bad investment and lost. We serve a God with countless means. Philippians 4:19 says:

> "My God shall supply all your need according
> to His riches in glory by Christ Jesus."

Notice that your needs will be met according to His riches, not your job, your boss, or the economy. If a millionaire gave you ten percent out of $1000, you would thank them. If a millionaire gave you ten percent *according* to his riches, you'd have won the lottery! How rich is God? This is why we can put our full confidence in Him. To put it in today's terms, this verse is a note drawn upon the bank of faith:

My God—the name of the banker
Shall supply—the promise to pay
All your need—the value of the note
According to His riches—the capital of the bank
In glory—the address of the bank
By Christ Jesus—the signature at the foot, without which the note is worthless.

Paul also puts the icing on the cake by saying in 2 Corinthians 9:8:

"And God is able to make all grace abound to you,
so that in all things at all times, having all that you
need, you will abound in every good work."

God will take care of us as we become vessels He can pour blessings through, so that we too can be a blessing wherever He places us.

THAT WAS OLD TESTAMENT, NOT NEW

We've been exploring Malachi 3:7–11 for a while now, and I feel it is important to say something about the fact that this large, life-long investment in giving is based on an Old Testament text. I know that there are those that dispute the fact that we are to give a ten percent full tithe of our gross income because it does not say anywhere specifically in the New Testament to do so. I'd like to address this, but first I'd like to gently ask, why are we disputing it? Would we be upset to find out that New Testament Christians are in error giving God 10% of their income, or would we be upset because we aren't the ones giving? If we are upset that a great many Christians are giving too much to God, we need to do some serious re-evaluating. Do you think God will mind if we accidentally give Him too much? Do you think that God isn't able to restore to us up and above that ten percent? It has been my experience that those who dispute tithing generally aren't the ones doing it. We must ask ourselves why we're upset.

> If you think about it, if they under the law were required to give 10%, how much more should we be giving, if we are now under grace!

Some people say that when Jesus came, He did away with the Old Testament law, but this is not true. In His parable about the wineskins, He said that new wine (the new covenant) shouldn't be poured into old wineskins (existing or old covenant) or it would burst and ruin both. He said rather, pour the new wine into new skins, so that both (the new and the old covenants) are preserved.

Jesus came to fulfil the Old Testament, not do away with it, so the Old Testament is valid in essence, if not in form. If the Old Testament is invalid, why do we have it? If only some of it is valid, which parts?

It's all God's Word to us. We don't make animal sacrifices anymore because Jesus became the one and only sacrifice to atone for sin, but the reasons for the Old Testament sacrifices and the New Testament one-time sacrifice both point to and address the condition of sinful humanity unable to approach a holy God. Therefore, they are both valid. Interestingly, the greatest law of the Old and New Testaments are one and the same: To love the Lord your God with all your heart, soul, mind, and strength (Mark 12:30).

If we still point to doing away with the regulations of the Levitical Law, which included tithing, it may help to know that tithing actually came about much earlier than the law as mentioned. Abraham began it by tithing ten percent to Melchizedek, God's representative who met with him; Jacob continued it by re-affirming giving the tenth in Genesis 28:22. Moses put it in writing when God brought the law, and Jesus Himself affirmed tithing in blasting the Pharisees that they gave a tenth of everything, but neglected justice, mercy, and faithfulness. In Matthew 23:23, Jesus Himself caps it by saying:

"You should have practiced the latter, without neglecting the former."

In saying this, He said tithing should be practised, but not without neglecting justice, mercy and faithfulness. And finally, Paul in 2 Corinthians encouraged the brothers to "excel in this grace of giving" and talks about giving a regular portion of our income, in keeping with our income.

If you think about it, if they under the law were required to give ten percent, how much *more* should we be giving, if we are now under grace!

I'M STILL NOT CONVINCED

If you're still not convinced that God's economy works, I'd like you to take a good look at some people. Examine the fruit (that is, the things that are coming out of the lives) of givers and non-givers (those who are not ignorant but say tithing or regular giving according to their income is not required). What do you see? I've done this and often you can see distinct differences between the two. Sometimes cranky Christians who criticize others for giving are the ones constantly in need. Their lives just don't run smoothly, especially in their finances. For givers, in addition to having God's favour and blessing pouring through their lives, I have seen them be generous in other areas too.

I like hanging around givers. Giving does something on the inside of us. It begins to chip away at whatever hold money has on us, and a spirit of greed begins to be replaced with one of generosity towards others. We begin to relax our grip as God shows Himself to be faithful. We begin to serve people with more ease. Have you ever seen a generous, joyful giver who doesn't open doors for people, or give up their seat on a bus? Giving has compounded benefits throughout our life. It truly is a lifestyle. It releases the blessings of God in and through our lives.

When we began being regular givers, I was surprised at the amount of joy that flowed my way through our giving. I didn't expect that. I was so used to being uptight about money that I thought I'd be even more wound up if I tithed.

There were times when giving was harder than others, but after having tasted the joy God gave me in meeting other people's needs, I'd never give that up. I've heard of people in need who received an anonymous financial gift from someone, and the person in need gave it away to sow it into the life of another, just for the joy of being God's secret agent. Don't you think He'll reward that?

On the topic of giving today and letting God take care of tomorrow, how and when we give our tithe is important too. We already know that because the tenth is His, it is holy and needs to be treated as such. We are to give it when we receive our wages, not six months later because we forgot or were careless. How would we feel towards God if He had a sloppy attitude towards meeting our needs?

> We need to be as careful with giving our tithe as we want God to be with meeting *our* needs, don't we?

Did you know too that as we give God His portion, it also gives us the right to expect Him to provide for us? Not out of arrogance or a demanding attitude, but out of a reverential expectation of God to fulfil His promise to us. Many people in the Bible reminded God of His promises to them and how they had been faithful. We honour God by expecting Him to keep His promises. A prayer that honours Him may look something like this:

"I thank you, Lord, that all my needs are met according to your riches in glory. I thank you that you are providing my needs today, and that you have given me seed to give. I ask you to bless that seed, and to multiply it in your Kingdom, and I thank you that as I give, you will more than meet my need. Thank you, Lord Jesus, for your wonderful principles and laws, which are not meant to bind me, but to bless me and set me free, to be a blessing."

I hope that these words have encouraged you to embark on a new adventure in watching God move in your life and finances as we excel in this grace of giving. It is important to remember that everything, be that money, talents, time, or acts of charity given to your Lord through devotion has not been used up by the need; it has been deposited in your heavenly bank account. You are not spending your money, time, or resources but investing them. What you give may leave your hand, but it will never leave your life! When we give to God, we are making an investment in eternity that will never spoil, rust, or be stolen. We're storing up treasure in Heaven, where our heart is anyways (Matt 6:19–21). In reference to our finances, everyone says that when you die, you "can't take it with you." Does it not then stand to reason then, that you should send it on ahead of yourself?

To close, an amusing story. There was a wealthy man who was not rich towards God but rather stingy. He had a large beautiful estate that required the services of a gardener. This gardener loved God and often gave liberally to the Lord's work. Eventually, both men died. The wealthy man made it into heaven and was given a tour of the mansions that were on the way to his permanent abode. As they walked down the gold streets, they came upon a large estate that housed a spectacular gold mansion, and the rich man asked who lived there. The angel responded that it was his gardener. The rich man was elated; surely if his gardener had such an abode, he could just imagine what his dwelling would entail. They continued down the street and came upon a small cottage. It was solid gold, but tiny. The angel said, "Here you go. Home sweet home!" The rich man was shocked and upset. He said, "You must be kidding! My gardener gets that big mansion, and I get this little cottage? That can't be right!" The angel responded, "I'm sorry, sir. It was the best we could do with what you sent ahead."

GOD, DID YOU BLESS ME OR DID I JUST WORK HARD?

We spend a lot of time working. With the exception of weekends, half of your waking time is spent at work. It is no wonder that God wants to be a vital part of our finances.

After we became established in our business and shared our testimony with people, we were asked if God was really the source of our abundance, or if it was just our hard work. After all, there are a great many wealthy people who don't even believe in God, never mind tithing, and appear to be prospering. Bill Gates was interviewed in November 1995 on PBS by David Frost and said, "The specific elements of Christianity are not something I am a huge believer in." Still, he has established the world's biggest charity with nearly $40 billion in its trust.

I do not know where Mr. Gates stands in his relationship with God, but clearly God has impressed upon him to give. Ironically, Bill Gates is about God's business in meeting huge needs in the world, whether or not he recognizes His hand! Do you think Satan wants people helped? I wondered about the wealth of those who don't believe in God too, until I realized that the riches they have on earth are perhaps to be the only wealth they will ever be in charge of, for all eternity. If we are faithful with whatever God gives us, His Word says we will be put in charge of more, in this life and the life to come. God will require an explanation of what they did with the wealth He gave them, just as He will require it of us.

I thought about the question. How much of our abundance was due to our own effort and how much was due to the Lord's blessing on our finances? God showed me Deuteronomy 8:17–18, which sufficiently answered my question:

> "You may say to yourself, 'My power and the strength of my hands have produced this wealth for me.' But remember the Lord your God, for it is He who gives you the ability to produce wealth."

Also, if God gives us the ability to produce wealth, it is not wrong then to produce it. If that were the case, then there are some big offenders in the Bible—Solomon, David, Abraham, Job, the wealthy men and women, tax collectors, and the honourable alike in the Old and New Testaments, who often financed the Gospel. David himself says in 1 Chronicles 29:12-17:

"Wealth and honour come from you; you are the ruler of all things. In your hands are strength and power to exalt and give strength to all. Now, our God, we give you thanks, and praise your glorious name. But who am I, and who are my people, that we should be able to give as generously as this? Everything comes from you, and we have given you only what comes from your hand... O LORD our God, as for all this abundance that we have provided for building you a temple for your Holy Name, it comes from your hand, and all of it belongs to you. I know, my God, that you test the heart and are pleased with integrity. All these things have I given willingly and with honest intent. And now I have seen with joy how willingly your people who are here have given to you."

There are two tests that God gives His children during life. He looks at how they act when they don't have money, and how they act when they do. Both convey a lot.

The apostle Paul likened greed directly to idolatry (Col 3:5) and for good reason; passages in Matthew 6:24 and Luke 16:13 say: "No one can serve two masters. Either he will hate the one and love the other, or he will be devoted to the one and despise the other. We cannot serve both God and Money." You'll notice in both passages that "God" and "Money" are capitalized. They are both names; one is the only true God, and the other is an idol, merely a substitute.

In saying all this about prospering, I feel I must also address those who serve and love their Lord who do not produce monetary wealth although God has led them. This is not to mean that God gives certain people wealth and deprives others. Mother Theresa had little money, but gave tremendously of herself and was known to the whole world. God has a specific plan for each of our lives, and if we follow it, we will be fulfilled because He will fulfil the desires He has given us. God needs extravagant givers, and they need to be in the position to earn that kind of coin.

People say Jesus and His disciples were poor, but if that were so, why did they need a treasurer (Judas) to handle their finances? It's true that while Jesus was on Earth, He didn't have much, but that wasn't because He was poor; it was because He was generous to a fault. At one point, Peter said, "Lord, we have left everything to follow you." There had to be an "everything" that Peter left in order to stay this. If someone makes the conscious choice to deprive himself of material wealth for kingdom purposes, and decides to live that way, God will honour him for his gift of servitude above all else. 2 Corinthians 8:9 puts it this way in relation to what Jesus did for us:

> "For you know the grace of our Lord Jesus Christ that
> though He was rich, yet for your sakes He became poor,
> so that you through His poverty might become rich."

In Heaven, Jesus had everything the Father had. He was rich in every way. This is what He gave up to come down to Earth and become like us, and so through His giving His life, we might become rich. The potential of these gifts are never ending; they are passed down from generation to generation. As you obey God, your kids see a life impacted, which creates the desire for them to have the same relationship with the Lord. Salvation bought us a life not separated from God. I don't know about you, but I certainly want everything Jesus died to give me! 2 Corinthians 9:12–15 sums it up nicely:

> This service that you perform is not only supplying the needs
> of God's people but is also overflowing in many expressions of
> thanks to God. Because of the service by which you have proved
> yourselves, men will praise God for the obedience that accompanies
> your confession of the gospel of Christ, and for your generosity in
> sharing with them and with everyone else. And in their prayers for
> you their hearts will go out to you, because of the surpassing grace
> God has given you. [15] Thanks be to God for His indescribable gift!

We will never out-give God. God gave His Son, and the Son gave His life, to give us His eternal life. For you. For me.

What will you give Him? What is He worth?

PART III

SPIRITUAL WARFARE: HOW TO DENY SATAN HIS PLEASURE

CHAPTER 18
How to Thrive, Not Just Survive, Depression

PAIN

Before I launch into Part III on spiritual warfare, I thought it appropriate to address the issue of pain, as it is closely tied to the topic at hand. We all experience and deal with it. Whether it's physical or emotional pain, it's simply a reality that we face on earth. In thinking about human suffering, escaping from life's trials and troubles is not God's purpose for anyone. Where does God fit in our lives when we are suffering? We cry out and plead with Him to be relieved of our painful situation. Heaven is silent, and we remain in pain. What happens next? Frustration, and perhaps even anger towards God. We cry out to our Heavenly Father, wondering how He could allow us to experience this. Why, God, why? When are you going to intervene? As a parent who loves her children, I would do anything to prevent them from being in pain, except if the ultimate reason for their pain will bring them a better gift than taking the pain away. For example, if I didn't want my daughters to ever be in pain, I'd advise them to never have a baby. But I know from experience that going through childbirth is worth the pain. As a side note, all three of our daughters are in the process of having babies this year! They'll need to go through that pain, because they'll end up with a new life. God clearly is no less of a parent than I am. It is through the lens of the highest form of love that we need to see why God allows pain in our lives.

> It is through the lens of the highest form of love that we need to see why God allows pain in our lives.

If God Himself allowed His only Son to be crucified because He loves us so much, surely He has reasons for allowing pain in our lives.

We've all been here and yet we are assured that God is aware of our situation, and that everything is subject to change, except God and His Word. There are seven words in the Bible that always comfort me during times of pain: "And it came to pass, that God..." Throughout the Bible, we read these seven words in response to God's people crying out. The problem didn't come to stay; it came to pass! But it took some time. God has heard your cry; He has already set in motion His solution for you, but it is up to us how we behave while waiting. Have you ever been in a doctor's waiting room with an impatient toddler? They will squirm, complain, whine, try to get out, and wreak havoc on anything that isn't nailed down. They're just immature babies, that's all. They'll grow out of it eventually. How do we wait on God? I can remember acting just like an impatient toddler in times past.

The book of Job gives us much insight. Remember all the terrible things that happened to him? He lost his kids, his fortune, his reputation, and if that wasn't enough, he lost his health when covered with painful boils from head to toe. Yet it says in Job 1:22, "In all this, Job did not sin by charging God with wrongdoing." Remember, he did not know why all these things happened to him. He was faced only with dealing with the emotional and physical pain. We know from God's Word that there was much going on behind the scenes; that there was a great debate going on between God and Satan over whether Job's loyalty and love for his God would stand up under the test of intense pressure. In allowing Job to go through all of that, God, his loving Father, was actually putting His faith in Job in believing that he would not turn away from Him.

God gave us the book of Job to show us what was going on behind the curtain and to encourage us. Although Heaven may seem silent, God is still in control of all things and our pain is for a reason. Everything that happens to us has gone by His inspection, and we need to trust His character and have faith in His love for us.

God always makes a way.

Job had been a highly esteemed and honourable man who had occupied a seat amongst the leaders of the town. Through all this hardship, he lost face with them. They assumed he was getting what he deserved through some secret sins he had committed. He humbly surrendered himself to God and took comfort in his integrity. His conscience was clear. His reputation with God was all that mattered to him, and he didn't care about his reputation with man.

He was, however, just as human as we are. His conduct and attitude throughout his trial demonstrate that it was okay to be frustrated. His frustration, though, was in the process and not with God. We need to vent and process our trials the same way to have patience with people who mean well. He promises not to ever give us more than we can bear. Job did just that, and don't forget what God did as a result. Just look at the reward Job received for refusing to blame God:

10 After Job had prayed for his friends, the LORD restored his fortunes and gave him twice as much as he had before.11 All his brothers and sisters and everyone who had known him before came and ate with him in his house. They comforted and consoled him over all the trouble the LORD [actually Satan, but God had allowed it] had brought on him, and each one gave him a piece of silver and a gold ring. 12 The LORD blessed the latter part of Job's life more than the former part. He had fourteen thousand sheep, six thousand camels, a thousand yoke of oxen and a thousand donkeys.13 And he also had seven sons and three daughters. 15 Nowhere in all the land were there found women as beautiful as Job's daughters, and their father granted them an inheritance along with their brothers.16 After this, Job lived a hundred and forty years; he saw his children and their children to the fourth generation.17 And so Job died, an old man and full of years (Job 42:10-13; 15-17).

When I am in pain and have no answers, I have chosen to say what Job said: "Though He slay me, yet will I hope in Him" (Job 13:15). Will you dare to hope in Him too? There isn't one minute of your pain that God is not aware of. Remember the Passion of the Christ? Why couldn't God's purpose in sending His Son to die be accomplished in allowing Jesus to be beheaded, like John? Why did Jesus have to suffer? God allowed it to show us the depth of His love for us. Are you willing to suffer to show the depth of your love for Him as you wait for your deliverance? Job said, "Indeed, this [his whole painful situation] will turn out for my deliverance." So too will yours.

THE PIT OF DEPRESSION

The following five sections convey a deeply personal part of my journey. I need to share this so that someone out there can find encouragement and hope. It has been used by God to define and refine me for His purposes, His glory, and my on-going growth. If you've not experienced what I'm about to share, note that I never thought that I'd be in these shoes either. Even if you never become seriously depressed, it's important to identify with those who experience it and offer hope and compassion to the many people who battle it daily. I pray and believe that this will bless you.

There is a world of information about depression and many opinions and methods in how to treat it, depending on your personal beliefs, background, and cultural upbringing. For example, an unbeliever might attribute depression to only physical factors such as chemical imbalances in the body, heredity, hormonal activity, menopause, mental illness, mid-life crises, or psychological problems. A Christian might attribute depression to only spiritual causes such as spiritual warfare, demonic oppression, an attack from the enemy, or perhaps a period of refinement allowed by God. What is the source of depression? How should we treat it? It could be any one or combination of these, or maybe something else. Everyone, even emotionally healthy people, at some time experience feelings of depression, and it is difficult to determine where the line is between normal and problematic.

As Christians, we believe that we are a spirit, we live in a body, and have a soul. Satan can't touch our spirit because we've been bought and paid for by the death and resurrection of Jesus Christ. Still, Jesus has yet to come and do away with sin once and for all, and because of that, we still live on a planet under the curse of sin. Our spirits have been reborn, but our souls—our minds, wills, and emotions need to be renewed daily to the truth of God. This is where Satan attacks us. Physical causes or manifestations of depression also attack our souls. The symptoms can be the same, but the treatment is different. As a Christian, which is it? As an unbeliever, which is it? This is what I believe makes an accurate diagnosis of depression so hard to treat. In the Bible, there were great men and women of God who were depressed, but they didn't let it keep them down. They also did not have modern medicine to determine the causes. There may be no answer to fully satisfy everyone. However, there is One who has all the answers, and He has been guiding me throughout this learning curve as I've been coming out the other side of it. This is what I want to share with you.

As a Christian, I believe that God is real and so I have chosen to believe that there is a war going on that we are in but can't see. However, we can see the results, both good and bad. The world does not acknowledge that there is a tangible enemy of our souls that seeks to do away with us. It doesn't acknowledge spiritual warfare as one of these methods, and as such, we often only treat the symptoms of depression and teach people how to cope with it, instead of acknowledging the transforming power of God that is available to heal its source. Of course, I thank God for the medical community and their ongoing research and many contributions to helping depressed people; but all healing, whether it's supernatural or through natural means, inevitably stems from God. However, treating depression as only a physical problem leaves out a large area to be identified and dealt with. I am not qualified to judge; I just want to bear witness to how God ministered to me.

> There is one common denominator to depression, whichever way you look at it and whatever your beliefs are: it's dreadful. Yes, it is full of dread.

There is one common denominator to depression, whatever your beliefs are: It's dreadful. Yes, it is full of dread. To me, it felt like all my hope had leaked out and was replaced with despair and dread. The family was good, the finances were good, everyone's health was good, and I hurt anyways. This confounded me. People looking at my life would have said I had absolutely everything going for me. I'm sure they'd have asked what in the world I had to be depressed about. I'm sure they might have told me to snap out of it, and that I was just feeling sorry for myself for no reason. As if I could just decide not to be depressed anymore, and not be. Anyone who has been depressed knows that although their intentions may be good, they're misguided. I did not know why I felt that way. What causes a person to be tormented day and night so thoroughly that life becomes a never-ending parade of despair for no reason? What causes a person to get up at 3:00 a.m. and hide in a bathroom and weep gut-wrenchingly for no specific reason until they fall exhausted back into bed? These were the questions I bombarded myself with for the better part of four long years. During this time, I went down many avenues. Was it a physical problem? Was it an emotional or psychological one? Was this spiritual warfare or was God trying to teach me something? I needed to ascertain the source of it because I couldn't pinpoint any reason for it. If I could figure out what was causing it, I could fix it—right?

I am an analytical and proactive person. If something breaks down, I exhaust myself figuring out why to avoid it next time. After trying to figure this out on my own for a long time, I finally gave in and went to my doctor. In the past he has commented that I was quite in tune with my body and gave good self-diagnoses over an ailment. I listen to what my physical body is telling me. I shared my feelings and thoughts with my doctor (who is also a Christian, by the way) and he sent me for tests to figure out if the problem was physical. Nothing showed up at the time. There was no physical reason or hormonal imbalance as the source during those early years.

Back to the drawing board. I was a Christian. Wasn't I supposed to be enjoying righteousness, peace, and joy in the power of the Holy Spirit? These feelings were foreign to me at this time. It was embarrassing. I was a care group leader in my church. How could I tell people that I was coming unglued? I shared my problem with a few solid Christian friends, who I asked to pray for me. What I found so frustrating was that this depression conflicted sharply with my gifting from my Lord. I was and am an encourager. It is in the fabric of who God created me to be as a Christian to encourage people and hopefully find some solutions; to tangibly help them—hence this book! If anyone is suffering, I want to give them a hug or a listening ear to ease their pain and be a source of refreshment to their weary souls. How could I give away what I no longer had myself? My hope was gone. It was tempting for me to withdraw completely from leadership and hole up in my house. I wanted to say, "You've got problems? Throw in the towel. I can't believe right now that God is going to help you." I didn't give in to that temptation because I knew that was not the truth of God's voice, but a lie from the enemy.

It was an intense war between what I knew was truth and the opposite of it. As a strong believer in the Lord, I knew these kinds of thoughts were not coming from God. Thinking about suicide in even the smallest way came from an intense desire to escape, but was definitely not truth or an option. I felt trapped; I couldn't die, and I hated living.

PERSEVERANCE IN OBEDIENCE

Have you ever tried to run in water? Have you ever had the nightmare where you try to scream, and nothing comes out? This is how I felt for a long time. There were days I told myself to breathe in and out and the day would eventually end. I couldn't carry any emotional weight. The littlest thing would put me on overload. It's like living with a constant panic attack, because you know you can't handle much and the last thing you want to do is fall apart in front of people. But I had one solid thing going for me, and I firmly believe this is a key to getting through with God.

Perseverance in Obedience.

It's not flashy. It's not easy, but it definitely has teeth. Despite how I felt, I decided I was going to obey my Lord, no matter what. I decided that I was not going to quit. It wasn't even faith that sustained me at this time. Faith is the substance of things hoped for, the evidence of that which is not seen (according to Hebrews 11:1), and I didn't have any hope. When I was asked if I would lead our Young Adults Care Group for another year, I wondered if I could do it. I decided that since God was the real leader anyways, He would simply have to provide what I needed to get through. I leaned heavily on Philippians 4:13: "I can do all things through Christ who strengthens me." I would be having a panic attack driving to the meeting, wondering if I could do it, and cry all the way home, beating myself up over how it went. However, to this day I am living proof that Philippians 4:13 is true and that God enabled me to lead during this time. We can do all things through Christ who strengthens us, but if we're not going to be obedient and do what is required, what can Christ strengthen? It doesn't take any strength to sit in a dark room. I began to see the

> "Pain without purpose is torture. But pain *with* purpose is a doorway to healing and renewal."

value of obedience in the hard place. It is a testament to God's provision. Few people knew the fight I was in. God always lifted me enough to minister to others, however exhausting it was. He was showing His faithfulness to me in a fresh way. I found that I didn't have to feel strong, to be strong. It was my obedience to God and His Word that started to put me back together.

I attended a women's conference during this time, where I heard the personal testimony of Lisa Bevere on a refining time in her own life that resonated with me. In not liking herself for the sin and bad attitudes in her life, she surrendered her whole self to Jesus and passionately prayed, "Lord, excavate me!" She continued, "What I should have prayed was: 'Lord, accessorize me!'" Women can appreciate the difference. The Lord honoured her prayer, and she went through a period of brokenness before God put her back together. I share this, and I can smile now, but that is exactly how I felt during my dark days. I felt I had been excavated on the inside and I was utterly smashed and broken. It took everything in me not to pray to die. You don't really fully appreciate the fact the world is spinning until you want to get off. I believe that had I not had God in my life, I may have been a casualty of suicide. It breaks my heart more now to hear of suicides. I know how they felt, and although I felt like all hope was gone, I knew that God's Word said that faith, hope, and love remained and that above all else, He was and is faithful.

You may be wondering why I didn't pursue antidepressants. Yes, the avenue of drugs was always in the back of my mind, but I resisted. However, if you are reading this and struggle with depression, my decision to look for other ways does not mean you should too. There is nothing wrong, humbling, or weak about getting medical help. I didn't at that time because, as a person publicly advocating that God will see us through whatever we face, I simply could not tell people I was full of joy and peace because God made me so, while relying on drugs to smile. I would feel like a hypocrite. I needed God to be my only source. If He was in control of my life, which I believed He was, I knew He had good reasons for allowing this. I had to find Him in it, and so I ruled out antidepressants. Either God was going to fix me, or I would languish. I also figured out that not all pain is bad. I had the acute sense that even though I was in emotional pain, God was accomplishing something I couldn't see. This was the only hope I had.

Shortly after the end of the worst part of my depression, I heard a preacher say something that I had already discovered: "Pain without purpose is torture, but pain with purpose is a doorway to healing and renewal." I have to agree.

THE VELVET BRICK

As mentioned, most people get depressed now and then. However, there is a huge difference between feeling low now and then and being depressed for an extended period. Anyone who's been depressed wants the hurting to stop. I believe that a lot of depression can be attributed to spiritual warfare, because if Satan can't have us, he at least wants to render us ineffective. Even if you are the strongest warrior, you won't accomplish a thing if you quit. I was sorely tempted to decline leading a home group, but then the enemy would have won, young people wouldn't have received instruction and been cared for, and I would have withdrawn. Secondly, it's important to fully realize that the words of God contain power. We must believe this first, or we won't have confidence in His Word to bring us relief. Isaiah 55:11 says:

"So is my word that goes out from my mouth: It will not return to me empty, but will accomplish what I desire and achieve the purpose for which I sent it."

If we are being led by the Holy Spirit and take the word He quickens in our hearts, something on the inside will begin to change. The supernatural will take precedence over the natural. That is what began to happen inside of me. I would be studying my Bible doing my morning devotions, when God's Word would jump off the page. It felt like I had been plowed between the eyes with a velvet brick. It didn't hurt at all; it was soft and lovely, but powerful. As it ministered to me, it was the Holy Spirit quickening that word to my spirit, for me in my time of need. That is when the word became living and brought change and relief. It wasn't

> I not only identified with these words, I began praying them right to my Heavenly Father as if I had written them.

a new word; it was my now word. Even if I didn't initially feel changed, I knew that changes were happening inside.

Psalm 143 ministered directly to my soul. The descriptions David uses are poignant. Verse 3 says, "The enemy pursues me, he crushes me to the ground; he makes me dwell in darkness like those long dead." When Satan takes this avenue to take us down, we feel crushed, and he makes us live in a dark place. We sense no life, just death all around us. Verse 4 says, "So my spirit grows faint within me; my heart within me is dismayed." We feel this way until we choose to obey verses 5 and 6: "I remember the days of long ago; I meditate on all your works and consider what your hands have done; I spread out my hands to you; my soul thirsts for you like a parched land. Answer me quickly ... my spirit fails." I not only identified with these words, I began praying them right to my Heavenly Father as if I had written them. I found that as I started meditating about how faithful God had been in the past and started to fill my mind with what He had done and not how I felt, I began to be lifted up.

Where the mind goes, the body will follow. Even if you're in a period of despair, you can visit hopeful places in meditating on the past deliverances of God. Reach out to God to water your dry, parched soul. I have found that as I did this, I left that darkness a little at a time, until I eventually came out. It can happen so subtly, you may not even realize it, but obeying the Word of God brings change a little at a time until you look back and realize that something has changed. Your focus is no longer on yourself, and you've begun to live in a world with windows, not mirrors. God began to put practical tools in my hands. If His Word brought results once, it will do so again.

David goes on to implore God, "Show me the way I should go, for to you I lift up my soul. Rescue me...for I hide myself in you. Teach me to do your will...may your good Spirit lead me on level ground." I bear witness that God did exactly all that, in my journey through my anguish and struggle. God showed me where my mind needed to go, He rescued me in my despair, He taught me how to obey Him, as His Spirit led me on a path I didn't stumble on.

One of the hardest things to do, when one is fighting, is to say God's promises, His solutions, out loud. To confess God's Word, we need to say it. Depression causes us to withdraw and become quiet. I always knew when I was really struggling because my family would ask me to repeat things, as I talked so quietly. I thought they should get their hearing checked, but saw eventually that it was me. Speaking with conviction is usually the last thing you feel like doing, but you must soldier on. We have to choose to say what we want to see happen, not what is currently happening. When you choose to speak God's Word, you've picked up your sword, and the enemy gets nervous.

> Never run at the devil with your mouth closed!

Again, obedience to God's Word came into play for me. I didn't feel full of faith—I felt emptied of everything—but I obeyed anyways, believing with blind faith God's Word would bring relief. If you're struggling with it, you need to let that truth fully sink in. He will bring you to a new place, even if you're feeling stuck. His love will sustain you from the beginning to the end. Whether it's a physical problem or spiritual warfare, God is the answer.

GETTING SPECIFIC

God's Word profiles many people who struggled with depression, including kings and prophets such as Jonah, Job, Elijah, Jeremiah, and even King David, so we're in good company. They too were not immune to the human condition. However, God never left them in that state, and this is reason enough to hope. If we give up, God's purpose for our lives is hindered; if we hang in there, it can be a means for God to reshape us into a more useful vessel for His purposes.

As I tried to cheer myself up, I attempted to drum up excitement over things I used to enjoy doing, but that now held no interest whatsoever. I finally realized that I was unable to fix myself and that I may as well get comfortable while God worked on me. When I finally resigned myself to quit trying to escape myself, I simply asked God to show me the way out of the woods in His timetable. It was at times like this that God's Word brought huge comfort, such as Paul talking about his weakness (2 Cor 12:9–10). We tend to take the position of "what can't be cured, must be endured," but Paul said, "What can't be cured can be enjoyed." Paul delighted in his weaknesses because God's power would be made perfect in it. He welcomed fresh occasions to draw on God's grace. This is what sustained me while I waited. I knew that at the end of it all, Christ would be glorified, and this made the wait palatable. I can't say I delighted in it, but knowing I was suffering for Christ's sake definitely helped. After what seemed like an eternity, God finally began to get specific with me.

In asking God to help me, He showed me that my thought processes were to blame for where I was. He showed me the triggers that pushed me into a downward spiral. I had low self-esteem to begin with, and the enemy used this to his advantage. Satan would whisper, "You're so useless at leading a Home Group. They're not getting anything out of it." Instead of immediately dismissing that thought, I believed he was probably right. I hate self-pity—I was not using these thoughts to throw a pity party. In being depressed, I had no fight left in me and took on the enemy's thoughts, which deepened it.

God showed me I was internalizing wrong (and sinful) thought patterns that caused my self-worth and value to plummet. This is why His principle of taking every thought captive and making it obedient to the Lordship of Christ is so important (2 Cor 10:5). What this means is if what the devil was whispering in my ear didn't agree with what God said about me, I kicked it out. We don't have to accept the negative thoughts the enemy presents to us. Internalizing wrong thoughts that exalt themselves against the knowledge of God will cause us to sink lower. However, the opposite is also true! As I began to take control of wrong thought patterns and say the opposite, I began to climb out of that bad head space. Instead of experiencing deflation when the enemy presented his agenda, I felt elevation when I simply told him that's not what God said and I'm not buying it. As I did this on a regular basis, I noticed a change in my outlook. It doesn't happen in one day, but the value is in going up, not further down.

Obeying God will bring results. I began to pay close attention to my thoughts at this point and when I'd slip, I vowed to do better next time. I had found a way out, and I wasn't about to let it go. I was finally gaining headway, and it also felt like it!

PRAYER

I mentioned earlier that I had asked solid Christian friends to pray for me. It's important not to hide your depression. This doesn't mean you have to tell everyone around you, but you do need to confide in solid Christian friends and loved ones, and let them know what is going on with you. That which is kept hidden in the darkness has power over us. When we disclose a personal struggle, it is no longer in the secret place. You expose it to the light for God to minister to you through others. I resisted this for a while and realized it was pride. I didn't want my friends to see me as needy. I wanted to be a strong spiritual leader and pray for others, but having them pray for me was humbling. When I recognized this, I simply gave up. I was hurting too badly to care. They laid hands on me and prayed. I didn't feel any different, but I know that feelings don't matter. They said a faith-filled anointed prayer and I know God used it.

God also used Jake, bless him. As a husband who dearly loves his wife, he too was on a mission to "fix" me. Being a man and logically minded, he had a plan. He was the husband, the umbrella and spiritual leader of the family. He felt the weight of responsibility that wasn't his. How could he do what only God could do? To his credit, he remained loving and understanding. He was a source of continual comfort to me. He listened patiently and tried to understand me, but the most important thing he did was to pray for me—a lot. When I was at my lowest and desperate, I'd frequently ask him to pray for me. He did, and I distinctly remember him praying along these lines: "In the name of Jesus, I take authority over the spirit of depression and command you to go. As the husband, I have a right; I am over my wife and command you to leave." He also prayed that God would minister to me and help me through. It was at these times when the spiritual warfare was the most acute, that I sensed a lifting of the heaviness; I actually experienced relief. Jake formed a habit of praying for me. In the early morning, before he got up, I often felt his hand on my shoulder. He was quiet but not sleeping. I knew he was already praying for me.

We must not underestimate the power of prayer. God's Word says that the effectual fervent prayer of a righteous man has great effect, so we can't do anything without it. All of life's challenges, no matter what they are, begin and end with prayer. It is giving earthly permission for heavenly interference in our affairs to effect God's will.

YOU ARE NOT THERE ALONE

Despite whatever challenge to your joy and peace you face today there is always one continual tangible comfort that you can rely on: In all of my struggles especially at the darkest moments, I always felt God's presence to be ever so near, so incredibly close to me, I'll cherish that forever. After having given up trying to fix myself, I remember at the lowest points going into my room and sitting down beside my bed, bowing my head and simply going to Jesus. I didn't pray or say anything. I just wept as I envisioned putting my head on Jesus' heart as He held me. I'll never forget those times. Even though He didn't remove the pain, He was with me in my pain and brought healing through it. Not only did I not stay in the same place, I *didn't stay the same.*

I am just beginning to see now some of the fullness of how God has transformed me. I know I have come through permanently changed in areas and extremely reliant on my Lord. My praying for people has also changed. There's something very freeing about praying for people with a crystal clear appreciation you are insufficient to meet their need, because that frees you up to pray for God's all-sufficiency to come through. I have been released to let go, and let God. I also have a far more acute sense of empathy for those who are hurting. For example, a Christian friend of mine told me she had broken up with her boyfriend, who was an unbeliever. She was clearly hurting. I simply conveyed my concern by saying, "I'm sorry for your pain." She looked at me and said, "You are the first person who didn't judge me and tell me it was best that we broke up because he didn't believe in God." She thanked me and hugged me. She already knew how God felt about that relationship but didn't need to hear it right then. She needed someone to empathize with her. Just like in me and in her, God uses these things to refine us and burn away the garbage. After having gone through this and coming out the other side, I'd like to close with something I know I will keep with me forever:

His grace is enough.

These words were and always will be, music to my soul. There is a praise and worship chorus that repeats this phrase throughout that I still simply cannot sing due to the lump in my throat. The lump used to be there due to pain and a sacrifice of worship as everyone else sung "Your grace is enough" as Jesus put His arm around my shoulder. Now there's a lump in my throat due to sheer joy as I know in my heart that His grace is enough through having experienced it. In my journey through depression, I began by trying to figure out why I became depressed and at the end of it all, the reasons why don't even matter anymore. He has restored me through the prayers of my husband and friends, persevering through obedience, feeding off of and relying on His Word, arresting triggers through taking captive errant thought processes, and remaining patient under the pressure the Potter's hands were putting on me as He re-moulded me into a more useful vessel. It's like God said, *this is what I wanted you to find— that my grace is enough.* I found that absolutely no matter what we face in life, His grace will be *enough,* for you to overcome too.

As I close this segment, I am encouraged by David's words in Psalm 42:

"Why are you downcast, O my soul? Why so disturbed within me? Put your hope in God, for I will yet praise Him, my Saviour and my God."

There is a future beyond our depression. Just keep moving forward through the night and morning will come, Praise the Lord. We are all in this thing called life on planet Earth together. If this has helped you in any way, it was worth it, because you are worth it.

CHAPTER 19
What We Need to Do to Deny Satan His Pleasure

RUNNING THE RACE TO WIN

God loves humankind so intensely that He sacrificed His own Son to save you and me. Satan hates God so intensely that he would stop at nothing to hurt Him. Since the Garden of Eden, he knew he couldn't win against Almighty God, so he chose the next best thing. What better way to hurt God than to hurt what He loves? All spiritual warfare is ultimately against Satan and our fallen flesh due to his deception and lies. Every time we lose a battle, Satan rejoices. It helps me to keep this filter at the forefront of my mind when I'm battling: "I will not give in. I will deny you your pleasure, Satan, as God enables me to, in His mighty strength."

The writer of Hebrews likens our life's journey to a race—not a sprint, but a life-long marathon. This verse is packed with good instruction that will give us a great payoff not only now, but in the life to come. Marathons involve training, sore muscles, exhaustion, mental discipline, and a reward at the end. Is it any wonder that the writer chose this metaphor? We can all relate to times in our Christian walk when this could apply. Let's take Hebrews 12:1 apart.

• "Since we are surrounded by such a great cloud of witnesses…"
This would seem that our race is being watched, but not so. The writer is talking about all the faith giants who came from before and bore witness to what *God had accomplished* in and through their own lives. We're in good company!

• "let us throw off everything that hinders…"
"Everything that hinders" can be many things and will no doubt look different to everyone. These can also be necessary components of our

lives, but our servicing of that thing can become out of balance. It could be anything from: a schedule that is too busy for God; putting material possessions ahead of God; the love of a comfortable lifestyle; even the love of a sport that takes a lot of time. The toys we buy need to be serviced. There is nothing wrong with owning a boat, but if it causes us to miss Sunday after Sunday of fellowship, soon our zeal will begin to wane. We simply can't spread ourselves too thin where our time spent running the race is compromised.

Spiritually speaking, this is a race of faith.

- "and the sin that so easily entangles…"

Satan is so clever. We're very short-sighted when it comes to sin, especially when we view them as "little" sins. Song of Solomon 2:15 says it's the little foxes that ruin the entire vineyard. We know the sins are there, but we don't treat them seriously. They may be thoughts of doubt, anxiety, or worry, or carnal thoughts or dirty jokes that we allow to linger and pollute our minds that Satan slips into our lives so subtly. Romans 14:23 says that whatsoever is not of faith is sin. The primary sin that so easily entangles is unbelief. Once we are no longer in faith, we take all sorts of detours that trip us up.

- "and let us run with perseverance…"

Think of a runner in the Olympics. Do they let anything get in the way of that finish line? For days, months, and years, they train with one goal in sight. The wonderful thing about the race in Hebrews is that there isn't just one champion; we all can win—provided we run.

Quitters never win, and winners never quit!

- "the race marked out for us…"

God has already road-tested your race course. You can win by running the race specifically marked out for you. If you don't know exactly where to go, He will show you. He may not show you the destination, but He will show you the direction (Prov 3:6). You can pray: "Lord, all I know is that I want to finish the race you have prepared for me, the purpose I was born for, for your glory and the advancement of your kingdom."

Let's do it! And when you fall down, don't get discouraged. The only thing that matters is how many times you get up and keep going. You will win your race!

TAKING POSSESSION OF OUR PROMISED LAND

Imagine that you and your countrymen—an entire nation—have been wandering a barren wilderness for forty years, waiting to get to the new home that God promised you, but your chief dies. As a result, you have been placed as leader over a large nation comprised of stiff-necked, obstinate people. You are to take them into a land populated by wicked nations much stronger and better at warfare than you are. This is where Joshua found himself. He had been given the charge of taking the nation of Israel into the land that God had promised them after Moses died. "A land flowing with milk and honey," it is called in Exodus 3:7-9. This was clearly a huge improvement over wandering in the desert. However, because they had been a stubborn and rebellious people, it took forty years for what should have been an eleven-day trip. Why did it take so long?

Sometimes children have to try all the wrong ways of doing things before they finally agree to do things the right way. This summed up the Israelites. God knew that the only way they'd survive in taking possession of the land was if they fully obeyed Him. They learned this during the forty years of discipline that God meted out because their parents had grossly disobeyed Him. If they had been a people who obeyed and embraced their God and His ways, they'd have entered their promised land right away. We can learn a lot from their example. I for one don't want to be in a wilderness for forty years, and yet it's amazing how many people choose just that. We've all had times when we've been in rebellion towards God. Did it ever work out well?

What is our "promised land?" I believe it is all God's promises, metaphorically speaking. We've inherited all of God's promises through Christ, but why then do we live in such failure so much of the time? Just like the Israelites had to go into the land and claim it, we too have to claim what Christ died to give us. There are so many of us settling for only a fraction of God's blessings. We all hope that our futures will pan out the best way possible, but life doesn't come with guarantees. The only thing that will never change is God, so it stands to reason that we'd be wise to pay attention to how to operate in His provision for our future. Just like a good parent, we don't just give our kids everything they want—they'd never learn anything that way. Instead, we teach them life lessons so they can go out and find their promised land, with their Saviour.

> It took forty years for what should have been an eleven-day trip. We can learn a lot from these guys.

After learning their lessons, the Israelites were about to finally enter their promised land. They came out from under oppressive bondage to the Egyptians to take hold of a new land with God as their leader. Likewise, we have come out of oppressive bondage to sin to take hold of a new life with Jesus. The Israelites were an inexperienced, wandering nation that faced huge and powerful adversaries. Have you ever had to do something that you know God needed you to do, with opposition that intimidated or overwhelmed you?

How will you respond when it happens? "Lord, it's too big. It's too difficult. I just can't see how I can do it." If there are problems in your life that seem too huge to handle or if you feel overwhelmed with what you know God wants you to do, take heart; God is aware of what it is going to take to see you through, and He does have a plan. I have learned so much in what God expects from me in studying the account of the Israelites. He instructed them how to proceed. That's why He wrote it down. God recorded His past dealings with His people to leave a record of Himself and His ways in the earth. If God gave His ancient children counsel of how to overcome giants, armies, and kingdoms, it stands to reason we can learn from them. The era may have changed, but God doesn't. He is the same yesterday, today, and forever. He gave them nine things to do to be successful in their mission. I believe these apply to me and you as well, and we'll take a good look at them.

SPEAK IT, THINK ABOUT IT, AND DO IT

"Do not let this Book of the Law depart from your mouth; meditate on it day and night, so that you may be careful to do everything written in it. Then you will be prosperous and successful.

I know what you're thinking, that the title of this section is in the wrong order. Shouldn't it be: "Think about it, do it, and then speak about it"? No. God doesn't make mistakes in His commands. Notice in Joshua 1:8, above, that He gave the Israelites instructions. Right at the end comes the juicy part: "Then you will be prosperous and successful." The *then* is important. It indicated they needed to do something else first. Remember, they were just on the verge of going in to take the land God had promised them. I believe these conditions apply to us as well. Let's look at it more closely.

- *"Do not let this Book of the Law depart from your mouth..."*

I believe God said it this way on purpose so that the first command as the Israelites were about to go into a foreign land and slay giants would be to speak His Word out loud. In other words, never quit speaking God's Word over your situation, so your own ears and others hear it. If it was good enough for us (or them) to simply meditate on it without speaking it, God would not have been so specific. God's words are containers for power.

When you've been given God's promise for your situation, God's Word needs to be in two places: in your heart first, and then in your mouth. When the heart is not filled with the Word, the force of faith is not there, and our confession will be only mental and will soon fail. Something tangible happens when we confess God's promises, especially in the face of insurmountable difficulty. He says in Proverbs 18:21 that the power of life and death is in the tongue (not the mind). He was talking about confession.

- *"Meditate on it, day and night, so that you may be careful to do everything written in it."*

> When the heart is not filled with the Word, the force of faith is not there; our confession will be only mental and will soon fail.

So how do we get anything else done if we're meditating on it day and night? God doesn't mean for us to sit in a dark room all day and night. He simply means for us to not just read our Bibles daily, but really ponder what He's saying to us. You can digest God's Word every time the Holy Spirit reminds you of it during the day and even the night. That's why worship choruses are so great; many times without even thinking about it I start humming a song while I'm driving or vacuuming. We need to know it to be careful to do what it says.

- *"Then you will be prosperous and successful."*

If we speak God's Word in faith, study it, and obey it, God makes this promise. I can personally state that over the past thirty years, God has not failed us as we obeyed Him in this regard. He has prospered us, and we've been more successful than I would have dreamed possible. Did we work hard? Yes, absolutely. But people can still work hard and lose millions. Was raising our three daughters tough at times? Yes, absolutely. But they have emerged as confident Godly women who are well on their way to a life blessed by being obedient to Him. Even when things haven't worked out as we planned, my consolation is always that I share the responsibility with God Almighty, who is never limited by anything. He can and does work out everything for our good!

I AM WITH YOU ALWAYS

"Have I not commanded you? Be strong and courageous. Do not be terrified; do not be discouraged, for the Lord your God will be with you wherever you go" (Joshua 1:8–9).

In the previous sections, we covered the three main conditions that need to be met to prosper and be successful. Remember that all the Israelites had to go on was the law that God had handed down through Moses. We now have the indwelling Holy Spirit to help us!

- *"Have I not commanded you?"*

Despite the challenges of speaking God's commands and having a lifestyle of meditating in His Word and obeying it, this is our ace in the hole. God's commands are His enablements. T. Austin Sparks says, "The real battle of faith is joined here. Not what we are, but what He is. Not what we feel, but His facts." We need to see our battle through the lens of God as our Supreme Commander. If we are able to do what He says with His help, we will have the victory.

- *"Be strong and courageous..."*

This is easier said than done. Courage is the quality of being brave; the ability to face danger, difficulty, uncertainty, or pain without being overcome by fear or being deflected from a chosen course of action. It is the willingness to invest who you are, what you have, what you want, for what you want to be. Faith is required to make the choice to go forward in God's strength because we don't have it. God says we can do all things through Christ who strengthens us, so we have no excuse to be weak. Joshua was facing strong, warrior nations who vastly outnumbered them. We can see that God was encouraging him because he needed it. We have to remember that God's Word recounts His faithfulness and we see it after the fact. Joshua did not know how it was going to play out, but he was told to be strong and courageous, and we know that God came through for them.

- *"Do not be terrified..."*

God's presence still demands human courage!

How effective are we when we can't move due to fear? This is the stuff nightmares are made from. I'm sure this is why God told them to not let fear paralyze them. We need to choose to not let terror control our actions. You can't be in faith for God's deliverance and in terror of your enemy at the same time. We need to service our faith, not our terror. Who you serve here will have an effect on the outcome. Joshua had good reason to be terrified, and this is why God told him to not be. His focus needed to be on God and not the vast armies before him.

- *"Do not be discouraged..."*

Discouragement is the opposite of courage, and this is one of the enemy's most effective weapons, as it often feels like we're carrying an elephant on our backs in the middle of the killing fields. To be discouraged is to be overcome by fear and deflected from a chosen course of action. It's like running in lead shoes, and the simplest things feel insurmountable. But we need to fight it, not wear it like a badge. We somehow feel we've earned the right to be discouraged and want sympathy when we feel overwhelmed. Again, if God told the Israelites to not be discouraged, we should obey that, despite how we're feeling.

- *"For the Lord your God will be with you, wherever you go."*

When Jesus was about to leave Earth to go back to Heaven, His parting comments to His disciples were of utmost importance. He said, "And surely I am with you always, to the very end of the age." Jesus died to give us our promised land. From the time Joshua stood on the brink of going in and taking it and the promised land that is before you right now, God has been with His children. Just look at the incredible beauty and symmetry of God the Father's words and Jesus the Son's in both the Old and New Testaments:

> "...for the Lord your God will be with you wherever you go..."
> (Josh 1:9)
> "...surely I am with you always, to the very end of the age..."
> (Matt 28:20).
> They're both saying the same thing. How can we lose?

CHAPTER 20
What We Need to Wear

THE ARMOUR OF GOD

What springs to mind when you hear the term "suit of armour"? Medieval knights jousting; protection from arrows and spears; chain mail; shields and heavy, bulky metal garb. How comfortable to do you think armours of past times were to wear? They would have first of all been heavy, and in the blazing sun or winter frost either uncomfortably hot or cold. As cumbersome and uncomfortable as they may have been, staying alive as opposed to dead definitely outweighed the discomfort. Is it any wonder then that God says we should wear an armour too, albeit a spiritual armour to protect and equip us against the enemy. The apostle Paul lived in the times of the Roman Empire. They were amongst the greatest warriors on Earth at that time. He tells us in Ephesians 6:10–18 to put on God's armour not once, but twice so we should keep in mind the dual emphasis.

If there's one thing that we are familiar with through the ages, it's fighting. God is very good at warfare for all the right reasons. The Old Testament is full of battles of one kind or another, so God knows what He is talking about. Just like in earthly warfare where there are positions of hierarchy among the ranks of soldiers, Paul tells us that there is a hierarchy of evil that is just as organized with spiritual enemies, rulers, authorities, powers and forces of evil in the heavenly realms. This warfare is not a matter of contending against godless philosophers, crafty priests, or cultists. The battle is against demonic forces, battalions of fallen angels, and evil spirits who wield tremendous power. Though we cannot see them, we are constantly surrounded by wicked spirit-beings. While it's true that they can't indwell true believers, they can oppress and harass them. We shouldn't be morbidly occupied with demonism or live in fear of demons. The armour of God is all we need to stand firm against their onslaughts. But how do we do that, especially when we don't relish the idea of going to war?

We have to first accept that we are in a struggle against Satan's schemes. We must also remember that on our own, we are no match for the devil. God's best soldiers are those who are conscious of their own weakness and ineffectiveness, and who rely solely on Him. Every true child of God soon learns that the Christian life is warfare. In fact, I would say that if we are never bothered by Satan, we may need to look at our lives to see why.

> God, actually, is very good at warfare for all the right reasons.

Satan usually tiptoes around Christians who are asleep because they're no threat to him. The hosts of Satan are committed to hinder and obstruct the work of Christ and to knock the soldiers out of combat. The more effective a soldier you are for Jesus, the more a target you become; Satan doesn't bother with nominal Christians. He already knows he's defeated, but that doesn't cause him to surrender. He still wants to do as much damage as possible. We need to be ready and properly dressed at all times. Let's look at the spiritual armour available to us:

1. The Belt of Truth: We are to hold to the truth of God's Word, but it is also necessary for the truth to hold us. This part of our armour keeps our covering in place. The truth won't ever come undone or be changeable. We can throw our full weight of confidence against the truth of God's Word; it is strong enough to withstand any pressure and will not break.

2. Breastplate of Righteousness: A breastplate protects your vital organs, particularly your heart, from the enemy's blows. The enemy can no longer accuse us, as we have a breastplate of right standing with God that protects us when Satan tries to condemn us as sinful beings. We point to Christ and say, "Take it up with Him!"

3. Our feet need to be fitted with the readiness that comes from the gospel of peace. When we know, understand, and are passionate about this—God's good intentions toward humanity—we are ready to go where God directs, invading the enemy's territory by spreading His message of peace toward all men.

4. The Helmet of Salvation: A helmet protects your head from injury. Let's face it; your brain is the seat of your mind. From it, we make sense of everything, and it controls the whole body. If that is taken out, you're as good as dead. So without salvation, we're spiritually dead too. The helmet of salvation deflects any claim Satan has on us. Our thought life is critical in relation to the battle. Satan attacks in this realm almost more than any other. The Bible speaks of battles where physical enemy forces would shout discouraging words to people who were on top of the city's fortified walls, in order to discourage them and encourage them to give up—to surrender. This was a direct attack on their confidence level of their faith in their king to defend them. They were told to ignore the enemy and stay true to their king.

My favourite piece of armour, yet one of the hardest to use on a continual basis, is the shield of faith, held up to put out the flaming arrows that would otherwise stab and burn us. Soldiers learn to keep their shields up in battle, but often we go through life with our shields dangling by our sides.

> There is no "shield of feelings." God is moved by my faith, not my feelings.

The shield of faith is made of the substance of things hoped for, and is the evidence of that which is not seen. It's invisible, but that does not make it any less effective. We still need to wield it! When we allow the enemy to hit us by doubting that God will rescue us, we've put our shield down. Instead of keeping our spiritual eyes focused on God and trusting Him, we allow what we are seeing with our natural eyes to determine how we respond to the enemy's arrows. We become the wounded instead of the victors and crumple down into a pile of discouragement. When we deflect the arrows with the shield by trusting God, we extinguish the enemy's doubts.

In my weakness, I have to choose to speak words of faith, even if I am afraid or discouraged. There is no "shield of feelings." God is moved by my faith, not my feelings. I have found that He has come to my rescue when I am in warfare when I choose to obey by trusting Him, despite how I may be feeling.

Second to last, the Sword of the Spirit: an extremely lethal weapon. It is the Word of God. When Jesus was tempted by Satan, He wielded this weapon: "It is written..." This is why it's important to know God's Word, for offensive and defensive use. Hebrews 4:12 says, "For the Word of God is living and active, sharper than any two-edged sword..."

> How can a sword be living? Jesus wielded and is the sword of the Spirit: the Word of God!

Jesus wielded His own words, and Satan left to return at a more opportune time. Satan retreated. He couldn't win against the Word of God, standing there in the flesh, wielding it. Jesus showed us the example we are to follow.

We have no power in and of ourselves; we just wield the sword that does. When we are wrestling with Satan, we need to wield the weapon of our warfare, the Word of God. This is why we need to deposit His Word in our hearts, daily. God will bring up in the bucket what is down in the well when we need it. We greatly underestimate this weapon because we often give up using it when we feel small and weak during a battle against the forces of darkness. We are small and weak, but God's Word and the weapons of our warfare aren't!

Finally, we must pray. How earnestly would we pray if we were in a foxhole with bombs raining down and bullets whizzing by? Like the saying goes, "There are no atheists in foxholes." This means that at times of extreme stress or fear, all people will believe in and call out for a higher power to save them.

We need to be connected with our Commander, praying all the time, and for everyone and everything in our situations. It is the atmosphere we are to live and breathe in. It requires vigilance, spiritual keenness, alertness, and concentration. We must watch against drowsiness, mind-wandering, and preoccupation. A good example of this was the disciples in the Garden of Gethsemane. Jesus told them to remain alert and pray because He knew what was about to happen. They fell asleep time and again and were completely unprepared for the crucifixion of their Lord.

Paul said we are to "pray in the Spirit on all occasions with all kinds of prayers and requests" (Eph 6:18). We are to pray inspired and led by the Holy Spirit. Formal prayers recited merely by rote without giving thought to their meaning have no value in combat against the hosts of hell. As soldiers, we should employ public and private prayer; deliberate and spontaneous; supplication and intercession; confession, praise, and thanksgiving. How can we win if we don't continually consult with the one who's running the show?

It's important to be fully dressed and ready for battle. One piece here and there won't be enough. We are to first get dressed for battle, pick up the weapons of our warfare, and be in constant communication with our Commander. This is how we "do everything, to stand, firm." God does have a battle strategy that will give us victorious life experiences with Him, and cause us to grow and mature. Satan is already defeated, and he knows it. His time is short, and he's getting desperate. Many times, we allow him to hurt us by going into battle without our armour. God desires to equip us, and if we won't obey His way, He won't make us. It's our choice to stand firm or retreat.

CHAPTER 21
The Battle is On!

FLEE! PURSUE! FIGHT! TAKE HOLD!
KEEP! COMMAND! GUARD!

These instructions weren't meant for us to use against the enemy; they were meant for us to use on ourselves to not become deceived through being lulled into lethargy, laziness, and apathy. They are a sober reminder that Satan can deceive us so subtly that we hardly know he's doing it. In 1 Timothy, Paul gives some strong commands that many Christians in a state of spiritual sleepiness desperately need to adopt as their way of life. Mediocrity will never please our Lord. If Satan can't get you into Hell, he'll at least try to render you ineffective to keep you from preventing others from going there. He'll do his best to lull us to sleep, ruin our witness, and keep us preoccupied, so we spend all our time trying to get out of the ditches of life instead of being the God-equipped warrior we can be. What is so interesting is that this passage resonates very clearly with the current state of affairs we deal with today, despite the fact it was written in AD 64.

Let's have a look at what we need to be on guard against in ourselves, and flee from:

- In 1 Timothy 4:1,2, Paul warned that in later times some would abandon the faith and follow deceiving spirits through hypocritical liars with seared consciences;
- In 6:4–5, conceited men taught false doctrines, loved controversy and quarrels, were full of envy and malicious talk, caused strife, promoted evil suspicions, brought constant friction, and thought that godliness was a means to financial gain;
- In 6:10, people who loved money more than God had wandered from the faith and in so doing, only hurt themselves;
- In 6:20, professing godless chatter and opposing ideas called "knowledge" caused them to wander from the faith.

Sound familiar? According to 1 Timothy 6:11–20, you and I have to flee from these diversions. Why would Paul give such a strong command? This may sound cowardly, but it is not. It is to emphasize the dangerously subtle way these things can trip us up.

Satan's primary weapon is deception, and he is very good at it. Remember Eve in the Garden of Eden? If she hadn't stayed to listen and consider his lies, she might not have become deceived. Far too often, we see Christians tinkering and dabbling in these things, thinking they're too strong to fall. We cannot sit under the counsel of the ungodly and not be affected. How can you touch fire and not get burned?

We are to flee from:

- Selective faith. Painting God's Word with our brush, instead of embracing the truth of God's Word, no matter what the cost or the loss;
- Prideful people superimposing their own interpretation of God's Word in order to get a following and money;
- Idolatry in the form of loving money or anything else over God;
- Worldly philosophy taking precedence over the truth of God's Word. In colleges all over North America, Christian students are falling away from their faith due to this.

Our radar should be tuned to the Holy Spirit, who will alert us when we're too close to danger. He leads us into all truth, and a flag will go up in your spirit if something is amiss. In fleeing, we are not just running away from something; we are pursuing something else.

According to 1 Timothy 6:11, we are to pursue:

- Righteousness: Do whatever it takes to maintain justice and integrity in our dealings with others and our Lord. Abolish unforgiveness.
- Godliness: We are to train ourselves to emulate and copy our Heavenly Father. Be God-like, as it has value for all things, holding promise for both the present life and the one to come.
- Faith: It doesn't just happen. Minute by minute, we need to make the choice to walk by faith and not by what we see, how we feel, and what we want.
- Love: Our love-walk is the most important witness to the world. They will know we are Christians by our love. It may be a cliché,

but sadly it is not always displayed. We need to pursue love in all things, at all times, forever.

- Endurance: How do muscles become stronger? When they are required to lift weights through regular exercise. Endurance is gained the same way. Don't resist a time of testing and refining fire. Work with it!
- Gentleness: We will never win souls with harshness. God values gentleness. He says in 1 Peter that the unfading beauty of a gentle and quiet spirit is of great worth in His sight.

With those qualities in mind and heart, we have these tasks ahead of us:

- Fight the good fight of the faith. We are to hold on to faith and a good conscience. This means maintaining an interdependent relationship with the Holy Spirit's unction.
- Take hold of the eternal life to which you were called. This doesn't mean we have to strive for salvation—that's been taken care of by Jesus. Instead, live out in daily practice the eternal life that is already ours.
- Keep your good confession of faith in Jesus. Let your life be a living testimony in full view of others and don't hide your relationship with Him.
- Command the rich (that includes an awful lot of us in North America) to put their hope in God and not money, and to be rich in good deeds. We are stewards of the wealth He has entrusted to us, and will expect an accounting of what we did with it.
- Guard what has been entrusted to you. Your faith is the most precious thing you have.

These are aggressive actions, and so they need to be! It's not going to be good enough to just know these commands. They only benefit us if we obey them and continually live them. You can start right now by making a solid decision this minute to be equipped for His purposes, His glory, and your fulfilment.

BEWARE THE FATHER OF LIES

In spreading the Gospel, the first Christians dealt with people who were as much under the devil's influence as some people around us today. They dealt with sorcerers, fortune-tellers, and idol worshipers, to name a few. Thanks to Hollywood and its depiction of sorcerers and the like, we've relegated these to whimsical myth and children's stories. It is Satan's method of operation. If we can laugh at what God expressly forbids us to stay away from, we're being sucked in by Satan's lies and are desensitizing ourselves and our kids, which should be of great concern to us. Our society tends to think itself too sophisticated to consider Satan a serious threat, but you can bet that all the oldest sins are still around, even if they take a slightly different form. You don't have to look far to find these in our society. So, what is the enemy largely doing through them, and how can we be aware of his tactics so we aren't deceived?

In Acts 13, Paul dealt with a Jewish sorcerer named Elymas who tried to stop a proconsul named Sergius Paulus, an intelligent man interested in hearing about Jesus, from putting his faith in the Lord. No doubt, he began to present the truth of the Gospel in a disparaging light. Paul looked straight at Elymas and said, "You are a child of the devil and an enemy of everything that is right! You are full of all kinds of deceit and trickery. Will you never stop perverting the right ways of the Lord?" (Acts 13:10).

Satan knows he's defeated. The only thing he can do now is to fool people into being deceived, and he is good at it. There are many who actively seek to bring down and discredit Christianity. We see this in our society everywhere, particularly on TV and in movies that undermine Godly standards and morals. "Perverting the right ways of the Lord" has become normal and acceptable. People inherently follow something, and as there's a vacuum in their life, they'll often follow whatever everyone else is doing and take the path of least resistance. This is why we need to warn them. It is a path to destruction, not life.

God is truth and love. Satan is lies and hate. Jesus Himself said about Satan, "He was a murderer from the beginning, not holding to the truth, for there is no truth in him. When he lies, he speaks his native language, for he is a liar and the father of lies..."

The only way he can win is to deceive us. If he can fool people into thinking Christianity is a crutch for the weak and that Jesus' followers are fanatics or narrow-minded bigots, then he's won. Satan's only avenue is to tempt us into believing a lie, and that we can't or shouldn't resist it. God has already stated that there is no temptation so strong that we cannot stand up against it. He has made a way out of every temptation.

> If we can laugh at what God expressly forbids us to stay away from, we're being sucked in by Satan's lies and are desensitizing ourselves and our kids.

Many people are under the devil's influence. However, we are not under his power, only his influence. As people made in God's image, we have the ability and responsibility to choose whom we will serve. You have not been programmed to fail. Although his influence can be strong, we can choose not to give in. God will always help us and support right choices if we deny Satan an avenue.

In looking at your own life, are there lies of the enemy that you have fallen for? What area do you not have victory in? Could it be that you are believing the lie that you can't triumph over a particular sin? How has the enemy wormed his way in? What form of Elymas has the enemy presented to you in order to deceive you and "pervert the right ways of the Lord"? God is a Lover and Satan is a Liar. You do the math.

CHAPTER 22
Taking Personal Inventory

ARE YOU FULL OF FEAR OR FAITH?

Are you generally a believer or a doubter? How is it that our faith sometimes disintegrates into fear? When I took personal inventory a while back and asked God to show me any building materials that I had been using on the foundation of Christ that were inferior, He showed me that many times I had sinned by being faithless. I was weak in this area, which in turn made my house weak too.

I'm not talking about being faithless in the sense of giving up believing in Jesus; I'm talking about the daily challenges of life that rob us of our peace and challenge our faith. Romans 1:17 says, "For in the gospel the righteousness of God is revealed—a righteousness that is by faith from first to last, just as it is written: 'The righteous will live by faith.'"

FEAR is faith in the enemy: False Evidence Appearing Real.

Living by faith from first to last is a tall order, but languishing in fear is definitely worse. All too quickly, our face gradually goes from a smile to a frown, we start to worry, and our joy evaporates like water on a hot tin roof. We begin to feel bad inside, and before we know it, anxiety and worry have replaced joy, peace, and faith. When I begin to worry or become anxious, I'm afraid something is or is not going to happen. This can lead to becoming cranky or angry, and those negative feelings spill over on those around us. Many times, anger is thinly veiled fear. Either way, we begin to express what's going on inside. This can cause us to be unhappy if we don't recognize that faith in God handling our lives is being replaced by fear.

I mentioned at the beginning that being faithless is sin. This was an eye-opener for me. I always thought that worrying was somehow noble because I was being careful, but the Bible says that any attitude we adopt that does not line up with faith in God is sin (Rom 14:23). Without faith, it's impossible to please God. He commands us many times to "fear not."

Fear is having faith in the enemy. For example, when you are afraid of a snake, you have faith in that snake's ability to hurt you. When you are afraid of losing your job, you have more faith in Satan's ability to make that happen than in God's ability to help you keep your job. Many times, what we fear doesn't even materialize! It just keeps us paralyzed, miserable, and preoccupied. That's when fear becomes "False Evidence Appearing Real." How much of our joy and peace do we sacrifice for things we fear that don't even occur? We believe false evidence that appears to be real, but isn't.

You and I have to make the choice. Are you tired of constantly being anxious, worried, and afraid? This is the first step. It takes place in the battlefield of the mind. If you've been faithless, repent now and ask God to forgive you and begin to change your default. Have a chat with yourself and start saying out loud what you believe, not what you feel. I'm certain you will begin to sense joy as you agree with God, and not the enemy.

HOW DO I WAGE WAR ON FEAR?

Did you know that your brain cannot differentiate between a perceived threat and a real one? We can obviously see a real threat, but our physical reaction to a perceived one is the same. If you are afraid of speaking in public and I told you that in ten minutes you would be giving a speech in front of a hundred people, your body would react. Your heart rate would increase, you might begin to sweat, and you might even faint at the thought. If there was no crowd and I was simply pulling your leg, you'd be hugely relieved, right? God has equipped us with adrenaline, which is the fight or flight hormone to aid us in real life-threatening situations. However, Satan is also clever at using perceived fear to his advantage. If he can get us to become afraid, he can control our actions. When fear manifests in our hearts and minds, we have to identify the root and deal with it properly by casting it right back into the lap of Satan.

The first step is to identify why we're feeling afraid. Ask yourself if the thing you're feeling afraid of is a real threat or just a perceived one. I have found that perceived fear has robbed me of too much peace and I'm simply not willing to put up with it anymore. I may not always win, but I'm not going to quit fighting feelings of fear. God knows exactly what we're feeling and when and why we're feeling it. That's why He keeps telling us to "Fear not!" He actually says it sixty-nine times in the ASV Bible. If you face a perceived threat, God has already provided the answer: The opposite of fear is faith!

Next, we need to do warfare the same way Jesus did. He used the Word of God as a weapon. This is why it's so important to know God's Word in context. You won't need to quote it perfectly or even know where the promise that gives you relief is written, but just that it's in there, and God said it! Philippians 4:6 in the Living Bible is one of the first passages I ever memorized and remains one of my favourites:

"Don't worry about anything! Instead, pray about everything! Tell God your needs, and don't forget to thank Him when He answers. If you do this, you will experience God's peace, which is far more wonderful for the human mind to understand. His peace will keep your thoughts and your hearts quiet and at rest, as you trust in Christ Jesus."

I have experienced the weight of fear or anxiety fall off me countless times, bringing instant relief. It has yet to fail me, but only when I've been obedient and done the things the verse tells me to. It doesn't always come easily or quickly; sometimes we need to persevere until we break through. This is how we grow in faith. Sometimes obtaining victory is simply outlasting the devil. Satan will bring pressure. He's going to test your resolve to see if you'll stick with God's promises and not your faith away. Hebrews 10:35–36 tell us to not throw down our faith or confidence because it has the potential for great reward, and that we need to patient, that after having done the will of God, we might receive what was promised. If He tells us not to throw down our faith, then it is very possible *to* throw down our faith. Anytime God tells us not to do something, it's for a very good reason! 2 Timothy 1:7 says, in the Amplified Bible:

"For God did not give us a spirit of... fear, but of power and of love and of...personal discipline (abilities that result in a calm, well-balanced mind and self-control)."

When fear tries to take hold, God's power can conquer it. 1 John 4:18 says, "perfect love drives out fear," so God's love gives us security in knowing we are safe. Why would God include self-discipline in His instruction about fear? Because He knows that fear is something we will face as long as we are on Earth, and we'll need self-discipline to see us through it.

1 Peter 5:7 says to "cast all our cares on the Lord, because He cares for you." We need to roll over or cast our concerns onto God and leave them there. Don't spend all your effort to hand your worry off to God and then take it back.

Finally, in my response to fear, worry, and anxiety, God's Word says that if we submit ourselves to God and resist the devil, he will flee from us. Did you know that as you submit and surrender yourself to God and resist Satan, that Satan himself will flee as in terror from us! Who's in fear now? One person with God has the majority in any situation. Remind Satan of these words the next time he tries to make you have more faith in him than in God.

I highly recommend going to biblegateway.com and looking up all the verses to do with fear. Then make up a small poster with God's promises to put on your fridge or a place where you will frequently see it. We need to remind ourselves time and again to let God's Word take root in us and grow, so it will spill out of us at our moment of need. My mom kept a little poster on her fridge for years, and I loved it each time I saw it. It said:

"When fear knocked on the door, faith answered, and there was nobody there!"

We cannot live in fear and in faith at the same time. You will service one, or the other. You will need to choose.

APATHY: SUBTLE DEADLY ENEMY NO. 1

Something has happened in the souls of many Christians. It is a subtle but deadly enemy to the heart of our personal relationship with Jesus. We're not excited about Jesus anymore. We've been lulled into an apathetic, desensitized spiritual slumber that soon becomes evident by our lack of response to God in any form. Is the teaching we receive about the Word continually boring? What happened to the excitement we used to enjoy? If we're no longer excited about the things that excite God, we've been lulled to sleep. Have you ever given someone good news when they're half asleep? When we live in the atmosphere of God's presence and blessings, we need to be careful not to become so used to them that we take them for granted. The Bible is full of accounts where people did exactly this, and it often took drastic action from God to shake them awake.

Can you imagine our reaction to God if we cried out to Him over a recurring problem and He responded, "That problem again? Oh well. I guess I'll help in a little while. I've got something else to do right now. After all, I've heard it all before. Nothing's changed. I'll get to it later." What kind of a God would He be? So, how do we avoid becoming sleepy-heads?

First, all relationships, with our Lord or others, require us to work at them on a continual basis if we want to grow forward together. It is like the analogy of being in a canoe paddling upstream on a gentle river. It's not necessarily hard to paddle, but it must remain continuous. The minute you quit, you begin floating back downstream instead of where you want to go. If you become apathetic in a canoe, you might wake up to find yourself going over a waterfall. Similarly, if we quit going forward relationally, we might find ourselves losing everything.

The second way is close to the first and lies in maintaining a close, intimate relationship with our Lord. This is the key. All throughout God's Word, He models His affection for us as a bridegroom towards his bride. This conveys excitement, passion, and an intenseness of devotion at the prospect of living together. It's how He feels about us. If we felt the same way towards Him, we would care about what He cares about.

If you've been asleep, the time to wake up is now. The time is short before the bridegroom will come to collect His bride. Fall in love with Jesus all over again. Get out that paddle and start moving upstream. Only you know what that looks like. Press into a new level with your Jesus. Life is too short to be bored. Go full blast with God, and you'll find that apathy has checked out and been replaced with a Holy Spirit fire that will be most rewarding and will continue throughout this lifetime and beyond.

PRIDE: SUBTLE DEADLY ENEMY NO. 2

God hates pride. It acts like yeast in bread. It puffs up so slowly bit by bit and permeates every part of the bread that we don't even notice it until our attitude is clearly reflected by it. You've no doubt heard the saying: "His head is so big I doubt he can get through the door!" There is much to say about this effective weapon used by the enemy and we need to be fully aware of how subtle this negative aspect of our fallen nature is and how it can rob from us, cripple us, and destroy us. I'm not being melodramatic; Heaven and hell hang in the balance. If we know the enemy's tactics, we can counteract them with God's help—but we need to recognize them first. The following is a sample of some of pride's characteristics.

Pride is so serious that Lucifer was literally kicked out of heaven because of it. He held one of the highest positions in Heaven, and yet that wasn't good enough. He wanted to be "like the Most High"; in other words, equal to God. Pride was his downfall—literally. He fell out of Heaven to be given the atmosphere around the Earth. This sets the stage for the next consequence of pride. Did you know that Adam and Eve's first sin was the same as Satan's? We always think it's about disobedience and a fruit, but why did they disobey? Eve wanted to be like God, knowing the difference between good and evil. Adam followed suit and they sinned through succumbing to Satan's lure (Gen 3:4), and all humankind inherited a sinful nature as a result. This should give us a picture of pride's serious consequences.

> Whose opinion of you matters most, yours or His?

Pride robs us of good relationships between people. How many times have you wanted to say you were sorry but your pride stopped you? Even if you feel the other person was at fault, God still expects us to seek reconciliation and take ownership of our actions. I've said this to my kids (and to myself), and they've never been too excited about it: "The more mature person will say they're sorry first." As much as we don't like humbling ourselves, yielding quickly and often is a good indicator of our spiritual maturity. Pride stops us cold. God called this being "stiff-necked" in the Old Testament. It is a posture that is the opposite of bowing one's head and humbly yielding.

Pride inflates our egos to make everyone else the problem. Looking at it closely, we can begin to see pride as the root of many relational problems between people. Proverbs 16:18 says, "Pride goes before destruction, a haughty spirit before a fall." If we're thinking we're all that and a slice of bread, look out! We might need to be taken down a peg or two. If we humble ourselves under the mighty hand of God, He will lift us up in His timetable (1 Peter 5:6). This is the key to everything. We must rest "under the mighty hand of God" to handle all our rights and wrongs. You and I don't have any rights if we've surrendered our lives to our Lord. Can you imagine what would have happened at Calvary if Jesus had exercised all His rights? He laid them down for His Father to mete out justice, and He expects us to do the same. Look how Jesus was exalted after the fact. He now sits at the right hand of the Father.

> I am not about to roll over and be a door mat. I want them to pay and I'm going to make them pay!

I know this is difficult to do. Our flesh will kick and scream at us to do anything but yield. Unfortunately, wanting to win or get revenge leaves us miserable. It's far more freeing to release it to God. When someone has unjustly offended me, it hurts, but I'm not about to park there. I immediately release my rights to myself and tell God He can handle it in His way and time. I go about my business, trying to be loving to the individual as best as I know how with God's help. He will heal my hurts. Jesus is immensely pleased when we bow our heads, humble ourselves, and seek to restore relationships. We are being Christ-like when we show love to people who we consider unlovable. After all, whose opinion of you matters most, yours or His?

Pride prevents God from healing us. 2 Chronicles 7:14 says, "If my people, who are called by my name, will humble themselves and pray and seek my face and turn from their wicked ways, then will I hear from heaven and will forgive their sin and will heal their land." Today, we are a nation in dire need of healing. If we as a church, province, or country arrogantly refuse to repent, we tie God's hands. He is not about to heal our church or land if those in it are arrogant and rebellious. We have to come with nothing save a humble spirit, crying out for His mercy to forgive us.

The largest consequence of pride is the most deadly of all: it keeps people from entering the Kingdom of Heaven. Humbling ourselves is not optional, but mandatory when we come to Christ to receive His forgiveness. There are multitudes on their way to Hell today because, after hearing the message of salvation, they think they are good enough to get into Heaven without Jesus. Or they refuse to budge in doing it God's way. The song "My Way" by Frank Sinatra is a sad song. Every time I hear it, I feel sorrow. The song's climax builds to a crescendo and emphasizes the line "I did it my way" in a positive key with a long sustained note to end. It should have been written in a minor key as a funeral song. There is only one way, and it's not my way; it's God's. Don't let pride rob you of the most important thing in your existence—your future in Heaven with Jesus.

Pride hides itself in nooks and crannies in our nature, and I find I need to regularly perform that check-up from the neck-up. A friend of mine once asked me, "If you say you're humble, are you?"

I Can't Wait Any Longer!

We are in a society that promotes immediate gratification. The value of waiting for things has greatly declined. Yet more often than we'd like, God requires us to wait, be it for a breakthrough, deliverance, or the fulfilment of a promise. He requires us to wait to prepare us for what is coming. We need to grow in the waiting room to fulfil God's purposes for our character development along the way. Do you think God might have some good reasons for making us wait? Absolutely.

Our society treats waiting for things like it's a plague. For example, we often hear, "You're waiting until you get married to have sex?" They look down their noses with scorn at these wise people who wish to stay within God's safe boundaries, honour His principles, and reap the rewards of obeying Him. We've all heard this one: "Buy now and don't pay for fifteen months!" Both shortcuts are dangerous. They promote instant gratification without counting the cost, which becomes apparent later. If I can't afford the couch now, what makes me think I'll be able to next year?

Take the people who do not wait until they are married to engage in a sexual relationship. It's almost a foregone conclusion with today's young people, Christian or not. If God specifically designed the sexual relationship to be engaged in within the boundaries of marriage, which is a huge commitment, then it stands to reason that He has good reasons. He's not looking to take away everyone's enjoyment, simply to protect His children.

There is a danger to jumping ahead of God's timetable. We can detour God's perfect will for us and undermine the good gift He has waiting. Already mentioned in Chapter 3, Sarah gets impatient waiting for God to deliver on His promise of a child, so she takes matters into her own hands and gives Abraham her servant girl Hagar to be his wife. But Sarah greatly underestimated the long-ranging consequences of her action. Hagar conceives and in Genesis 16:10 the angel tells Hagar, "I will so increase your descendants that they will be too numerous to count." The angel was backing up the promise made to Abraham that his seed would be great. This is not to say that Abraham received God's best by detouring, but that the detour itself would eventually create the Arab nations. We see how that is working out for the nation of Israel!

God gave His promise and confirmed it by cutting a covenant with Abraham. He doesn't break His promise over human error or impatience. Look at the huge responsibility and privilege humanity has been given through God's design. If we meet God's requirements but are out of His timing, we often assume that He will intervene and alter His promises and conform them to our plan. However, the power of our free will to mess it up will be honoured because of the iron-clad unchangeable greatness of God's promises.

I don't want to lay a burden of remorse on those of us who have ignored or barged ahead of God's plan. The good news is that He is bigger than any mistake you or I can make, but you may have to work with Him for a while. Either way, you may still have to wait until He has fixed what we messed up. Ishmael, Abraham's detour, was thirteen years old when the promised Isaac finally arrived to Abraham and Sarah. God can make all things beautiful in His time and work them out for out good.

We need to be careful to obey His commands and see the value of waiting for Him to lead us. God asks us to wait not because He wants to withhold good things, but because He has better things in store. Psalm 27:14 says, "Wait for the Lord; be strong and take heart and wait for the Lord." Remember, there is always something good waiting on the other side of your obedience. It will always be worth it. He hasn't forgotten about you; He's simply lining everything up!

CHAPTER 23
How to Wage War on Sexual Immorality

GUARD YOUR THOUGHTS!

Practically everything to do with sex practices, with the exception of rape, child pornography, abuse, and trafficking, seems to be accepted in today's society. This is not okay with God. His Word has much to say on this, and before I go any further, we need to determine what our core beliefs are on this. Are the boundaries God has set up in respects to our sexual conduct valid today? If you say no, I sincerely hope you continue reading anyways. My hope is that God's reasons for his boundaries will convince you otherwise.

Sexual sin has caused untold damage and has been around since the beginning of time. The tragedy is that the church seldom openly talks about it, thereby allowing Satan to keep it shrouded in misconception, deception, and lies. Satan has taken the good thing that God created and twisted it into something that causes marriages to fail, diseases to run rampant, children to be born illegitimate, people to be hurt, and more. As a result, God's best plans for His children have often been detoured. Even in the early church when the Gentiles who knew very little about God's laws were receiving Christ as their Saviour, the disciples gave them guidelines which included "to abstain from sexual immorality" (1 Thess 4:3). There must have been good reason, and it shows the misuse of our sexuality is as old as humanity.

Sexual immorality is made of what I call sticky sins. They cling to us as other sins don't. Since we were created to be sexual beings, sex is unique because, within His boundaries, it is encouraged by God. Outside of those boundaries, however, it is condemned. There are few things we engage in that can be both a blessing and a curse. Sex is something we need to be a master over, and not let it master us. As we adhere to God's way, we learn to exercise restraint as we choose to remain within His boundaries, mastering and controlling our desires in our actions and our thought life. If we adhere to Satan's way, we let go of all restraint, and this sin begins to master us. That isn't freedom; it's bondage packaged as freedom. Once Pandora's box is opened, it's difficult to close.

The first thing we all need to do is to guard our thought-life. All sin begins in our mind. Rarely do people sin without thinking about it first. Jesus said that if a man even looks at a woman lustfully, he has already committed adultery with her in his heart. Just as the brain cannot tell the difference between a real and perceived threat where fear is concerned, it also cannot tell the difference between real and perceived sexual stimuli. When a person fantasizes about a sexual situation, the heart rate goes up, the body begins to sweat, breathing becomes irregular and shallow, and chemical responses occur. Why? Your brain believes it is in that situation. You know you aren't, but your body will tell you otherwise. This is why it is critical to "take captive every thought to make it obedient to Christ" (2 Cor 10:5). As I have said, where the mind goes, the body will follow.

We must learn to resist the flesh's inclination and the devil at his onset. That means that the second you have a sinful thought, you have not sinned ... yet. When we see people that are scantily clad or semi-pornographic advertisements, we stand at a fork in the road. What will we do? Linger, or look away? What we do with that thought causes us to sin or have victory?

God has wired us this way for marriage partners to desire and enjoy one another, but that does not include the misuse of this attribute. Satan and your flesh will present you with all sorts of sinful thoughts; it is then that you have to take them captive and cast them down. God's power will accompany your actions when you choose to be obedient instead of sinning. You will have to take the first step every time, but then God will step up to the plate to help you do the right thing.

Remember, Satan may not simply go away after you resist him once or twice, especially if the problem is a stronghold. You may have to grow in exercising God-given authority and provision to resist. God will enable you to do so as He makes you stronger in the power of His grace to resist sexual immorality in all of its forms.

WHAT ARE YOU THIRSTY FOR?

The thing about sex is that it is a primal need for all of us. This alone is justification for many engaging in sexual activity outside of marriage. The attitude is perhaps, "if God doesn't want me to engage in sex outside of marriage, He shouldn't have made me this way. It's not my fault." But this goes back to what you choose to believe. God does not program us for failure. Many people think themselves to be too strong to be bound by the power of this sticky sin. What began perhaps as experimentation can end up as something that is a deep need to be met at any cost. Does this sound like freedom? At the end of the day, this lifestyle keeps you bound to it. Playing the field, exchanging one partner for another makes you no longer free to enjoy sex with only one person for a lifetime. It's not enough, because the nature of this sin is that the more you feed it, the bigger the need for that type of immorality becomes. One partner satisfies until you grow bored with them and want the titillating newness of a different person.

> When your flesh presents a sinful choice, don't let it vote!

God seeks to fulfil our sexual needs as He Himself created them, and you to need them. Don't you think He knows the best way to do so?

Romans, chapter 6, summed up deals with slavery to sin, particularly with sinning with "parts of our bodies." I highly recommend meditating on it. Verses 12–14 say, "Therefore do not let sin reign in your mortal body so that you obey its evil desires. Do not offer the parts of your body to sin as instruments of wickedness, but rather offer yourselves to God, as those who have been brought from death to life; and offer the parts of your body to him as instruments of righteousness. For sin shall not be your master..."

How do we begin to be masters of sin? When our flesh presents a sinful choice, don't let it vote! Who we obey determines who or what we are a slave to. You may say, "I can't obey God. I want to, but I can't resist my flesh. I just don't have the power or the strength." Paul explains in verse 7 that sin no longer has power over anyone who has died. This is easily understandable. If I'm dead, I can't sin, correct?

If we have received Jesus as our Saviour, our old self died along with Him (verses 6-8), so that we too should no longer be slaves to sin. You were born again without sin.

Since Jesus rose from the dead, death no longer has power over Him, and we too are raised to have victory over death and sin. We can conquer sexual sin, because Christ conquered all sin! When Satan tells you that you can't resist, reframe his picture. You can. Look at the passage again. Progressive, consistent obedience is the key.

I saw a TV ad for soda that used this line commanding all who were watching: "Obey your thirst." In other words, if you're thirsty, obey it and fulfil it. Where sex sin is concerned, you need to decide which appetite you're going to obey, because whatever you feed becomes stronger. If you equate sex sin to a large dog, who is forever crouching at the door demanding to be fed, just don't feed him! As you feed your obedience to Jesus, he'll eventually become so emaciated, he'll leave your door and go elsewhere.

Will you obey Jesus or your flesh? What do you thirst for? Who or what do you love more? Everything always comes back to that intimate love relationship with Jesus. Plus, whatever you sacrifice for becomes more dear to you. The more you love Him, the more you want to obey Him. The more you obey Him, the more victory you'll have, and you'll eventually be free. Don't worry if you fall. Jesus will pick you up, forgive you, and help you begin again. I like what one preacher said in respect to her struggle with sin: "I may not be where I need to be, but praise God, I'm not where I used to be!" As you obey, you will get there, one step at a time.

> When Satan tells you that you can't resist, reframe his picture. You can!

GOD EXPECTS ME TO WAIT?

I mentioned earlier that in today's churches there is a lack of good Godly teaching on the subject of sex. Past generations of Christians often gave the perception that all sex was somehow sinful when, in fact, it is something God created and said is good. Since there is this lack, there exists a gap that the world will quickly fill in. I've seen so many people who have fallen in this area for a number of reasons, but the primary one is that they are constantly bombarded by the sexuality encouraged on TV and films that say casual sex is acceptable. Pretty soon, "everyone is doing it." The enemy gets far greater airtime in today's world than God does.

In today's age, many people fall for Satan's lie that they need to be sexually active before marriage. They argue many things, including the need to see if they're sexually compatible. Let me assure you, God made Adam and Eve sexually compatible, so there are no two people who genuinely love each other and desire to serve one another in the realm of the marriage bed that will not be compatible. Or they may say, "I'm not planning on getting married until I'm thirty. God can't expect me to wait that long to abstain from sex." Whose choice is it to wait, yours or God's? If He asks us to wait, He will provide a way for us to wait and not sin. If you're in a season of waiting for God to bring you the perfect girl or guy, my advice is to concentrate more on becoming the perfect girl or guy, instead of looking for them. They'll find you! There's nothing more unappealing than a needy, insecure, desperate person looking for a mate. Let God make you secure in His love for you, and you will exude that to all around you, which is very attractive.

How about: "I just want to feel loved, and giving my boyfriend/girl-friend sex is the only way he/she will stay with me; surely it can't be wrong to want to feel loved." No, it's not wrong to want to feel loved, but God should be the one meeting your need to feel loved, married or not. He will *never* fail in this regard. If this is your primary reason, I recommend spending time with God. In fact, our God is a jealous God (Exod 34:14). If there's something or someone taking His rightful place in your heart, He may let things fall apart to get your attention, in order for you to give Him His rightful place.

Here's a compromise that the enemy uses that often does not pan out the way you think it will in the end: "We're getting married anyways..." There is a trend of late that appears to lend itself well to this compromise. Many couples now get engaged with the wedding date set years later. I think this is unwise. It infers that you're almost married and so it is somehow less sinful to engage in premarital sex. Many things can happen to end a relationship between the time you have sex and actually get married, and then your primary reason for yielding amounts to regret. Even if you do get married, premarital sex is still sin. Never forget that if someone is willing to have sex outside of marriage, then that someone is willing to have sex outside of marriage. Did you catch that? Will the marriage vows to remain true to you alone really count later if the person was willing to have sex outside of marriage previously?

Then there's the all too famous line that teenage young women have been given: "If you love me, you'll let me." The response to that one should be a very firm: "No, actually. If you really love me, you'd be willing to wait."

In pondering these things, they all amount to compromise. What you compromise to have now, you risk losing in the end. I do not desire to lay a burden of guilt on anyone, especially if they have paid a hefty price and are hurting because of it. God will heal your hurts and start restoring to you what the enemy has stolen. I desire to uphold God's ways of handling the sexuality He has given us in order to avoid these pitfalls and spare us pain. I feel a heavy burden to impress upon all people that we desperately need to look at sexual immorality through God's eyes, and get this thing turned around. It's such a huge problem today, and as a society, we'll all end up paying a price that will affect not only us, but all the generations following. God designed sexual purity for our wholeness and well-being. We just need to do things His way to have it.

He parallels His relationship to us many times as that of a virgin bridegroom and a virgin bride, which leads to the reason God instructs us to wait to have sex. At the altar, the couple are at the height of pure innocent love, eagerly anticipating being together forever from this point on. This is the picture I have of Jesus as the Bridegroom and His bride, the church—us. There will come a day when we also will be together forever with Him, and we also eagerly anticipate it. Jesus is trying to convey His feelings for us.

Hence a decision to be with one another for an entire lifetime needs to come before a sexual relationship. We've got it all backwards. Our society says that we need to have sex first, and then develop the relationship. God says exactly the opposite, and the sexual union occurs only after the two are married, and then the two become one. God knows us. Much of the fallout due to sexual immorality is avoided when two people choose to take an oath to stay true to one another for a lifetime. This sets the stage to provide a secure place to raise a family. As out-dated as many may think this is, God's reasons always come from a place of love and what will give us and our families the best life we can have.

SEXUALLY TRANSMITTED DISEASES

The world says that casual sex with multiple partners is perfectly fine and not dangerous, yet the truth cannot be ignored. STDs are rampant. On the news just last night, I heard a report that even though "safe sex" and sexual education are both being promoted more than ever, sexually transmitted diseases are on the rise. The world assumes and promotes the erroneous agenda that people are going to have sex with multiple partners, so the answer has to be to educate and promote safe sex. God's answer of abstinence until He joins two people together in holy matrimony isn't even a viable solution, or even mentioned. Two virgins getting married, committed for a lifetime is the best formula to avoid STDs.

The average person who has contracted a STD has had sex with few partners. If people are sexually active and not using condoms they are at high risk of getting STDs and it is quite likely they have a disease, according to kidshealth.org. Because many people who have STDs do not have obvious symptoms, they believe they're "clean" and safe to have unprotected sex with. Statistics tell us otherwise: A staggering six out of ten young people with HIV don't know they're infected. Even if someone has only had one sexual partner, that partner could have a disease. Years ago, I met a lovely young woman through an acquaintance we'll call Mark who didn't know the Lord, and they were dating. After three or four dates, Mark complained to Jake and I that his girlfriend wouldn't have sex with him (clearly he came to the wrong people for sympathy). Soon after this, the two broke up. Jake asked Mark what had happened and was told that she had confided in him that she had contracted herpes and hadn't wanted to pass it on. Mark immediately ended the relationship. The tragedy is that this young woman had contracted herpes from the first man she'd ever slept with, who not only took her virginity, but left her with a venereal disease. She had been naïve and trusting, and simply fell into the world's ways of having casual sex with her first boyfriend.

What people fail to realize is that outside of marriage between two virgins, there is no such thing as completely safe sex. The measures we take to be safe may prevent pregnancy, but few people realize that some sexually transmitted disease cells, including HIV, may be smaller than the smallest hole in natural membrane condoms, which are porous as opposed to latex. Also, the first drop of semen can contain the HIV virus before a condom is even put on prior to intercourse. You may be safer, but completely safe is a myth when you're having sex with someone who has had multiple partners. God says in His Word that when two people get married, "the two shall become one flesh." He infers that this is a spiritual union as well as a sexual one. This was given as a huge privilege for us to procreate. The union has borne God fruit—a child in the image of God Himself, a blessing from the Lord. This child has characteristics of both mom and dad.

Just as this union bears fruit, so do sexual unions outside of God's boundaries. I'm not talking about the wrath of God or judgement here, but a literal transfer: for example, if a person has contracted herpes, he or she has tangibly received something from the infected person that has now become a part of their own body. The symptoms can be treated, but the virus remains intact in the new host. I recently saw ads on TV that make light of having an incurable disease by joking and offering commercial remedies. The people in the commercial were happy and carefree, frolicking in a wheat field with smiles on their faces, saying that it's really not that serious that they have syphilis. Any child or teenager watching would think, "I thought STDs were serious. I guess it's not that big a deal." They're lulling unsuspecting people into a trap! They don't mention one thing about being careful with one's conduct.

Using preventive measures does lower, but not eliminate the risks; but just how much risk do we want to gamble with? If a person has had six sex partners, and we have sex with that person, we now contain in our body the material of all seven of those people, including all the people *they* slept with. Can you see why God put our boundaries in place? He doesn't seek to steal your fun, only to protect you from the consequences of sexual immorality.

We are not meant to judge one another, but to judge sin and magnify the truth; to bring us to repentance; to arouse righteous anger at Satan and the world for promoting something as safe when it's spiritually, emotionally, and physically detrimental to all of us. It is meant to save and prevent people from untold suffering; to hold up the God-standard that society deems prudish and is too sophisticated to embrace.

There is still hope for those of us that have fallen victim to this, Christians and unbelievers alike. God's mercies are new every morning. Even if you have an STD, He will make a way. He is the Great Physician who still heals today. Ask Him to forgive you and make a new beginning. I've heard of some church groups promoting something called "secondary virginity" whereby people who want to make a fresh start draw a line of purity and cross it with the resolve to wait for marriage to engage in any further sexual activity. He will wash you as white as snow and help you do what's right for your own benefit and future.

SEXUAL STIMULI:
DISTANCE YOURSELF FROM THE CHOICE!

The Western world is preoccupied with sex. As advertisers know, sex sells. Put sexual tension in an ad, and people sit up from whatever they were doing and pay attention. It fascinates us, and we identify with it at a primal level. We tolerate a great deal of it, desensitizing ourselves because there's so much of it around. Even if we look away, a continual response is needed to deflect the choice to sin.

It is better to continually deflect even the choice to sin than to wrestle with sexual temptation. If I know I want to do what's right more than I want to sin, why torment myself? There is so much illicit sex on TV it's almost inescapable. Would it not be better to have a plan of action beforehand? If we have an action plan to immediately change the channel, we won't be hypnotized and tempted to linger. I am grateful for the warnings before movies and the fact we can lock certain channels from our kids, but the minute we put a safeguard on something the world comes up with another way to get around it. The Internet alone is a huge avenue.

> If I know I want to do what's right more than I want to sin, why torment myself and create an inner war?

Making a solid decision to not give Satan or our flesh any ground to stand on can be that easy. Distance yourself from the choice! Make up your mind to uphold a high standard for yourself, your family, and your God.

Perhaps you don't think looking at a *Playboy* magazine is sinful, just as long as you end up having sex with your spouse. Here's the reality: as a father, would you want other men to look lustfully at your naked daughter in a magazine? That girl you are looking at and lusting after is God's daughter also. How do you think He feels? The same goes for women. Men are now being portrayed in sexually stimulating ways and women are also responding in lustful ways. Although we've had male sex symbols for a long time such as Robert Redford and James Dean, my generation did not know the phrase "He's a hottie" or "look at that six-pack" in a blatant reference to how those men were making women feel. Many people defend their reaction by saying they can't help how their bodies react. That is partly correct, but you can control allowing what your eyes take in and what your thoughts dwell on.

We are told that King David was once relaxing at the end of the day on his roof, when he saw Bathsheba bathing. He had a choice to make: Look away and take control of his reaction, or continue to look. He was married. He could have immediately looked away and cast down thoughts of Bathsheba and gone to his wife and gazed at her body, and consummated his desire God's way. God doesn't want us to burn with desire. He wants us to be master over it and fulfil it without sinning. Instead, we often linger and pause, weighing the pros and cons of what we will let our minds entertain. This is why the Apostle Paul said to flee sexual immorality like our life depended on it. This is where David got caught. As king, he figured he could just take another man's wife, even though he knew better. God loved and forgave him, but not without painful discipline and huge consequences.

> That girl you are looking at in that way, is God's daughter too.

We will not escape God's loving discipline any more than David did. There is a process involved in resisting sexual temptation. We need to have a plan. Only you know what that means for you. We must recognize and implement it, and victory will be ours as God backs up our obedience to "resist the devil at his onset." As God's child, He will not let you sin in peace. Skip the torment of the inner struggle. Remember, when you flee sexual immorality, you are not running from Satan's power, but to God's power.

SEXUAL STRONGHOLDS

The truth hurts, sometimes a lot, but unless we face the truth about ourselves and admit that to God, we won't grow or prosper. It's not the truth about someone else that sets us free; it's the truth about ourselves. I am not a professional counsellor. I'm an ordinary person with a high school education who became convinced that involving God in everything, including our sexuality, ultimately ensures victory. I just want us to have the freedom Jesus died to give us. I've been married for over thirty years, having been born in the sixties during the sexual revolution, and I've seen the result of the eighties era and the increase of sexually transmitted diseases. I've seen the breakdown of marriage, even in my own extended family, as a direct result of infidelity.

There's a term out there that we're repeatedly hearing lately called sexual addiction that somehow infers that it is a sickness instead of sin. It's far easier to say that we are sick instead of sinful. Believing we have a sickness means we don't have to admit we are sinning. We conveniently side-step the number one requirement of God.

This is probably one of the biggest strongholds the enemy has on people, crippling their walk with God and their relationships: a long-term entrenched lifestyle of sex sin that is kept carefully hidden. So much is currently under wraps that we often see the problem only after the wheels have come off of the marriage and the divorce is pending. It is kept hidden because the individual is embarrassed by it, but cannot leave it because they are bound to it. They believe the lie that Satan has ingrained in them that it is the only way to fulfil their desire.

We also see it in the lifestyles of young Christian men who don't seem to find the right gal to marry. They get older and older while their girlfriends get younger and younger, all the while engaging in sexual activity. They have fallen for the motto, "Why buy the cow if you can get the milk for free?" I'm not saying it's wrong to be older and single—just older, single, and sexually active. This has had a ripple effect on the young women out there, desiring to get married and have a family. There appears to be an acute shortage of men desiring to get married. Young men are no longer so inclined, as casual sex keeps them preoccupied with a lifestyle that is completely self-serving and in truth robs them of the whole rewarding wife, children, and long-term family package, which is a direct blessing from the Lord.

Satan has many traps set for all people with sexual sin, especially when it's so deeply ingrained that we can't even imagine what a wholesome sexual relationship or response looks like. None of us are exempt. We are all capable of any sin. I'm not pointing a finger. It's like a hidden cancer that afflicts our souls.

HOW DO WE BECOME FREE?

The first thing we need to do is acknowledge that sex outside of God's boundaries, is in fact, sin. If you don't agree with this basic fact, the next action won't mean anything. The next thing we need to do is repent. If you're genuinely sorry and want to change, God knows it. Make a solid decision that with God's help, you'll not go back to that lifestyle or way of thinking. Slam the door shut; draw a line in the sand and cross it. From a spiritual vantage point, you've just given Satan a mighty blow to the head. God's forgiveness and the blood of Jesus pours over us and cleanses us. Never forget that. You belong to God, and He says, "No temptation has overtaken you except what is common to mankind. And God is faithful; He will not let you be tempted beyond what you can bear. But when you are tempted, He will also provide a way out so that you can endure it" (1 Cor 10:13). What He is saying is that you're not the first person to be tempted the way you are, and He will provide a way out.

Next, we need to get God's provision and foundation to conquer this deeply established on our insides. Galatians 5:16 says, "So I say, live by the Spirit, and you will not gratify the desires [lust] of the sinful nature." We need to realize that we cannot do this on our own without the indwelling life and power of the Holy Spirit. It doesn't cost us anything to believe, so I say, believe big. Ask God to show you how you should live by His spirit. We have everything to gain and nothing to lose.

Galatians 5:25 tells us what to do next: "Since we live by the Spirit, let us keep in step with the Spirit." God is not going to ask us to do something we aren't capable of doing, but He will always show us the next step. When Jesus died, the law of sin that had kept everyone bound was demolished. Romans 8:1 and 2 say that there is therefore now no condemnation for those who are in Christ Jesus, so even though you may feel condemned because of your problem, you aren't. The characteristic principle of the Holy Spirit is to empower the believer for holy living, while the indwelling sin is to drag a person down to death. It's like the law of gravity, equaling sin. When you throw a ball up into the air, it comes down because it is heavier than the air. A living bird is also heavier than the air, but it can fly because the life in the bird overcomes the law of gravity. The Holy Spirit supplies the risen life of the Lord Jesus to us, making us free from the law of sin and death, enabling us to break the power of Satan to drag us down. Always remember that the life in you is the life of Christ and it has already done away with the power of death.

Give God complete permission and freedom to change you, no matter what. He will never violate your will. Once you've done that, God now has free reign to change you from the inside out. Your job is not to deflect or ignore Him when He shows you the way out. He doesn't expect you to do this all on your own, but He does expect you to obey the steps He presents. I believe that getting entrenched in sex sin is progressive, so you might have to get out one step at a time. If you've been engaging in it for a long time, it won't be easy to extricate yourself, but it is possible with the power of God. God can and may dramatically deliver you, but chances are, if you are in this place, there are other character traits and weaknesses He wants to address along the way.

"A great lover is not a man who has loved many women; rather, it is a man who has loved only one woman for many years."

Once we've repented, surrendered, given God permission to change us, and realized that it may take some time, where do we go from here? The world has filled our minds with its brand of what it considers appropriate sexual behaviour. We need to counteract them and start replacing those with God's principles of wholesome fulfilment within His boundaries. What we haven't been taught is that it is up to us to monitor what we allow our minds to dwell on. If the problem is in your thought life, it's a fact that the more you don't want to think about something, the more you will anyway. Suppressing sexual thoughts won't work, and giving in to them is not the answer. The next thing you need to do is take authority over the sinful thoughts and replace them. Taking those thoughts captive and making them obedient to Christ is key (2 Cor 10:5). I quote God's Word back to my flesh and the devil when I'm being tempted. We've been wired with a sex drive that responds to visual stimulation. When tempted, I immediately say to myself, "I don't take that thought. I put it under my feet and make it obedient to you, Jesus. I love and desire my husband only." I say the opposite of what I'm feeling, but what I know is the truth. We are then:

- Responding in a way that pleases Jesus;
- Not giving the temptation any room to torment us or grow into action;
- Reaffirming our desires are within God's boundaries;
- Strengthening ourselves each time we resist;
- Maintaining a clear conscience before God.

We are then being transformed by the renewing of our mind, so we may prove the perfect will of God. This has often been when God's Word has broken the power of sin over me. I tell the devil the opposite of what he's trying to get me to do.

If you're not married, the Bible is clear that we are not to burn with lust for the opposite sex, and since God ordained marriage specifically to procreate and fulfil these desires, then perhaps it's time you consider getting married. If you are serious about wanting to get married, then inviting God into that arena will get the wheels moving in the right direction. We must keep things in the right order: courting, marriage, sex, then kids. It's not that difficult, and yet we see these components being exhibited completely out of order in today's society. God may need to get this thing turned around one person at a time. It begins with you and me.

My favourite weapon against my flesh and Satan is confessing Psalm 19:13: "Keep your servant also from willful sins; may they not rule over me; then will I be blameless; innocent of great transgression." Don't forget who said these words. They were uttered by David, who committed adultery with Bathsheba. He knew what he was talking about. No doubt he had learned his lesson when he wrote this. He was well acquainted with the price he paid in his own suffering and that of his kingdom.

God knows how difficult sexual immorality is to overcome. Jesus identified with all of our weaknesses, yet was without sin. Although Jesus was fully God, He was also fully man, so He knows what it's like to continually face temptation. He can keep us from succumbing to those sins, and with His power break the bondage of them.

HOW DO WE STAY FREE IN PRACTICAL WAYS?

The previous points cover the battle that goes on in the soul and how to do spiritual warfare, but there are also beneficial practical things we can do:

- Find a rock or symbol and place it where you can always see it, to remind you of your resolve.
- Keep away from the places that present the choice to sin;
- Take steps to protect yourself from temptation;
- If you're weak at a certain time of day, or in a certain place, change your routine.

For example, if you're on a diet, don't choose to go into a bakery when you're hungry, or stock your cupboard with junk food. Instead, buy fruit and vegetables and have a plan when the hunger pangs strike. Why tempt yourself? The same is true with sex.

If you are a single guy who used to sleep around, you simply can't go to a nightclub or places that you previously picked up girls. You may need to make some serious lifestyle changes. If buying pornographic magazines is the problem, go to stores that don't sell them. Support from your church body is also helpful; perhaps your care group or pastor can encourage you and regularly pray with you. I met a fellow who knew his weakness was illicit TV programs. He traveled frequently and would watch sex channels when he was lonely. Now he only rents rooms that don't have a TV or asks to have it removed. He doesn't want to torment himself, so he simply removes the vehicle that presents the choice. We'd probably find this extreme, but whatever works, works. He's serious about conquering the problem.

If the Internet is the problem, put inspirational verses on sticky notes all around your screen, so you have to take them off if you want to sin. The more obstacles you have to go around, the more time God has to help you do the right thing. If you're weak on your own, hang out with a solid Christian friend and make yourself accountable to them. Don't forget that you are not the only one who deals with this specific stronghold and temptation—many men and women do as well. It would be especially helpful if someone who has overcome your issue is your mentor. Tell them your problem and set up an avenue whereby you can call them in a moment of weakness. If you're too ashamed to tell someone, remember, that which is kept in secret or darkness has power over you. In confessing your sin and challenges to another person, you've brought it out into the light where Satan no longer can torment you with that terrible secret. As you step out in faith for God to provide the avenue from temptation, He will soon begin to fill your heart with peace, joy, and confidence.

To sum up, we need to:

1. Acknowledge our sin
2. Truly repent
3. Make a solid decision to leave those sinful ways
4. Live by the Spirit and stay in step with Him
5. Surrender our will and give God permission to change us from the inside out
6. Realize it may take some time and remain patient
7. Take authority over sinful thoughts and make them obedient to Christ
8. Replace those sinful thoughts with your "now" word and confess out loud what you really desire by faith
9. Keep yourself away from the areas and places that present the choice to sin
10. Have a backup plan
11. Make yourself accountable to someone
12. Pray!

Pray, pray, pray. It began with repentance and will end with rejoicing! Prayer is the power conduit between you and God. Don't let long periods of time lapse between communicating with Him. It's amazing how quickly the enemy will try to shut this down first. As long as you stay connected to Him, His power will flow to you and through you to have victory. Jesus declared the response to being a slave to sin in John 6:36: "...if the Son sets you free, *you will be free indeed!*"

We Must Equip the Next Generation

I mentioned earlier that our world is preoccupied with sex and personal gratification at every level, and it bombards us at every turn. Sex sells, and so the god of money promotes this heavily. Satan gets a two-for-one as he binds people with sexual addiction and those promoting it with the lust for money. I'm sure I don't need to tell you that an incredible amount of illegal and legal money is made from the sex trade. How exactly do we equip our children to handle it?

That which was meant to be kept behind the veiled curtain of an intimate marriage relationship is now splashed freely about almost everywhere you look. I am concerned for our young boys and girls, who are growing up seeing things they ought not to see, especially for those whose parents are letting them experience sexual development with no boundaries. I can only imagine the fallout we will need to deal with when all the pre-adolescent boys and girls who have been viewing pornographic sites in the privacy of their own homes via the Internet grow into young adulthood. Satan has made it phenomenally easy to get bound to sexual sin. All their premature sexual reactions are being ingrained when they are still young and tender. That's exactly when Satan likes to strike, when they're not yet equipped to handle such strong reactions. I've heard that the average age children hit puberty is getting younger. It used to hit at fifteen or sixteen, though I remember a girl in my class who was ten years old and began her monthly cycle not knowing what was going on. She thought she was dying. There are now children in some schools who are dating as young as ten, and the parents don't see the danger! They think it's cute and innocent. As the age drops for these activities and they become more aware of dating dynamics, we must start talking to our kids about these things before they develop sinful habits. Get over your initial embarrassment! Kids will receive your instruction as no big deal if you naturally explain things to them.

When is the right time? Some feel that explaining what happens between mommy and daddy to an eight year old is too early and that they're not even thinking about it yet. However, this is the best time to start, when their own hormones aren't raging yet, it's not shrouded in mystery from their friends' errant views, and they've not been dealing with sexual responses on a regular basis. You don't have to sit them down for a two-hour lecture, but you can begin. As a parent, you'll know when your kid can handle the information and what he or she needs to know at that time. You won't have to look far for an opportunity to talk about it. Watch a half hour of TV and take the time to talk about what you see. This will begin to shape their views about sexuality. I'm concerned to see the degree that some mothers take to make their lovely five-year-old girls look "beautiful" with makeup in beauty pageants, and enrol them in dance classes in how to dance in a sexually provocative way. Having raised three daughters, I've seen the damage it does. For example, one of my neighbours had two daughters who she raised to be extremely conscious of their bodies, including what they wore, their weight, and their physical appearance from kindergarten onwards. She taught them that all their value and self-esteem came from their outward appearance. Her oldest daughter was the same age as my youngest daughter, and because I let my little girl just be a little girl with scuffed knees, pigtails, and glasses, I got the sense that she felt sorry for me, when I felt the same for her. She didn't speak English so I couldn't convey the damage she was doing. Since we were neighbours, our daughters grew up through elementary and high school together.

When senior year came, the damage had been done. My neighbour's oldest daughter became bisexual, and her sister was known to be promiscuous. I'm sure our Heavenly Father was extremely grieved, and although they ended up this way, there is much grace available for them to turn from these lifestyles. I believe this stemmed from their mother placing much pressure and importance on how sexually attractive her daughters should appear. This programmed these innocent girls to go down the wrong path with their sexuality.

The mechanics of sex are simple, but what we need to teach our children at the appropriate time to keep their feet on the right path is the nature of their responses. They need to know why they respond the way they do and how to handle those responses at regular intervals during their development. An eight-year-old girl or boy may find your lecture embarrassing or boring, but as they mature and begin to deal with their own maturing sexuality, they'll remember you talked about it. They will come back later and perhaps question you further, as you have already opened the door of communication regarding this delicate subject. If you treat it as taboo that should be hidden, not-talked-about, and closed, they'll treat it that way too. This is where parents often feel awkward, but you will be surprised at how natural kids can be, and after you broach the subject and present it from God's point of view, it will be accepted and understood when their reasoning is not clouded by sexual urges and hormones. You will be equipping them for future responses, and they will be better able to master the control of their own bodies, and recognize the dangers of our sexually predominated society.

Moms should talk to daughters, and dads should talk to their sons. It's important for moms to convey to their daughters the importance of dressing appropriately when they begin to mature. Young ladies need to dress in such a way they don't cause young men to sin in lusting after them if their breasts and butts are half-exposed. This may compete with a young woman's desire to show off her developing body and exercise the power and desire that is growing in her to control a man. This needs to be explained because our sexually inexperienced daughters may not have a problem with a little exposure and don't understand boys yet. Teaching them that all attention, is not good attention is very important.

Dads need to talk to their sons about the powerful involuntary rush of testosterone they experience upon visually seeing a young woman with half-exposed breasts. Dads need to instruct their sons in how to deal with this so that they learn to control their reactions. They also need to teach their sons to respect young women and see them as God's daughters and not as sex objects. If you are a single dad and find it awkward to talk to your daughter who's blossoming, perhaps a female elder in the church or Godly role model can talk to her. The same could be true if you're a single mom. I know there are excellent Godly role models in my church who wouldn't mind hanging out with the son of a single mom who needs some help.

I remember what my sex education consisted of. I was brought up in a conservative church that did not talk about it, and my parents never talked about it, but we did have a yearly family camp that many went to for a weekend. I remember sitting between my father and mother as the pastor presented the basics of sex, complete with diagrams. I was really hoping the floor would open and swallow me alive as they painfully went through each definition of the sexual parts of our bodies. To my church's credit, at least they addressed the basics, which I already knew from school. However, they didn't address the relational issues between boys and girls like dating, raging hormones and what that meant, and the different physical and emotional sexual responses that boys and girls have. We all were young once, and you know your own child. Just think back to the things that puzzled or concerned you, and you'll begin to discern what you need to be talking to your kid about. God will help you in this.

We have to model good and Godly behaviour to our children. They will hold you accountable for your own actions. For example, the TV and Internet bring a lot of questionable entertainment into the home. If it's not okay for them to watch it, then you shouldn't watch it either. Sin is sin, no matter how experienced or inexperienced one is. If your child sees you shoo them out of the room because of a racy show, they will assume it's okay for them to watch it when they're older. Why not set the example of leaving them in the room and changing the channel for a few minutes? You then teach them how to appropriately respond to the garbage the world tries to feed you.

The key is to be proactive with their sexual education. Equip them beforehand, instead of doing damage control later. We have to promote awareness through God's eyes, and convey this not only to our children and young people, but to a needy, hurting, impoverished, bound world. It's never too late to start upholding God's standards in this area. As long as there is breath in our bodies, each new day brings fresh hope that we can start again and begin taking advantage of the opportunities God gives us to share good counsel with our kids.

CHAPTER 24

What did Jesus mean when He asked us to follow Him?

AM I A WORTHY FOLLOWER?

As I wrap up the final section of this book, every topic covered ultimately was to arrive here—following Jesus until we step into Glory. What did Jesus mean when He gave this charge to His followers in Matthew 10:38? "Anyone who does not take up his cross and follow me is not worthy of me." What kind of picture does this invoke? I've been a Christian for almost all my life, and I'll tell you that when I heard this verse over the years, it often made me feel uncomfortable. I thought about what Jesus could have meant by this. Surely, He wouldn't expect me to be as strong and determined to be able to do what He did. He had to have meant something else. This challenged me greatly, and hopefully, it will shed some light what we need to be about.

Herein lies what we often do to Jesus' clear to-the-point instructions by our own interpretation. We water them down. Who in their right mind would embrace the concept of picking up the heavy crossbar of a crucifix, knowing they were headed to their own execution? We are so far removed from this, we can hardly relate on any level. How do we go about obeying this verse? It helps to remember the era that Jesus lived in. We often think that Jesus' crucifixion was a singular event, that it was a special horrible death, exclusive to Him and a few others.

> It is our *attitude* that matters. When Jesus said we were to pick up our cross and follow Him, He was asking us to declare publicly that we identify with His death and lay down the love of one's own life, to Him.

But that's not true. The Romans used crucifixion as a form of capital punishment reserved for those they wanted to make an example of, as routinely as the need came up. As a Jew living under Roman rule, they would have been highly motivated to avoid that form of death at all costs; the Romans routinely crucified people one after the other along major routes so that all people would see them dying and read the sign above their heads noting their crimes. The new believers would have had first-hand knowledge of what Jesus meant. If following Jesus meant taking up a cross, they knew where they could wind up. When Pilate presented Jesus to the people and asked them what should be done with Him, they all shouted, "Crucify Him!" This says to me that it was a well-known form of death. Had it been reserved for a precious few, they might have had to think about it and hesitate, but that was not the case.

In light of this, Jesus' mandate to you and me, to "pick up his cross and follow me" must cause us to pause and weigh how that translates to us. Jesus died for us so we wouldn't have to, but we need to be willing to follow in His footsteps and carry His message of salvation, even if we're headed to the same fate, to be worthy of Him. Jesus said exactly what He meant, and meant exactly what He said. There are no padded crosses.

In thinking about this, how does Jesus' expectation affect our responses to being persecuted in our society today? Many Christians are even embarrassed to bow their heads in a restaurant to pray—I know because I used to be one of them! Something is way wrong here. We should be grabbing every opportunity to bear witness that presents itself and saying grace in a restaurant and then leaving a big tip is a regular way to do so. I had to ask myself why I was so afraid to say grace in public. At that time, my fear came from not knowing what to say if I was questioned, yet the answer is so simple: "I believe God gave me this food, and I'm simply thanking Him for it." It opens a door of opportunity. What are we so afraid of? In publicly bowing your head, you're sprinkling spiritual salt all over the place. Bring flavour to the table and be different, because you are! No one is going to drag you before a horrid government that will crucify you for praying. Not here, anyway. Our forefathers fled tyrannical governments and came to North America so that we could sit in a restaurant and freely pray. At the end of each day, we need to ask ourselves this question: If I was put on trial for believing in Jesus, would there be any evidence to convict me? Unless we can say yes, something is wrong.

It is our attitude that is critical. When Jesus said we were to pick up our cross and follow Him, He was asking us to declare publicly that we identify with His death, that we lay down the love of one's own life to Him. However, we often don't want to even suffer a disparaging look from people. If this is the case, there is a chasm between what we're doing and what He expects from us that needs to close.

In our culture, no-one is crucified, let alone for their faith, yet there are more Christians today physically suffering for their Lord than in all the past ages put together. In our safe country, we can barely identify with these people, and yet it is happening. They are literally sitting behind bars or dying for their Lord, and we must continually remember them in prayer, as well as pray for, guard, and protect our freedoms. Satan is sly and subtle; little by little the situation could be ours, tomorrow.

If you're looking inside and know you couldn't do it, don't fret. I'm sure I couldn't do it either. I wouldn't be strong enough. But then, none of us are. We are not meant to walk this line in our own strength. He will enable us to do whatever we are called to do for His sake. We just have to make sure we soberly embrace an attitude of dying to self and remain passionately in love with our Lord with all our heart, soul, mind, and strength. It's important to be open to the fact that we are all called to follow Jesus, and that may not always be comfortable; in fact, it may be painful at times. To be worthy of our Lord Jesus, taking up our cross, and following Him is the greatest achievement we can attain.

WHAT IS MY CROSS?

By God's design, I just happened to write this segment for Good Friday on what it means to follow Jesus. All that you do for the sake of Jesus, He notices and is incredibly pleased with you. We have the capability of bringing Almighty God pleasure by giving Him our life, our all, such that it is, warts and all. A life of devotion fuelled by love. This thrills me to my core. Even if we blow it time and again, He will never quit loving us.

"If anyone would come after me, he must deny himself and take up his cross *daily* and follow me. For whoever wants to save his life will lose it, but whoever loses his life for me will save it" (Luke 9:23–24).

What does it mean to follow Jesus? What is our cross? It means to deliberately choose the kind of life He lived. It means sacrificing what we want for what He wants. It might mean we have to suffer rejection from friends, go to church when we'd rather be doing our own thing, or proclaim an unpopular message in the midst of sophisticated, worldly people who might look down on us. It may mean you'll be lonely at times and left out of events because you live out God's standards and remind friends that they're not living right. It is an attitude of servitude that becomes the filter through which we do life. It is waking up each day with the prayer: "Lord, please help me to do today that which you've called me to do." It means living our lives on purpose, for His purposes, not ours.

It looks like a hard road to follow, because it is, but it also means that we are laying hold of life. If that sounds like hollow compensation, let me assure you it isn't. It means finding the reason for our very existence. If the pursuit of wealth, power, and fame are keeping us from surrendering our life completely to Jesus, and cannot bring lasting fulfilment, why do we chase them? God created us to have relationship with Him and to serve Him; all else will simply create a bigger void. It means we bring pleasure to our Heavenly Father as we learn to enjoy Him and receive an eternal reward. Most of all, it means we honour the death of Jesus, God's own Son, our Lord and Saviour.

> Following Jesus means denying ourselves and taking up our cross for His sake.

We instinctively recoil from a cross-bearing life. Our minds are reluctant to believe that this could be God's will for us. Yet what did Jesus say? "If anyone desires to come after me, he must deny himself." This means that nobody is excused, nobody is excepted, and "must" is not an option. I'm not talking about salvation, which is free; I'm talking about seriously living out the fullest purpose God has in store for our lives, in serving Him daily. He'll not force us; that's why Jesus spelled it out. He even says to count the cost before you begin (Luke 14:27–28). Sadly, many Christians have Jesus as fire insurance only.

Their lives don't stand out and make a difference; they blend in with a world that is also consumed with everything but Jesus.

Where does this leave you and me? Jesus never meant for this word to condemn us for failing to carry out His mandate, but to convict us and re-frame our picture for this life and the one to come. Remember, there is an incalculable amount of time on the other side of this life, and what you do here will determine your position there. This sounds like I'm advocating working to be exalted later, but I'm not; there will simply be a distinction in heaven between a life laid down sacrificially for Jesus and one that was lived for self (1 Cor 3:12–15).

Jesus said in Matthew 10:39, "Whoever finds his life will lose it, and whoever loses his life for my sake will find it." In order to win, we need to lose. In order to live, we need to die. Paul said, "I have been crucified with Christ, and I no longer live, but Christ lives in me. The life I live in the body, I live by faith in the Son of God, who loved me and gave Himself for me" (Gal 2:20). In the fullness of his faith in God, Paul considered his life to have been crucified along with Christ, so that Christ's life could live in and through him.

The same is true for us. He doesn't expect us to be anything other than what He can be and do through us. The pressure is off to perform; we simply need to trust and obey. The reality is, when we lose our agenda for His, we become winners! When we die to self, we begin to truly live!

JESUS, WHAT YOU ACTUALLY DID, JUST FOR ME. WHAT I NOW CAN DO, JUST FOR YOU

I was tempted to leave you with a lighter meal, but I would be doing you a disservice. Every page in this book is related to the sacrifice of Jesus Christ and our response to it. On that day when we stand before the Father, He will ask us only one question: "What did you do with my Son?" We need to answer well. Because Jesus rose from the dead, we are forever sealed and saved, but the cost He paid to redeem us to have an intimate relationship with us deserves more than we can ever give, save a lifelong response.

Paul said, in Galatians 5:24, "Those who belong to Christ Jesus have crucified the sinful nature with its passions and desires." In meditating on this, the Lord brought me an interesting thought. Notice he said we have "crucified" the sinful nature, but it still desires to dominate us. Why would he not say "killed" or "subdued" the sinful nature? Because crucifixion is painful. It will hurt, and it won't be over quickly. In an age when crucifixions were regularly practised, they'd have fully appreciated what Paul was saying.

What did Jesus experience when He was physically crucified? If we were to draw a parallel and our response to it, it might look something like this. I implore us to take an honest look at ourselves, because His sacrifice merits it.

His feet...
They were pierced through with spikes. His weight no doubt rested on His feet and His arms and hands in such a way that He could never find a second of respite from the horrific agony. The cross was designed to be as uncomfortable as it could be with no place to rest, even for a moment.

Our feet...
Where does Jesus desire for us to walk to daily? What direction are our feet pointed in? Where are we going that we know we shouldn't be, or where are we not going that we know we should? How do we walk? Do we rush into sin, or do we drag our heels when God asks us to walk towards obedience? This is important. If you're moving, you will move in the direction you're walking. Have we crucified our walk to go where He needs us to? We are His feet carrying the message of His great love, and they bear the scars of untold agony so we could do so.

His hands...
They were pierced with nails. The hands that stilled the storm, that gave sight to the blind, healed the sick, and raised the dead. The hands that created the universe were mangled, bleeding, and full of pain.

Our hands...
What do we put our hands to each day? What tasks do we perform? Are the daily tasks we do going to make a difference in someone's life for all eternity? Have we crucified our hands to do what He needs us to do? We are His hands reaching out to those who are suffering

and perishing to help them and show them we care, and that God loves them.

His head...
He wore a crown of thorns that pierced His scalp, and He was beaten on the head whilst He wore it. I imagine He didn't even pull the thorns out to relieve His pain, even if given a chance to do so. The King of all Kings wore a crown of thorns causing His blood to flow.

Our head...
What do we allow our minds to dwell upon each day? Where is our focus? Do we allow the world to conform our minds, or do we renew our minds daily through God's Word for Him to transform us? Have we crucified our fleshly thought life and allowed our minds to be controlled by the Spirit?

He wore a crown of thorns so we could wear a crown of righteousness.

Jesus said of Himself on the cross in Psalm 69:20, "Scorn has broken my heart and has left me helpless; I looked for sympathy, but there was none, for comforters, but I found none." He was left utterly alone; His disciples had fled, and His Father could not look on the Son of His love with the collective sin of humankind on Him. When Jesus was on the cross, His heart broke over the scorn He received from those He came to save.

He was left alone for a time so we would never be left alone.

Surely He is worthy of walking where He guides us, of doing what He enables us to, and letting Him renew our minds. Only God knows the incredible potential you have, if you'll let Him have all of you. One life lived on purpose for God will make a lasting difference now and for all eternity, for you and all those whose lives you touch.

The Journey will be well worth it!

Printed in Canada